Consumer Australia

Consumer Australia: Historical Perspectives

Edited by

Robert Crawford, Judith Smart and Kim Humphery

CAMBRIDGE SCHOLARS

PUBLISHING

Consumer Australia: Historical Perspectives,
Edited by Robert Crawford, Judith Smart and Kim Humphery

This book first published 2010

Cambridge Scholars Publishing

12 Back Chapman Street, Newcastle upon Tyne, NE6 2XX, UK

British Library Cataloguing in Publication Data
A catalogue record for this book is available from the British Library

ISBN (10): 1-4438-2270-1, ISBN (13): 978-1-4438-2270-1

TABLE OF CONTENTS

List of Illustrations

Illustrations are reproduced by kind permission of the following: State Library of New South Wales, Unilever Australasia, State Library of Victoria. Every effort has been made to locate rightful copyright owners

ACKNOWLEDGEMENTS

In preparing this collection we have incurred many debts. We would like to express our sincerest thanks to Kathy Lothian for her gracious assistance with the production of the manuscript. This project was also aided by a Dissemination Grant from the Faculty of Arts and Social Sciences at the University of Technology, Sydney. We are also grateful for the assistance and support of the State Library of New South Wales and the State Library of Victoria. Finally, we would like to thank each of our contributors for participating in this project and, indeed, for their patience.

INTRODUCTION

ROBERT CRAWFORD, JUDITH SMART, AND KIM HUMPHERY

In their polemical account of contemporary Australian life, Clive Hamilton and Richard Denniss assert that a growing number of Australians have been by gripped by an insatiable desire to consume goods and services in ever-increasing quantities:

> The problem is not that people own things: the problem is that things own people. It is not consuming but consumerism we criticise; not affluence but affluenza ... most Australians acknowledge that our society is too materialistic and money driven.[1]

While Hamilton and Denniss explore the social, cultural, and political ramifications of "affluenza," their study is silent when it comes to identifying the social and historical forces that have shaped our propensity to consume. It is as though these consumer impulses suddenly emerged from a vacuum and are merely a product of individual greed. Noting that "Contemporary consumer culture applauds freshness and obliterates traditional life," Susan Strasser offers a partial explanation for Hamilton and Denniss's silence.[2] This collection of essays begins to redress this neglect of history, by tracing the roots of Australia's consumer culture.

Before we begin to trace these beginnings, it is perhaps worth pausing briefly to reflect on what is meant by consumer culture. The growth of research in this area during the last two decades has inevitably produced a proliferation of viewpoints.[3] At its most fundamental level, consumer

---

[1] Clive Hamilton & Richard Denniss, *Affluenza: When too Much is Never Enough* (Sydney: Allen & Unwin, 2005), 17.
[2] Susan Strasser, "The Alien Past: Consumer Culture in Historical Perspective," *Journal of Consumer Policy* 26, 4 (2003): 376.
[3] For some recent overviews see Eric J Arnold & Craig J Thompson, "Consumer Culture Theory (CCT): Twenty Years of Research," *Journal of Consumer*

culture or consumer society can be defined as the product of the "historical shift from an economy dominated by production to one strongly influenced by consumption,"[4] and we take this as our starting point. As such, consumer culture is continually in flux, where new practices coexist with the old.[5] This dynamic relationship lends itself to historical analysis, and our collection of essays therefore adheres to what Eric Arnould and Craig Thompson label the sociohistoric patterning of consumption, whereby "the driving research problematic is set by the question: what is consumer society and how is it constituted and sustained?"[6]

Historical accounts of the origins of the culture of consumption are divided. In her examination of its historiography, Roberta Sassatelli documents the shift away from productivist explanations focusing on the role played by organised production in determining what was available towards consumer-orientated accounts that emphasise the primacy of consumer desires in deciding what was produced.[7] The date and location of these origins are similarly equivocal. For some, the foundations of the culture of consumption can be traced back to Western European and North American homes and stores of the 17th and 18th centuries, whilst others contend that its true beginnings can be observed in the emergence of department stores in the late 19th century.[8]

Research 31 (2005): 868–82; Monroe Friedman, "The Consumer Culture Research Landscape," *Journal of American Culture* 30, 1 (2007): 1–5; Frank Trentmann, "Beyond Consumerism: New Historical Perspectives on Consumption," *Journal of Contemporary History* 39, 3 (2004): 373–401.

[4] Friedman, "The Consumer Culture Research Landscape," 1–2.

[5] Strasser, "The Alien Past,", 377. See also Lizabeth Cohen, *A Consumer's Republic: The Politics of Mass Consumption in Postwar America* (New York: Vintage, 2003).

[6] Arnold & Thompson, "Consumer Culture Theory (CCT)," 874.

[7] Roberta Sassatelli, *Consumer Culture: History, Theory and Politics* (London: Sage, 2007), Chapter 1.

[8] Peter N. Stearns, *Consumerism in World History: The Global Transformation of Desire* (London: Routledge, 2001); Neil McKendrick, "Commercialization and the Economy," in *The Birth of a Consumer Society: The Commercialization of Eighteenth Century England*, ed. Neil McKendrick, John Brewer & John M. Plumb, (Bloomington: Indiana University Press, 1982), 1–33; Colin Campbell, *The Romantic Ethic and the Spirit of Modern Consumerism* (Oxford: Basil Blackwell, 1982); Susan Strasser, *Satisfaction Guaranteed: The Making of the Mass American Market* (New York: Pantheon Books, 1989); Hamish W. Fraser, *Coming of the Mass Market 1850–1914* (London: Macmillan, 1981); William Leach, *Land of*

The emergence of the culture of consumption in Australia is perhaps more straightforward. In *Economics and the Dreamtime*, Noel Butlin explores the nature of Aboriginal economies prior to 1788. As hunter-gatherers, members of Aboriginal societies consumed their own products. Although they manufactured and traded certain objects such as axe heads and pelts, any widespread flow of trade was limited by factors such as isolation, restricted scope for storage, and the broad similarity of supply conditions. Butlin, however, concedes that the true flow of these patterns may not have been fully understood and certainly there is evidence in Western Victoria of goods exchanged having travelled thousands of kilometres.[9] Nevertheless, the First Fleet would fundamentally alter this way life.

In addition to its cargo of convicts, the First Fleet also imported new cultures—including the culture of consumption. For many of the convicted thieves on board, transportation had been the direct result of giving in to their consumer desires and needs. As the fledgling colony found its feet, the culture of consumption began to take root. The first stores, shops and public houses quickly found a market that was eager to consume their assortment of wares—a growing proportion of which had been produced locally. As Jane Elliott has shown, high wages in the colony allowed convicts access to more and better clothing and other goods than had been possible in Britain, and expenditure on these items served to reduce the outward signs of social difference and status between free and unfree.[10] Over the next decades, the desire to consume scarcely abated and, by the second half of the 19th century, had become ingrained in everyday Australian life. A small but significant number of shop owners capitalised on these desires, using them to convert their modest stores into department stores.[11] The urge to consume, as well as the increased capacity to do so, not only provided a boost to local retailers, manufacturers and other

Desire: Merchants, Power, and the Rise of a New American Culture (New York: Pantheon Books, 1993).

[9] N.G. Butlin, *Economics and the Dreamtime: A Hypothetical History* (Cambridge: Cambridge University Press, 1993), 84–8.

[10] See Jane Elliott, "Was there a Convict Dandy? Convict Consumer Interests in Sydney, 1788–1815", *Australian Historical Studies* 26, 104 (1995): 373–92.

[11] See also Beverley Kingston, *Basket, Bag and Trolley: A History of Shopping in Australia* (Melbourne: Oxford University Press, 1994), 27–8.

associated industries, it also helped recast Australia as an "urban, commercial, and partly industrial society."[12]

Scholarly research on the foundations of the culture of consumption in the Australian context has been fragmentary. Charting the growth and development of the Australian economy, economic historians have traditionally viewed consumption as something of a by-product of economic development rather than a central driving force. In *Making the Market*, Greg Whitwell places consumption on centre stage, though, in positing that the real beginnings of Australia's consumer society lay in the post–Second World War boom, he ignores the degree to which consumption is driven by cultural imperatives. A similar criticism can be levelled at many of the earlier histories of Australia's leading manufacturers and retailers. Equating vision, hard work, and service with success and progress, these hagiographical accounts have all too frequently interpreted healthy ledgers and the expansion of the company's premises as reflections of consumer attitudes. This imbalance in the historical scholarship has, however, been partly redressed in more recent years.

Since the early 1990s, historical accounts of shopping have led the way in developing a more multifaceted perspective on the ways that Australians have embraced consumption. Beverley Kingston's *Basket, Bag and Trolley* provided a short yet important overview of shopping in Australia since 1788. More detailed accounts of shopping, such as Gail Reekie's examination of interwar department stores and Kim Humphery's cultural history of supermarkets, have also deepened our understanding of consumption and its inherent complexity.[13] Archaeology has added further insights into past patterns of consumption as well as the consumers themselves, whilst the discipline of cultural studies has provided additional perspectives on more recent patterns.[14] The increased attention paid to the

---

[12] Richard Waterhouse, *Private Pleasures, Public Leisure: A History of Australian Popular Culture since 1788* (Melbourne: Longman Australia, 1995), 85.

[13] Gail Reekie, *Temptations: Sex, Selling and the Department Store* (Sydney: Allen & Unwin, 1983); Kim Humphery, *Shelf Life: Supermarkets and the Changing Cultures of Consumption* (Melbourne: Cambridge University Press, 1998).

[14] See Penny Cook, "Shopping and Historical Archaeology: Exploring the Contexts of Urban Consumption," *Australasian Historical Archaeology* 18 (2000): 17–28; Mark Staniforth, *Material Culture and Consumer Society: Dependent Colonies in Colonial Australia* (New York: Kluwer Academic/Plenum Publishers, c.2003); John Fiske, Bob Hodge & Graeme Turner, *Myths of Oz: Reading*

interaction between consumers and retailers has also resulted in an increased interest in the ways that consumer activism has affected consumption in Australia.[15]

Linking manufacturers, retailers, and consumers, the media has played an equally important role in both the creation and the maintenance of a culture of consumption in Australia. While audience studies have long been an integral part of media and communication studies, historical accounts of the media appear to have only recently paid attention to the consumer. Bridget Griffen-Foley's "From *Tit-Bits* to *Big Brother*: A Century of Audience Participation in the Media," as well as the more recent special edition of *Media International Australia* focusing on participation, illustrate the growing interest in this field.[16] Although the historical literature on advertising, marketing, market research and public relations industries has tended to focus on these industries and their activities more than their consumption, researchers have nevertheless been attuned to the pervasive presence of the consumer and have recognised his/her impact.[17] Even so, while consumers and the culture of consumption they inhabit have begun to receive increased attention from scholars, the

---

Australian Popular Culture (Sydney: Allen & Unwin, 1987), Chapter 5. The growing maturity of Australian archaeological studies of consumption is evident in the large project currently being undertaken by Tim Murray, Susan Lawrence, Andrew May, S.C. Hayes, and Linda Young on "Suburban Archaeology: Approaching an Archaeology of the Middle Class in 19th-Century Melbourne."

[15] Judith Smart "Feminists, Food and the Fair Price: The Cost of Living Demonstrations in Melbourne, August/ September 1917," in *Gender and War: Australians at War in the Twentieth Century*, ed. Joy Damousi & Marilyn Lake (Cambridge: Cambridge University Press, 1995), 274–301; Amanda McLeod, "Quality Control: The Origins of the Australian Consumers' Association," *Business History* 50, 1 (2008): 79–98. See also Simon Smith, ed., *In the Consumer Interest: A Selected History of Consumer Affairs in Australia 1945–2000* (Melbourne: SOCAP, 2000).

[16] Bridget Griffen-Foley, "From *Tit-Bits* to *Big Brother*: A Century of Audience Participation in the Media," *Media, Culture & Society* 26, 4 (2004): 533–48; *Media International Australia, Incorporating Culture and Policy* 130 (2009).

[17] See Robert Crawford, "Emptor Australis: *Emptor Australis*: Constructing the Australian Consumer in Early Twentieth Century Advertising Literature," *Australian Economic History Review* 45, 3 (2005): 221–43; Amanda McLeod, "The Lady Means Business," *Melbourne Historical Journal* (2003): 54–73; Susie Khamis, "Thrift Sacrifice and Bushells Tea: One Brand's Strategy in the Early 1930s," *History Australia* 6, 1 (2009): 07.1–0.7.10.

comparatively small body of published research remains at odds with the impact that they have had on Australian history.

***

"The cultural history of consumption," observe Geoffrey Crossick and Serge Jaumain, "has found a world in which consumers, distributors and producers symbolically came together, and out of whose encounter emerged not only new methods of selling and to some extent production, but also what might be designated a 'consumer culture'."[18] The diverse contributions in this collection not only seek to reflect this world, they also offer a response to Frank Trentmann's call for a "more ambitious and ecumenical view of consumption, no longer limited to shopping and the market."[19] The following chapters have been divided into three sections: selling, buying, and exchanging. These categories are not intended to be mutually exclusive and there is obvious slippage between these different aspects of the consumption process/es. However, they do provide an opportunity to explore the different components of consumer culture and its development in Australia.

Chapters contained in the first section focus on selling and the issues associated with it. Selling is a defining element of consumer culture that differentiates it from other systems such as bartering. Far from viewing this process as a simple exchange of capital for goods or services, the chapters in this section explore the ways that selling has developed as well as its impact—on both the seller and the purchaser. Susie Khamis's overview of the means by which the Bushells brand was established during the late 19th and early 20th centuries provides an insight into the tactics manufacturers used to cultivate a position for their wares in a marketplace saturated with like products. As Khamis reveals, the quality of Bushells' product ran second to the quality of its selling, whereby "Bushells promised consumers not 'just' tea, but some purchase into a better and more modern way of life." Such dreams were also cultivated by Sir Harold Clapp, the subject of John Sinclair's chapter. Charting the extraordinary range of initiatives implemented by Clapp in the interwar

---

[18] Geoffrey Crossick & Serge Jaumain, "The World of the Department Store: Distribution, Culture and Social Change," in *Cathedrals of Consumption: The European Department Store, 1859–1939*, ed. Geoffrey Crossick & Serge Jaumain (Aldershot: Ashgate 1999), 1–2.

[19] Frank Trentmann, "Beyond Consumerism: New Historical Perspectives on Consumption," *Journal of Contemporary History* 39, 3 (2004): 373–401.

period to increase patronage of the Victorian Railways and, indeed, extend its services, Sinclair contends that Clapp was selling much more than train tickets: 'Clapp's significance is not so much in the particular forms of consumption that he introduced ... but more in the fostering of a move to a mass consumption in general'. While the statistics certainly reveal that levels of consumption had escalated rapidly during the first decades of the 20th century, they also show that consumption was brought to a sudden halt by the Great Depression of the 1930s and then the Second World War. In his chapter on the ways that Australia's manufacturing, retail, and advertising industries dealt with the shift from a seller's market to a buyer's market, Robert Crawford highlights the deep-seated fear that Australians might have forgotten how to consume. By charting these industries' efforts to "convince consumers that consumption was necessary, normal, and beneficial," Crawford's chapter underscores the degree to which consumer culture needed to be sold before it could be embraced. However, once consumers embraced this culture, they were defined by it. This is reflected in Natasha Campo's chapter on the emergence of the "24-Hour Woman" in the pages of *Cleo* and *Cosmopolitan*. The 24-Hour Woman of the 1980s was celebrated as the modern embodiment of the liberated woman, free to live her life, on her own terms, 24 hours a day. Concluding that "collective knowledge about feminism was shaped by consumerism, advertising, and other global discourses in the popular media," Campo reveals that the 24-Hour Woman was little more than a convenient image that could be packaged and sold to female consumers. Here, as in each of the other chapters from this section, it is apparent that the development of a consumer culture in Australia (and indeed elsewhere) owes as much to the selling of these dreams as it does to the selling of consumer wares. As John Brewer and Frank Trentmann note in *Consuming Cultures, Global Perspectives*, "People have dreams and desires of consuming long before they reach a shop counter to purchase a particular item."[20]

The chapters contained in the second section focus on the flipside of selling—buying. Synonymous with consumption, buying inevitably occupies a central position in consumer culture. The chapters in this section view buying as an ongoing and active process that is not restricted to the act of purchase or shopping. Within this process, the consumer

[20] John Brewer & Frank Trentmann, "Introduction: Space, Time and Value in Consuming Cultures," in *Consuming Cultures, Global Perspectives: Historical Trajectories, Transnational Exchanges*, ed. John Brewer & Frank Trentmann (Oxford: Berg, 2006), 3.

occupies a central position, and the chapters by Judith Smart and Amanda McLeod analyse the emergence of a consumer identity. Smart's chapter on the Housewives' Associations between 1915 and 1950 charts the rise of Australia's first consumer organisations and suggests reasons for their decline after the 1960s. It reveals how consumer identities were forged in relation to other identities, in this case, women's roles as homemakers. While these common interests effectively united them as consumers, Smart also reveals that their long-term fragility was responsible for the Housewives' Associations' demise. Competing economic identities "as wives and daughters and sisters of working men, employers and businessmen, or as members of regional communities" made it difficult for these organisations to sustain agreement on issues over time and maintain a stable platform for action. Similar tensions can be discerned in McLeod's survey of the Victorian Consumers Protection Council in the late 1960s. Here, the struggle is located within government ranks, as legislators seek to define what exactly constituted the "consumer interest" and how it should be met. Observing the ways that government interests did not necessarily equate with consumer interest, McLeod underscores the impact of broader influences on the conceptualisation of the consumer. Such influences prompt her to conclude that "attending to the consumer interest will always be complex, controversial and contested." Both Smart and McLeod pay heed to Trentmann's assertion that studies of the consumer should explore the "processes of identity and knowledge formation that criss-cross the market or occur altogether outside its domain."[21] The remaining chapters in this section similarly highlight these influences, albeit in different settings. Matthew Bailey's chapter on the reception of regional shopping centres in the 1960s reveals that buying was not the only practice to be altered by these new complexes: "People came to shop ... and meet up, spend time together, chat, browse, enjoy a meal, work, pass the time ... and shop again." As a social activity, the act of buying (and the conceptualisation of consumer identity with it) came to be influenced by a new range of issues. In his survey of wine consumption in the 1950s through to the 1980s, David Dunstan contends that "patterns of consumption do not change overnight." Illustrating how the increasing levels of wine consumed "coincided with population growth, increased wealth and leisure and new demands for social activities such as entertaining and dining out," Dunstan similarly underscores the impact of

[21] Frank Trentmann, "Knowing Consumers—Histories, Identities, Practices: An Introduction," in *The Making of the Consumer: Knowledge, Power and Identity in the Modern World*, ed. Frank Trentmann (Oxford: Berg, 2006), 5.

"wider demographic, technological, economic and cultural contexts" that have affected, and, indeed, continue to affect, the ways that Australian consumers buy and behave.

Exchanging is the theme of our third and final section. The chapters contained in this section focus on broad, consumption-generated changes, whereby old habits, routines and traditions have been exchanged for new ones. While it could be argued that each purchase has an impact on the consumer's day-to-day existence, the chapters here develop a macro-perspective as they follow the course of these changes and exchanges over an extended period of time. Moya McFadzean thus charts the changing contents of women's glory boxes between the 1930s and 1960s. '[A] tangible expression of female transition, from single to married state', the glory box is also used by McFadzean to illustrate the transition from producer to consumer at an individual level. In observing that the contents of these glory boxes 'gradually shifted from an emphasis on women's own hand-made production to the purchase of the ready-made', this chapter reveals that this process of exchange was not sudden. The exchange that forms the basis of Tony Dingle's chapter also concerns time. Looking at the experiences of Australian housewives from the 1920s to the 1980s, Dingle explores the ways that time-saving appliances (such as vacuum cleaners, dish washers, etc) affected housekeeping activities. Significantly, Dingle observes that the shortened hours devoted to housekeeping came to be counterbalanced by time-using technologies (such as television). He also observes further exchanges that were altering suburban life, noting that "Recreation was becoming increasingly privatised and domesticated ... consumerism was keeping the family together in the home." In Seamus O'Hanlon's chapter, it is the home itself that is ultimately being consumed. However, the exchange here returns to the shift from production to consumption. O'Hanlon analyses the "Red Tulip warehouses" and the transformation of this site "from a place of industry, employment and production in the first half of the twentieth century to one of residence, leisure and consumption today." His study underscores the degree to which modes of consumption—both past and present—reflect broader social, cultural, and economic trends and developments. Kim Humphery's chapter similarly traverses the past and the present in order to reflect on the uniqueness of Australia's consumer culture. Searching for the roots of Australian materialism that lie in its colonial beginnings, Humphery questions the degree to which Australians had exchanged one lifestyle for another. In positing that historical antecedents have indeed informed "the material practices that characterise the life-world we now inhabit [as well as the] practices that remain still to be confronted," Humphery not only establishes a consistent thread between the past and present modes of consumption in the Australian context, he also provides a rationale for each of the chapters contained in this collection.

PART I:

SELLING

CHAPTER ONE

CLASS IN A TEA CUP: THE BUSHELLS BRAND, 1895–1920

SUSIE KHAMIS

In January 1895, readers of the *Bulletin* were introduced to Alfred Thomas Bushell by way of an advertisement. It featured a striking portrait of the bearded, balding 61-year-old, drinking from a cup stamped with his namesake—Bushells Tea. The simplicity of the image was matched by the brevity of the pitch: "None pure and genuine without this signature upon each package of tea."[1] Since its introduction two years earlier, the Bushells brand had showcased the essence of modern marketing practice; the product, a staple of everyday Australian life, was now being imbued with a new range of ideals and associations. Thus, with its appeals to glamour, prestige and progress—all in the semiotic space of a single tea cup—Bushells proved a fitting harbinger of contemporary brand culture. If the right tea could offer cache and class, there was virtually no limit to the transformative powers of the branding process, or, indeed, the extent to which brand logic could mesh with the pace and character of modern life.

Twelve years before his appearance in the *Bulletin*, Alfred Bushell had commenced business under the name Bushell & Company, selling Bushells Tea (and, on a smaller scale, Bushells Coffee) throughout Queensland. Since its humble beginnings, the brand's growth and development has closely paralleled the changing character of Australian consumption. As the separate colonial economies matured into a single, more sophisticated and internationalist economy, Bushells imbued an otherwise unremarkable product with the airs and inclinations of an emerging demographic: the urban middle class. This chapter considers those processes that transformed Australia's consumer culture in the late 19th and early 20th centuries to the point that, by the 1920s, this brand of

---

[1] *Bulletin*, June 5, 1895, 18.

tea was offering not merely superior taste and value but also the myths and motifs of modernity.

A maturing marketplace

Bushells fashioned an image closely tied to a distinctly middle-class mindset, as this was the most compelling force in the 19^{th-}century Australian marketplace.[2] The brand's ascent signalled an important shift in the nation's economy. Prior to the mid-19th century, most Australian households had a rather indiscriminate approach to sourcing basic provisions. Many still retained some connection to the land, usually by way of fruit trees or a vegetable patch. Cows were also kept for private supplies of milk, butter and cream. Itinerant salespeople offered fish, bread or ice, whilst the local grocery store, which was usually within walking distance, stocked the other household requirements. From the closing decades of the 19th century, though, the rise and influence of an educated and propertied class helped recast the nature and direction of the Australian marketplace. To this end, two processes were especially important. First, between 1831 and 1850, the Australian colonies admitted over 170,000 immigrants from the United Kingdom, a third of whom had paid their own fare. This group contained a core of highly qualified and ambitious professionals. While many had struggled to make a mark in British society, they were of "respectable" standing nonetheless. For these "new chums," Australia provided a second chance.[3] Second, the gold rushes had an equally profound effect on the size and make-up of Australian society. The discovery of alluvial gold in both New South Wales and Victoria in 1851, and the subsequent spike in the number of gold-seekers arriving in the colonies, not only multiplied Australia's export earnings; they also boosted its labour force, stretched its skills base, and fostered material conditions that far outlasted the boom itself.

This influx of migrants effectively laid the groundwork for an advanced state of consumer capitalism in the Australian colonies. After 1850, capitalist production was the nation's pre-eminent economic imperative, with the expansion and diversification in commodity production and distribution. Andrew Wells thus notes, that from the mid-

---

[2] Andrew Wells, *Constructing Capitalism: An Economic History of Eastern Australia, 1788–1901* (Sydney: Allen & Unwin, 1989).

[3] K.S. Inglis, *Australian Colonists: An Exploration of Social History 1788–1870* (Melbourne: Melbourne University Press, 1993), 23.

19th century, a combination of domestic needs as well as the requirements of British and world markets helped transform the Australian economy into a predominantly capitalist one. Gold and wool had been the principal Australian commodities sold on the imperial and international markets between 1850 and 1890. By century's end, "a wider range of pastoral, agricultural, mineral and processed primary commodities" were being traded, reflecting the expansion of intra-colonial and inter-colonial trade.[4] Colonial capitalists, particularly those working with merchants and finance capitalists in Britain, were well positioned to direct and exploit lucrative opportunities in the growing economy. As early as 1891, almost two-thirds of the Australian population were living in cities or towns, a proportion that was not matched by either the United States until 1920, or Canada until 1950.[5]

With commercial trade growing and the middle class occupying an increasingly central place in urban development, a necessary change occurred in the way that advertisers addressed consumers. Increasingly, points of status, prestige and distinction were woven into all kinds of commodities. This was not done in any tangible, quantifiable way but at a connotative, associational level. Turn-of-the century advertisements in the *Bulletin* illustrate how Australia's tea traders deployed this dynamic. The copy in these advertisements relied more on allusions and imagery than attributes and availability—what the tea "meant" effectively mattered more than what the tea "did." With the rate of tea consumption in Australia growing, the nation's tea traders understood that tea "meant" profit. As Michael Cannon notes, "many comfortable middle-class importers' and retailers' fortunes were being founded on the habit."[6] Tea advertisements reflect the habit's spread. Highlighting its distribution networks, one advertiser stated: "The London & Sydney Tea Co.'s Tea—Chests delivered free to any RAILWAY STATION or PORTS in NEW SOUTH WALES."[7] Colonial borders were no barrier to another advertiser: "Drink Cup Blend Tea. Unrivalled in quality. ALL storekeepers in NSW

---

[4] Andrew Wells, *Constructing Capitalism: An Economic History of Eastern Australia, 1788–1901* (Sydney: Allen & Unwin, 1989), 2.

[5] N.G. Butlin, *Investment in Australian Economic Development, 1861–1900* (Cambridge: Cambridge University Press, 1964), 181.

[6] Michael Cannon, *Life in the Cities: Australia in the Victorian Age—3* (Melbourne: Thomas Nelson, 1974), 183.

[7] *Bulletin*, October 15, 1892, 17.

and Queensland."[8] Other advertisements illustrate the growing competition between the different brands. "Every variety of TEA! And each of unrivalled excellence, delivered free by Atcherley & Dawson," exclaimed one advertiser, as its competitor emphatically declared "Globe Teas have NO equal."[9] The breadth of tea's appeal was such that, in an increasingly nuanced marketplace, the scope for profit was considerable.

Class-conscious branding

For the Bushell family, the post-Federation period provided the perfect opportunity to expand the company's operations and boost the brand's up-market image. In 1902, Alfred Bushell entered a partnership with his sons, Alfred Walter and Philip Howard. By 1912, their firm had become a public company, Bushells Limited, with a paid-up capital of £15,000 and Philip as chairperson. As it happened, the brand's growth already owed much to the siblings' efforts as the "Tea-Men of Australia." Their extensive nationwide travels to promote their father's brand meant that they were sufficiently informed to assume its control. In 1913, the company's headquarters were established on Sydney's George Street, and further land was bought on Harrington Street in the neighbouring Rocks area in 1919. Over the next few years, the brand spread into Western Australia, South Australia and Tasmania. The Victorian operation recommenced in 1922, having been closed in 1904 to allow concentration on the New South Wales market.

The increased urbanisation of Australian society during the 19th century had a direct impact on the ways that brands like Bushells imagined their consumers. Mindful that middle-class mobility turned attention to all signs of rank, advertisers pitched quality, taste and distinction to prospective consumers. Such traits were attributed to products as pedestrian as laundry powder, shoe polish, mouthwash and tea. The Bushells brand was situated within this shiny new world, and its advertisements tempted fashionable Australians to follow suit. Significantly, this cued a thematic break from other popular tea brands of the time, like Swagman Blend, Pannikin Blend, and Billy Tea. Whereas these brands had espoused the rustic charm of the "the bush," a motif that had wide

---

[8] *Bulletin*, May 25, 1895, front cover; June 1, 1895, front cover; June 8, 1895, front cover.

[9] *Bulletin*, May 29, 1897, 3; June 5, 1897, 3; August 4, 1900, 12; August 18, 1900, 12; August 25, 1900, 14.

populist appeal in the late 19th century, the Bushells brand of the early 1920s forged a far more glamorous image. Its cultural debt was to a very different ensemble of influences; it quoted New York and Art Deco, matinee shows and jazz.

Modernity and the *Sydney Mail*

Several Bushells advertisements appearing in the *Sydney Mail* during the early 1920s illustrate how the advertiser eschewed the rustic charm of bush populism in favour of courting the avaricious middle class. Bushells integrated the pace and glamour of the "Roaring Twenties" into these advertisements in order to project a sophisticated, discerning and modern image. The company attracted the status-seeking suburbanite by incorporating associations that already enjoyed middle-class approval, and its advertisements in the *Sydney Mail* from this period reflect the brand's growing identification with a particular middle-class consumer: the discerning, discriminating female. The vignettes considered here feature two recurring motifs that both point towards a specific cultural and aesthetic disposition: the beautifully groomed female, and the exotic glamour of the Indian sub-continent. A more nuanced understanding of these images can be obtained by examining the influences informing them, especially the extent to which Bushells took its promotional cues from America's Madison Avenue—the venerated "home" of advertising.

In several of the Bushells *Sydney Mail* advertisements, the product is almost sidelined by the centrality of a well-groomed and attractive woman. Moreover, it is clear from the accompanying copy that this figure inhabits a specific social arena, the middle-class household, and readers are prompted to identify with her. Whether these tableaux position this female looking out into the front garden ("Proud of the Tea You served your Guests?"[10]), awaiting a housemaid ("Tired! Languid! After Shopping, Matinee, or Household Duties"[11]—Figure 1 above), or in a hotel lobby ("Peggy from Sydney has 'Pink Tea' with Betty in New York"[12]), the message remains consistent: Bushells tea befits the elegant, fashionable lady. (The nod to New York is telling: such imagery placed Bushells alongside American brands that used scenes of glamour and prestige for similar effect.) These women are all suitably coiffed and accessorised, with

[10] *Sydney Mail*, July 7, 1930, 20.
[11] *Sydney Mail*, June 23, 1920, 32.
[12] *Sydney Mail*, October 20, 1920, 24.

FIGURE 1.1 Bushells' class-conscious consumer. Advertisement for Bushells. *Sydney Mail*, 23 June 1920. Image courtesy of Unilever Australasia.

bob-cuts and pearls, and their elongated, slender figures reflect the period's preference for the streamlined form. However, it is their overriding concern for social propriety that most vividly underscores their acute class consciousness.

This series might well include another three Bushells advertisements: in these the glamorous consumer seems absent, yet her class sensibility remains very much present. All three make oblique reference to the relatively high price of Bushells tea, but resolve this concern by subsuming it to the more urgent consideration of social respectability. The first of these advertisements has two formally attired men seated at what appears to be a restaurant table: "My Wife Says Tea is Higher Tom. What Sort of Tea Does Your Wife Buy?"[13] In the second, "Mrs Macluran," a "manageress" from the Wentworth Hotel, offers "Advice to Housewives on the Cost of Tea."[14] The third advertisement depicts two sets of hands; one is clutching a nameless canister, the other a tin of Bushells. "Do You Guess or Do You Know?" it asks, before explaining the quandary that is literally at hand: "Decide to make your hands resist that temptation to 'guess' at the quantity the teapot needs."[15] Bushells may have been more expensive, but consumers could take solace in the fact that their purchase was worth it.

Alternatively, several Bushells advertisements reference the Oriental allure of Ceylon, which had become one of Australia's main sources of tea. Some of these figures are male, such as the turbaned tea-curer ("When Rama Swami Smiles His Pleasure—You'll Smile Your Pleasure, Too"[16]) and the bare-chested tea-picker ("Young, tender leaves, picked fresh and cured slowly and gradually, so as to hold their juicy sap"[17]). Others are female and are discernibly younger, curvier, and more nubile than the Anglo-Australian consumers featured in the aforementioned series. Such images include the long-limbed beauty peering over her shoulder and raising a single tea leaf ("Freshly Picked Tea—Slowly Cured—Holds that Delicious Tea-Sap Flavor That You'll Love"[18]); the bejewelled, wide-eyed girl, kneeling beside a small tea plant, baring both her knees and her décolletage ("This Little Tender Leaf Drinks the Sunkissed Dew for its Lovely Flavour"[19]—Figure 2 below); and the voluptuous "Napuli," with her back arched and eyes closed ("Come pluck your leaves ere the Sun steals off with the Flavor of the Juicy sap"[20]).

There is an obvious dichotomy here between blue-eyed cultivation and dark-skinned naturalness. On the one hand, Bushells was promoting the

[13] *Sydney Mail*, February 18, 1920, 33.
[14] *Sydney Mail*, March 31, 1920, 29.
[15] *Sydney Mail*, May 19, 1920, 13.
[16] *Sydney Mail*, October 6, 1920, 26.
[17] *Sydney Mail*, November 17, 1920, 21.
[18] *Sydney Mail*, November 3, 1920, 24.
[19] *Sydney Mail*, April 7, 1920, 30.
[20] *Sydney Mail*, May 5, 1920, 30.

credentials of its source. Ceylon is defined as a place of exacting and uncompromising standards, and therefore worthy of middle-class patronage. On the other hand, its foreignness is overtly sexualised. Bushells effectively reconfigures the tantalisingly taboo into a product that can be respectably incorporated into the suburban milieu. The Bushells consumer can thus enjoy the best of both worlds. She can rest assured that the tea she serves her guests is comparable to the tea served in New York. The product's quality alone deserves a few extra pence—not to mention her husband's approval. At the same time, she could also enjoy the enduring aura of a seductive "dark" land and the sensual mystique of its people in the comfort of her own home.

Bushells' depiction of Ceylonese workers as both obedient and sensual was far from atypical. Between the 1890s and the 1920s, Lipton's, one of the leading tea brands in the United Kingdom, had used a similar montage to advertise its tea—from the serenity and order of idyllic plantations, to the eroticised servility of Ceylonese women. Anandi Ramamurthy contends that this approach satisfied a range of interests. First, the only country to export tea before 1838 was China. Indeed, until the 1880s, 84 per cent of tea exports still came from China.[21] With the growth of tea cultivation in India and Ceylon, there emerged a new need to combat the commercial and associative advantages that China enjoyed. Organisations such as the Planters' Association of Ceylon and the Indian Tea Association therefore sought to foreground their products' country of origin. As Ramamurthy writes:

> [T]he image that was constructed was therefore in tune with what the planters wanted to see—a place of rich natural resources, but to a degree wild and therefore productively tamed through European intervention.[22]

It was, in other words, a picture of imperial triumph—and consumers appeared to be eager to lap it up. By 1900, only 10 per cent of the tea consumed in Britain was imported from China, while 50 per cent came from India and 33 per cent from Ceylon.[23]

---

[21] Dan M. Etherington and Keith Forster, *Green Gold: The Political Economy of China's Post-1949 Tea Industry* (Oxford: Oxford University Press, 1993), 25.

[22] Anandi Ramamurthy, *Imperial Persuaders: Images of Africa and Asia in British Advertising* (Manchester: Manchester University Press, 2003), 98–9.

[23] Lizzie Collingham, *Curry: A Biography* (London: Chatto & Windus, 2005), 194.

FIGURE 1.2 Bushells and Ceylon. Advertisement for Bushells. *Sydney Mail* 7 April 1920. Image courtesy of Unilever Australasia.

In its normalisation of what were notoriously exploitative conditions, this depiction of labour reflected a clear racial hierarchy. Its projection of the Ceylonese woman thus completed the Orientalist logic. Embodying the traits that Britons associated with the East (organic, spiritual, decorative and passive), this figure embellished imperialist advertising perfectly. Ramamurthy thus notes, "She is framed and contained in contrast to the European consumer. She is the worker in contrast to the leisured European woman."[24] This image did not merely naturalise the labour conditions under which the tea was produced. By affirming a division of the world that was gendered, racialised and imperial, this image reconfigured its workers so that they flattered the consumers preoccupied with status. Bushells' advertisements in the *Sydney Mail* present an antipodean extension of this philosophy. Despite their differences, the Lipton's and Bushells advertisements reveal that, insofar as status is always relational, the middle class (in both the United Kingdom and Australia) saw in Ceylon a site of appropriate difference.

Through this imagery, Bushells fused the political economy of the tea trade with the cultural economy of Australia's middle class. To spotlight the sub-continent not only exploited the sexual allure of Oriental exotica; it also played to Australian consumers' perception that tea from this region was superior to that from China. While wild tea plants had been discovered in India's Assam highlands in 1823, it was not until 1867 that nearby Ceylon turned to tea cultivation when disease wiped out its coffee crops. A key part of the concerted campaign to extol the virtues of tea from the sub-continent concerned the product's purity. Up until the early 1900s, Australians had been subject to rampant adulteration of foodstuffs; from the late 1800s, tea from China came under particular attention for its sometimes questionable quality. As such, Bushells' Ceylonese backdrop was not just an aesthetic gesture; it stressed the brand's alignment with this "better" source. Bushells was neither the first nor the only Australian tea brand to use tea from the sub-continent; tea merchant James Inglis had orchestrated that change in the nation's tea supply. However, Inglis's star brand was Billy Tea, most famous for idealising the lone outback swagman through advertisements in the *Bulletin*; this figure was humble, stoic and male. So, where Inglis borrowed from "the bush" for Billy Tea's brand, Bushells was aimed at a very different sensibility and therefore utilised very different imagery. The Ceylonese scenes achieved a perfect compromise for Bushells' perfect housewife: they flattered consumers for whom prestige outranked price. At a time when "modern" development was still imbued with imperialist ideals, an Orientalist sub-text was both culturally astute and a strong point of difference from the likes of Billy

---

[24] Ramamurthy, *Imperial Persuaders*, 123.

Tea; it was a brand strategy tailored for the subtle geometry of middle-class aspirations.

From Madison Avenue to middle-class Australia

In their unabashed glamour and ambition, Bushells' advertisements of the 1920s were on par with the kind of advertising that was becoming standard overseas, particularly in the United States. These advertisements sought to usher consumers to an exciting new age. International trade and industrial production had not only revolutionised the manufacturing potential of the modern world, they had also redefined how this new world was to be understood and appreciated. This redefinition found its most dazzling expression in American advertising. America's advertising industry had finessed its techniques to such a degree that it set an advertising benchmark that inspired not only Bushells in the 1920s, but also numerous other brands for decades thereafter.

The influence of American advertising in the 1920s was largely the result of specific developments from the 19th century that had radically transformed the US. Within the space of a few decades, three key features distinguished the US economy: the astonishing scale, scope and speed of American manufacturing and distribution; the concomitant size and sophistication of the American advertising industry; and the growing prominence of an accommodating media apparatus. From the turn of the century, companies like Colgate-Palmolive, Heinz, Coca-Cola, Procter & Gamble, Campbell's Soup, and Carnation had actively adopted and applied new ideas about design and promotion. The "soft-sell" approach was especially popular. Juliann Sivulka observes that this resulted in advertising content being progressively weighted towards "feel-good" associations.[25] Copywriters therefore overlaid advertisements with the signs and symbols of middle-class correctness: good taste, good housekeeping and good manners. Manufacturers had more than immediate sales in mind. As Richard Ohmann contends, they sought to establish a nexus between the demands of modern production (high-speed, conveyor-belt assembly) and the reshaping of people's habits and lives as compliant.[26] To achieve this, advertisers played on consumers' paranoia;

[25] Juliann Sivulka, *Soap, Sex and Cigarettes: A Cultural History of American Advertising* (Belmont, California: Wadsworth Publishing Company, 1998), 55.
[26] Richard Ohmann, *Selling Culture: Magazines, Markets and Class at the Turn of the Century* (London: Verso, 1996), 91.

like the economy, consumers had to be rationalised. Advertisements for everyday products like processed food increasingly displayed what Jackson Lears deems "an almost panicky reassertion of culture over nature—an anxious impulse to extirpate all signs of biological life from one's immediate personal environment."[27] Whatever the commodity, the cultural sub-text was the same: social approval was possible, but always at a price, and only with the right brand. Of course, advertisements rarely admitted as much explicitly. Rather, inspired by Parisian poster artists like Jules Cheret, Eugene Grasset and Henri de Toulouse-Lautrec, and le modern style of Art Nouveau, American copywriters of the 1890s had brought a nuanced understatement to advertising. As such, American advertising from the early 1900s defined the aesthetics of consumption.

By the 1920s, one of the most pronounced ideals in American advertising was modernity itself. Roland Marchand argues that advertising effectively schooled Americans in a new language, one that "established and disseminated a vocabulary of visual images and verbal patterns that acculturated people into life on a complex urban scale."[28] Americans had to be eased into the pace and pressure of the modern world, with all its technological innovations. Indeed, they had to be coaxed to embrace these changes with enough enthusiasm to sustain the economy. Advertisers took up this responsibility with missionary zeal. Copywriters thus became modernity's "town criers" who brought "good news about progress."[29] This "good news" also had an essential class dimension. Commodities were pitched as portals to status, and often positioned within settings of affluence and accomplishment such as hotels, ballrooms, club verandahs and restaurants. It was the 20th-century solution to an age-old pursuit: prestige. As Marchand explains, "the pursuit of modernity offered fulfilment only if it brought secure social status in reasonable proximity to an authentic social aristocracy."[30] This proximity was now obtained via superficial externals, rather than by hard work, perseverance, and diligence. Consumers were encouraged to scrutinise themselves through society's eyes, scared, as it were, into self-consciousness. In this modern society, people looked for quick clues to one's character. So:

---

[27] Jackson Lears, *Fables of Abundance: A Cultural History of Advertising in America* (New York: Basic Books, 1994), 171.
[28] Roland Marchand, *Advertising the American Dream: Making Way for Modernity 1920–1940* (Berkeley: University of California Press, 1985), 335.
[29] Marchand, *Advertising the American Dream*, 1.
[30] Marchand, *Advertising the American Dream*, 194.

> [if] they found these in the cut of your clothes, the brightness of your teeth, the age and taste of your furniture, your inept choice of silverware, or the closeness of your shave, they judged appropriately in a world of quick decisions.[31]

In other words, advertising promised middle-class consumers an irresistible short-cut to status and respect. It was a lesson that Bushells had learnt well.

Conclusion

In the opening decades of the 1900s, Australian tea merchants enjoyed one of the most robust tea markets in the world. Australia was one of the sub-continent's top export regions for tea. In 1929, it laid claim to being the world's premier tea-drinking nation, when its per capita consumption of tea briefly eclipsed that of the United Kingdom.[32] With such high stakes, the cultural significance of the leading tea brands was serious business indeed. In the early 1920s, Bushells framed representations of the "good life" as perfectly suited to a burgeoning middle-class sensibility. These were born of processes and dynamics that had shaped the nation's material environment, as well as the popular imagination, and spoke of an exciting and bountiful modernity. The Bushells consumer, idealised in the form of an elegant and class-conscious woman, was pictured within this glamorised circuit; every consumer choice she made could convey her keenness to impress and her comfortable place within this complex web of political economy.

Herein lay the awesome potential of 20th-century marketing: as long as consumers "bought into" the curious promise of any given brand, the likes of Bushells would grow and prosper. Branding presupposes a realm of anxiety and desire that is quite separate from whatever criteria consumers use to determine a commodity's quantitative usefulness. It rests on the belief of a qualitative difference—a sensitivity to the images associated with the brand, as distinct from any attributes that are, for all intents and purposes, identical to whatever alternatives are also marketed. Brands exist at this associational level; they are imagistic constructs that make most sense when viewed through whatever contemporary conditions made

---

[31] Marchand, *Advertising the American Dream*, 210.

[32] Robin Walker and Dave Roberts, *From Scarcity to Surfeit: A History of Food and Nutrition in New South Wales* (Sydney: University of New South Wales Press, 1988), 133.

one configuration of symbols and allusions more compelling than others. Given the formidable position of tea in the late 19th century as an item enjoyed broadly and often, the brand did well to turn the everyday into the remarkable: Bushells therefore succeeded in promising consumers more than "just" tea; it also promised purchase into a better and more modern way of life.

CHAPTER TWO

MAKING THE MARKET MODERN: SIR HAROLD CLAPP, ENGINEER OF CONSUMPTION*

JOHN SINCLAIR

For all the different possible accounts of the genesis of consumer culture in Australia, there should be little dispute that the period between the world wars was crucial in its diffusion. Although the bourgeoisie kept to themselves the benefits of the wealth that their control over industrial and commercial development had brought them, the possibilities of enjoying a life beyond subsistence was opened up to urbanised white- and blue-collar workers, at least until the onset of the Depression. Such were the structural conditions that internationally gave rise to the social critique of "mass society" and "mass culture" from thinkers on both the left and right at the time. However, this chapter explores how a particular individual, given a certain background, worldview and position of influence, can act to realise the immanent potential in historical forces that would otherwise be blind indeed.

As Chief Commissioner of the Victorian Railways from 1920 until 1939, Harold Winthrop Clapp (1875–1952, Sir Harold after 1941) was able to deploy the key sector of state infrastructure under his command so as to facilitate a major social transition from pre-war subsistence living to the incipient consumer society of the 1920s. Clapp was a committed

---

* This contribution is an output from an ongoing ARC Discovery project, DP0556419, "Globalisation and the Media in Australia," funded 2005–2009. The author gratefully acknowledges the ARC's financial support, and research assistance provided to the program by Dr Rowan Wilken. It is a slightly revised and updated version of the central segment of a previous publication "Agents of 'Americanisation': Individual Entrepreneurship and the Genesis of Consumer Industries," *Journal of Australian Studies* 90 (2007): 17–33.

moderniser who had a particular impact on food marketing and the development of the transport and tourism industries in Australia, but who was also influential in a much wider sense for the mass-market methods of distribution and sales he established.

Although born in Melbourne, Clapp was profoundly formed by an American background. Both of his parents were American born, the father, Francis Boardman Clapp, having come to Victoria in the gold-rush years. After becoming involved with stagecoach services, Clapp Senior went on to found the Melbourne Omnibus Company, which in turn became the basis of Melbourne's sophisticated cable tram network, adopting the cable technology from San Francisco. Clapp Senior remained as managing director until his company became absorbed into the public Melbourne and Metropolitan Tramways Board after 1916.[1]

Very much his father's son, Harold Clapp went from a private school education to an apprenticeship in engineering, and then to his first job, with the Brisbane Tramway Company, in which his father was a shareholder. Clapp oversaw the transition from horse to electric power, and is credited with having driven the city's first electric tram in 1897. In 1901, he left for the US to take up a position with General Electric, which involved him in the building of the subway in New York.[2] Thus began a career in urban electrification and transcontinental railway management that took him to posts in California and the mid-West. After nearly twenty years in the US, and when in line for the presidency of Southern Pacific Railroad at £35,000 a year, he chose instead for his own reasons to accept £5000 a year to return to Melbourne as Chief Commissioner of the Victorian Railways.[3]

In an era when most people still travelled by public transport; when the railways formed the main link between the cities and the regions, but were beginning to be threatened commercially by competition from road transport; and when the processing and distribution of primary produce was relatively undeveloped, Clapp saw how the railways could profit from bringing the producers into more direct contact with consumers. He

---

[1]Michael Angelico, "'Only Ten Per Cent Iron': Sir Harold Winthrop Clapp," http://www.kepl.com.au/gobyrail/clapp.html (accessed 2 March 2006).

[2] Phil Belbin and David Burke, *Changing Trains: A Century of Travel on the Sydney–Melbourne Railway* (Sydney: Methuen, 1982).

[3] "Rebel in the Railways: The Career of Harold Clapp," *Newsrail*, April 2005, 104–05.

marked his arrival with his first "Eat More Fruit" campaign. The rationale was that, "If the demand for fruit can be stimulated, more will be required, consequently more will be grown, and so more transportation will be demanded."[4] This mission, to sell as well as carry produce, meant that Clapp had to extend the scope of his Victorian Railways activities well beyond their technical management, although that was certainly not neglected. Clapp was so much a publicist and entrepreneur that it is easily forgotten that he was, after all, an engineer. He soon completed the electrification of the suburban lines, and expanded and upgraded the state network.[5] At a much later stage, following a trip to the US in 1935, he imported equipment from there and adopted design concepts that enabled the Railways to build, under his personal supervision, the first steel-enclosed, air-conditioned and streamlined passenger train in the southern hemisphere, the thoroughly modern and tellingly named "Spirit of Progress."[6]

Clapp preached to his "Fellow Railwaymen" that the "aim and ambition of everyone of us in the railway family is to GET THE BUSINESS [*sic*]."[7] Consistent with this, he brought the Railway's advertising in-house,[8] and took a personal interest in devising slogans such as "Citrus fruit is nature's way To keep you fit for work and play,"[9] and "Everyday—in Everyway RAISINS [*sic*]."[10] On one occasion, Clapp admitted, "Of course it sounds silly, but it sells."[11] As well as advertising with banners, hoardings, posters and pamphlets at railway stations, Clapp took up the new medium of radio with weekly talks from 1925.[12] He was not just in step with, but setting the pace for, the historical process by which advertising became, by 1930, what Raymond Williams called "an

---

[4] Quoted in Michael Symons, *One Continuous Picnic: A History of Eating in Australia* (Adelaide: Duck Press, 1982), 124–5.
[5] Patsy Adam-Smith, "Clapp, Sir Harold Winthrop," *Australian Dictionary of Biography* (*ADB*) 8 (Melbourne: Melbourne University Press, 1981), 1–3.
[6] Belbin and Burke, *Changing Trains*; "Famous Train 21 this Month," *Victorian Railways News Letter*, November 4–5, 1958.
[7] Patsy Adam-Smith, *Romance of Victorian Railways* (Adelaide: Rigby, 1980), 101.
[8] Ken McGarry, "Tea for Two Million," cited in *Romance of Victorian Railways*, Adam-Smith, 130–9.
[9] Adam-Smith, "Clapp, Sir Harold Winthrop," 2.
[10] Marc Fiddian, *Flinders St Station: Melbourne's Taj Mahal* (Hastings, Vic.: Galaxy Print and Design, 2003), 27.
[11] Quoted in "Rebel in the Railways," 105.
[12] Adam-Smith, "Clapp, Sir Harold Winthrop," 2.

organized system of commercial information and persuasion, as part of the modern distributive system in conditions of large-scale capitalism."[13]

While Clapp continued by various means to promote fresh primary produce, particularly in times of glut, such as when "Peach Week" became "Peach Fortnight," he went on to involve the Railways in light food processing and retailing ("value adding"). The Sunraysia district, with its soldier settlement farms producing grapes and citrus fruits on lots irrigated by the Chaffey brothers, the Canadians from California,[14] would have reminded Clapp of his own time in California. Moreover, the line to Mildura was the longest in the state, and Clapp could see the benefits in promoting citrus and not grapes but raisins.[15] Consistent with later attempts to bring primary production and secondary industry together, Clapp's strategy was for the Railways to carry the produce at a loss, but profit from higher freights on manufactured goods being carried back from the city to farmers made prosperous by the sale of their produce.[16]

Thus, when the Railways opened its own bakery in 1923, it was distinguished not so much by the pies it helped to make into a national dish but by the raisin bread. Backed by what Clapp himself called "propaganda," and with the innovation of machine-wrapping the bread, the first bakery in the state to do this, raisin bread was so popular that scores of other bakeries throughout Melbourne were soon also making it, as they still do. Similarly, Clapp gave a fillip to milk consumption by selling "pasteurised milk in sealed bottles" at Railways "refreshment rooms,"[17] an innovation in packaging that added the essentially modern qualities of standardisation, hygiene and convenience to a product, which, in those days, was generally fetched from the local dairy in one's own billy. Ice-cream was also offered as a feature of train travel, particularly in the summer months. As to the citrus fruit, Clapp opened a fruit juice stall at Flinders Street Station, the city terminus for all the suburban lines, which was a total innovation. As Michael Symons describes it in his *One Continuous Picnic: A History of Eating in Australia*,

---

[13] Raymond Williams, *Problems in Materialism and Culture* (London: Verso Editions and New Left Books, 1980), 179.

[14] Peter Westcott, "Chaffey, George (1848–1932) and William Benjamin (1856–1926)," *ADB* 7 (Melbourne: Melbourne University Press, 2006), 599–601

[15] Fiddian, *Flinders St Station*, 27.

[16] Adam-Smith, *Romance of Victorian Railways.*

[17] Symons, *One Continuous Picnic,* 125.

FIGURE 2.1 Serving Melbourne's thirsty commuters. Unacknowledged. Image reproduced from Patsy Adam-Smith, *Romance of Victorian Railways* (Adelaide: Rigby, 1980), 103.

> Behind the counter of white vitrolite, with black edging, stood a line of 10 uniformed attendants, each at her Sunkist fruit juice extractor, the first in the country. Customers purchased fourpenny tickets at a cabinet, presented them at the counter and selected orange or lemon. The attendant cut the fruit, squeezed the juice and added sugar, syrup and soda from an American-looking fountain.[18]

Again, this was a great success, with 27 such stalls five years later becoming the biggest outlet for the state's citrus growers.[19] However, poultry, eggs and meat were a different matter. Rather than freight them in from producers, the Railways had its own poultry farm and butchery, the latter being supplied by usual wholesale channels. By the end of the 1920s, Clapp had integrated the fruit and juice stalls, bakery and butchery, along with refreshment rooms, bookstalls and other platform services, into the

[18] Symons, *One Continuous Picnic*,, 126.
[19] Symons, *One Continuous Picnic*,, 126.

"Refreshment Services Branch." The Railways' own advertising agency, as well as its guest house at Mt Buffalo, were also part of this burgeoning empire.[20]

Clapp's strategies as a moderniser went beyond the consolidation of these various enterprises into the one state organisation dedicated to "GET THE BUSINESS" from private road transport competitors. First, he sought to give a general stimulus to trade between country and city with an annual special service that began in 1922, the Victorian National Resources Development Train. Soon known as the "Reso Train," it provided first-class accommodation for city business people wanting to spend a week visiting rural projects. Then, in 1924, the Better Farming Train was inaugurated. This was not only an agricultural show on wheels, displaying agricultural science and farm technologies, but also came to include a "domestic economy" carriage demonstrating household skills, a mothercraft and child welfare carriage, and another again for public health.[21] In this way, Clapp was putting the railways to the purpose of what is still called "agricultural extension" in the US, specifically implementing an approach that post–Second World War theorists would later advocate as the "diffusion of innovations," a deliberate strategy for achieving "modernization."[22] Similarly, the rationalisation of child-rearing practices that the train brought to rural women gave further reach to the role of government in this era in "producing the modern model baby."[23]

Clapp's further contribution to modernising babies and child-rearing was the establishment of a crèche at Flinders Street Station, where mothers, brought into the city by rail to shop, could leave their children in the care of professional staff,[24] and incidentally, surrounded by the modernist interior design of Stephenson and Turner. These were architects specialising in health facilities, but who, later, towards the end of Clapp's term of office in 1939, were also commissioned to install a massive mural featuring the Spirit of Progress in the Victorian Government Tourist

[20] McGarry, "Tea for Two Million," 131.

[21] Leo J. Harrigan, *Victorian Railways to '62* (Melbourne: Victorian Railways Public Relations & Betterment Board, 1962), 266.

[22] Everett Rogers, *Diffusion of Innovations* (Glencoe, NY: Free Press, 1962).

[23] Kerreen Reiger, *The Disenchantment of the Home: Modernizing the Australian Family, 1880–1940* (Melbourne: Oxford University Press, 1985), 138.

[24] Harrigan, *Victorian Railways to '62*, 189.

Bureau, an entity operated by the Railways until 1959.[25] Another huge mural was featured at the country terminal, the former Spencer Street Station; depicting a century of transport to 1935, it too very much reflected both the modernising mission and modernist taste in public art of the Chief Commissioner.[26]

Clapp was a moderniser in labour relations who paid close attention to current American models. In employing rhetoric about the "railway family," he saw himself as its patriarch, and resented union challenges to his attempts to implement "scientific management" techniques, or "Taylorism," the labour management theory associated with Ford's innovations in mass production. Though "progressives" in Australia had been actively interested in Taylorism and other American modernising ideas since before the war, [27] Clapp took his personal commitment to Taylorism within the Victorian Railways a step further by sending senior officials to see it in practice in the US.[28] More benign was his support for workers' self-improvement initiatives. Evidently valuing these activities as much as efficiency in his employees, Clapp encouraged them to study and to take advantage of the library, sporting, and social facilities on offer at the Victorian Railways Institute.[29] Against opposition, he also opened up employment in the Railways to hundreds of women. Indeed, his biographer, Patsy Adam-Smith, came from a family of "station mistresses" who owed their jobs to him.[30]

As well as admiring Taylorist efficiency, Clapp was imbued with several other values and beliefs that provided an ideological foundation to capitalism in the US at the time. His commitment to sales, service and showmanship was also fused with notions of personal uplift deriving from that characteristically "American" version of the Protestant ethic and the spirit of capitalism first formulated by Benjamin Franklin and popularised in the 1930s by Dale Carnegie. Clearly, Clapp saw individual moral virtue as the path to commercial success when he wrote to staff:

---

[25] Philip Goad, Rowan Wilken and Julie Willis, *Australian Modern: The Architecture of Stephenson & Turner* (Melbourne: Melbourne University Publishing, 2004), 40.
[26] Adam-Smith, *Romance of Victorian Railways*, 113.
[27] Philip Bell and Roger Bell, *Implicated: The United States in Australia* (Melbourne: Oxford University Press, 1993), 41.
[28] Eddie Butler-Bowdon, *In the Service? A History of Victorian Railways Workers and their Union* (Melbourne: Hyland House, 1991), 48.
[29] Angelico, "'Only Ten Per Cent Iron'."
[30] Adam-Smith, *Romance of Victorian Railways*, 104.

> A pleasing personality is worth more than money in the bank. The first step is the abolition of selfishness and complacency. Replace these with consideration of others and cheerfulness. And always observe the rules of cleanliness and neatness. This will help to improve railway salesmanship.[31]

The belief here in cleanliness, which for him was "almost … a religious cult,"[32] earned him the public nickname of "Clever Mary," after a brand of household cleanser widely advertised at the time. Yet, for all his efforts to improve the Railways, Clapp was not a popular figure. He himself had more "pep and hustle"[33] than "a pleasing personality." His green Stetsons and the American accent he never lost marked him out as a "Yank"[34] amongst the people and the press of Victoria, which labelled him as "a 'megalomaniac', or a person who thinks big, especially of himself."[35] Ironically, since he was applying the methods of capitalist competition to a state instrumentality, he was also denounced as a "socialist."[36] This epithet derived partly from the wide diversification of activities under the Railways Refreshment Services Branch, which his critics saw as properly the domain of private leases, if indeed they were to be associated with the Railways at all. It also stemmed from his aggression towards private enterprise, evident in the Railways bus fleet he established to compete with a private service on the Melbourne–Geelong route.[37] Another time, questions were asked in Parliament about Clapp having said that his private road transport competitors "wouldn't have a feather to fly with" by the time he was finished with them.[38]

It would be easy to dismiss Clapp as a "booster," in the style of the self-promoting small-town businessmen's brotherhood of Sinclair Lewis's novel of the time, *Babbitt*. But, although he shared their firm belief, which has become today's conservative orthodoxy, that social development is generated by commerce, he had none of their smug provincialism. Rather, Clapp's modernising outlook included a truly national vision, evident in two of the fields in which he intervened actively in his later years, namely tourism and railway unification. Understanding the intrinsic value of

---

[31] Adam-Smith, *Romance of Victorian Railways*, 104..
[32] Belbin and Burke, *Changing Trains,* 110.
[33] "The Story of Sir Harold …," *Victorian Railways*, June 1975, 86.
[34] Adam-Smith, *Romance of Victorian Railways.*
[35] Angelico, "'Only Ten Per Cent Iron'," 7.
[36] "Rebel in the Railways," 105.
[37] Butler-Bowdon, *In the Service?*, 48
[38] Adam-Smith, *Romance of Victorian Railways,* 101.

domestic tourism to the Railways, especially in the era before buses and cars, Clapp took a series of initiatives in tourist development well before the establishment of the Victorian Government Tourist Bureau.[39] His vigour in promoting tourism in Victoria included popularising the chalet at Mount Buffalo, which the Railways took over in 1924,[40] but he also saw tourism in a national context; Clapp was a nation-builder as well as a moderniser.

In a report to the Commonwealth in 1927, the Chairman of the Victorian Railways Betterment and Publicity Board, Charles Holmes, together with T.E. Moorhouse of the joint Commonwealth–State Development and Migration Commission, argued for a national coordinating agency and "greater zest in salesmanship" to promote domestic tourism on a national basis. In addition, they recommended circulating "propaganda," mainly through offices in the "English Speaking world," to attract tourists from overseas. The Reso Train was mentioned as a model for domestic tourism, while, on the overseas front, reciprocal farmers' tours and group tours of industrialists were envisaged.[41] It is difficult not to see Clapp's hand in this, and not surprising that, when the Australian National Travel Association (ANTA) was subsequently established in 1929, its offices were set up in the Victorian Railways building in Flinders Street.[42] Clapp was Chairman, a position he held until his death in 1952, and Holmes was "chief executive officer" until 1957. The ANTA overseas offices, which were opened during the 1930s and represented a wide range of Australian interests, were, at the onset of the Second World War absorbed into the Department of Information, one of whose directors wrote of Clapp as "the prime instigator and founder" of ANTA.[43] The Melbourne office meanwhile devoted itself to "promotion and propaganda;" it commissioned posters from the likes of Percy Trompf and James Northfield, and, inspired by the successful *National Geographic* from the US, it also published the

[39] Harrigan, *Victorian Railways to '62*; Richard White, *On Holidays: A History of Getting Away in Australia* (Melbourne: Pluto Press, 2005), 65–7, 79.
[40] Adam-Smith, "Clapp, Sir Harold Winthrop."
[41] Jim Davidson and Peter Spearritt, *Holiday Business: Tourism in Australia Since 1870* (Melbourne: The Miegunyah Press, 2000), 77.
[42] Davidson and Spearritt, *Holiday Business*, 77.
[43] Quoted in Edward L. Vickery, "Telling Australia's Story to the World: The Department of Information 1939–1950," (PhD diss., Australian National University, 2003), 149.

monthly magazine, *Walkabout*. ANTA was eventually succeeded by the Australian Tourist Commission in 1967.[44]

As well as having made such a durable contribution to modern nation-building with tourism, Clapp was instrumental in bringing about the ultimate unification of the railways of the nation. Clapp left the Victorian Railways with the advent of the war in 1939, and held various executive posts in aircraft production and land transport under the Commonwealth, before being asked in 1944 to report on railway unification. Exasperated by the "State-mindedness" that had led to three different rail gauges across five States, Clapp characteristically argued in favour of rail unification, rather than road transport development, both for defence and for economic reasons. The Commonwealth accepted his recommendations in principle, but there was resistance amongst the states, so that it was not until 1962, a decade after Clapp's death, that it became possible to travel between Melbourne and Sydney without changing at Albury.[45]

Clapp was well placed to bear out Marx's dictum that "The country that is more developed industrially only shows, to the less developed, the image of its own future." His unique American experiences, values and beliefs enabled him to see opportunities for innovation, and to be sustained by a guiding ideology in pursuing them. However, he could only capitalise on his individual qualities and fulfil the prophecy to the extent that there were actual or potential similarities between the US and Australia. Michael Symons suggests that Clapp had seen in California how publicity could be used to clear the glut of agricultural production created by irrigation. He also understood that such publicity had to emphasise "family goodness" and welfare in an age of Prohibition in the US and ascendant wowserism in Australia.[46] Thus, it was citrus fruits, raisins and milk, rather than wine grapes, that suited the era. The discovery of vitamins before the war, together with the ensuing publicity about their importance, made both national populations receptive to the idea that food should be good for you and that this was especially important for children.

---

[44] Davidson and Spearritt, *Holiday Business*, 79.

[45] Adam-Smith, *Romance of Victorian Railways*, 108; Adam-Smith, "Clapp, Sir Harold Winthrop," 3; Harrigan, *Victorian Railways to '62*, 196–7.

[46] Symons, *One Continuous Picnic*, 128. 'Wowserism' was evident in Australia in the widespread incidence of six o'clock closing after the First World War and a long tradition of sabbatarianism.

Political conditions in Australia favoured Clapp's mode of promotion. For all the personal criticism he bore, Clapp's support of primary production would have won favour with rural interests, including the government-supported "single desk" marketing boards, and the two Country Party Premiers under whom he served. More than fruit, Symons identifies the promotion of milk as being of enduring consequence, not just in building a local dairy-based consumer culture in Victoria, but in providing the basis upon which the overseas food corporations then beginning their operations in Australia could develop national markets.[47] Cadbury's advertised the "glass and a half of full cream milk in every half pound" of their Dairy Milk chocolate from 1928, "one of the all-time greats of British advertising;"[48] Peter's ice-cream, a company established in Melbourne by yet another American, was "the health food of a nation;" Nestlé (or "Nestles" as it was then known colloquially) was claiming as early as 1914 that its condensed milk was "the best substitute for the mother's milk;"[49] Kellogg's introduced their cornflakes, made to be consumed with milk, to Sydney in the 1920s; while Kraft processed cheddar cheese was brought to Melbourne in 1926 by Fred Walker, a local food manufacturer whose greater claim to fame was the development of Vegemite.[50] Furthermore, Clapp's promotion of milk and the fruit juice bar arguably laid the basis for the advent of the "milk bar" as a form of modern, local distribution in the following decade.[51] In all, as Symons concludes:

> Clapp was at the top of a powerful public service elite, consciously manipulating an entire population. He arose when the crisis of world war had welded the modern State apparatus … for keeping the troops in line. The new 'mass society' flocking twice daily beneath Clapp's Flinders Street clocks was to be moulded into a nation of consumers.[52]

Thus, Clapp's significance lies not so much in the particular forms of consumption that he introduced, such as the regimented fruit juice bars,

---

[47] Symons, *One Continuous Picnic*, 129–31.
[48] Cadbury Schweppes, "Cadbury Dairy Milk," http://www.cadburyschweppes.com/EN/Brands/About/Confectionery/factsheet_dairymilk.htm (accessed 31 October 2006).
[49] Quoted in Symons, *One Continuous Picnic,* 130.
[50] Quoted in Symons, *One Continuous Picnic,* 130.
[51] Nanette Carter, "Milk Bar Modern," in *Modern Times: The Untold History of Modernism in Australia*, ed. Ann Stephen, Philip Goad and Andrew McNamara (Melbourne: The Miegunyah Press, 2008), 120–7.
[52] Symons, *One Continuous Picnic*, 128.

bottled milk, or packaged raisin bread, but more in the fostering of a move to mass consumption in general. In this regard, his mission was very much in accord with the manufacturers, retailers, and other "captains of consciousness" in the US during his era. These were the men who, as Stuart Ewan notes, sought to "Fordize American business and industry" with a "general strategy to consumerize the worker," especially through advertising.[53] On the production side, the strategy involved lowering costs with efficiencies achieved via "scientific management" and the application of mass-scale production techniques, so that, on the consumption side, workers could be paid better so as to be able to afford to buy the manufactured goods advertised to them. For many theorists of capitalism, this is seen as an epoch-making transition that gave capitalism its form for most of the last century, when Fordism was "the centre of modernism."[54] Clapp was one of the engineers of this transition in Australia, or, as a railway shunter's graffiti put it, "Kant on pure reason is nothing compared to Clapp on pure raisin."[55]

---

[53] Stuart Ewen, *Captains of Consciousness: Advertising and the Social Roots of the Consumer Culture* (New York: McGraw-Hill, 1976), 24, 28.
[54] Robin Murray, "Fordism and Post-Fordism," in *Modernity and Its Futures*, ed. Stuart Hall, David Held and Tony McGrew (Cambridge: Polity Press, 1992), 184–95.
[55] Adam-Smith, *Romance of Victorian Railways*, 110.

CHAPTER THREE

FROM A SELLER'S MARKET TO A BUYER'S MARKET: ADVERTISING LOOKS FORWARD TO THE 1950S

ROBERT CRAWFORD

Opening the Top Management Conference in 1948, chairman Malcolm Moore outlined his view of the conference's central theme, "Meeting the Buyer's Market:"

> [W]e are in the transition stage between a seller's and a buyer's market. Doubtless each one of you has a clear idea of the two terms, but doubtless each of you would define them a little differently. I feel inclined to define a **buyer**'s market as one where you takes your choice and pays your money; and a **seller**'s market as one where you pays your money and you takes what they'll let you have—if it's in stock.[1]

While the manufacturing, retail, and advertising industries understood that this transitional stage was temporary, the future was still uncertain. In addition to asking when this transition would end, these industries were also wondering how they would fare in the new climate. The latter question posed a real quandary. A decade of unstable and inconsistent conditions made it difficult to ascertain how consumers would react. Would the enforced thriftiness of the recent years continue or would they discard these frugal habits altogether and consume with abandon? In order to realise the latter, they would have to convince consumers that consumption was necessary, normal, and beneficial.

Although the 1940s mark a key point in the history of consumption in Australia, the period has been overshadowed by the events that took place

[1] Malcolm Moore, "Chairman's Opening Address," in *Meeting the Buyer's Market: Proceedings of the Sixth Australian One-Day Top Management Conference* (Melbourne: Institute of Industrial Management, 1948), 5.

in subsequent decades. In her examination of the Long Boom from the late 1950s through to the 1970s, Amanda McLeod posits that Australia only became "a mass consumerist society from the post-war period, and particularly after 1955, as it is not until this time that most Australians experience affluence and abundance."[2] Greg Whitwell's *Making the Market* offers a similar perspective.[3] Looking at the American experience, Stuart Ewen pays greater attention to the past, arguing that the activities undertaken during the inter-war period laid the foundations for the consumption of the 1950s.[4] The 1940s, however, remain absent from these accounts.

This chapter seeks to redress this shortcoming by examining the ways the manufacturing, retail, and advertising industries cultivated consumer dreams during the 1940s, particularly in the latter half of the decade. Their marketing strategies were informed by hopes of an impending golden age of consumption as well as the deep-seated fears that recent hardships could return at any moment. Such strategies were also forged by broader economic, political, and social conditions. By examining the ways Australians were being conditioned to consume at a time of scarcity, this chapter explores a seminal moment in the emergence of a culture of consumption in 20th-century Australia.

Maintaining the desire

For Australia's manufacturing, retailing, and advertising industries, the Second World War threatened to upset the consumption patterns that had been improving for almost six years before 1939. Weathering this storm was now their priority. Norman Rydge, the editor of *Rydge's: The Business Management Monthly*, thus outlined the new duties of business:

> In these critical times every businessman has the obligation of preserving our economic morale and maintaining the stability of our internal conditions. This is a patriotic duty we all owe to Australia and the Empire.[5]

---

[2] Amanda McLeod, *Abundance: Buying and Selling in Post-war Australia* (Melbourne: Australian Scholarly Publishing, 2007), 2.
[3] Greg Whitwell, *Making the Market: The Rise of Consumer Society* (Melbourne: McPhee Gribble 1989).
[4] Stuart Ewen, *Captains of Consciousness: Advertising and the Social Roots of the Consumer Culture* (New York: McGraw-Hill, 1976).
[5] Norman Bede Rydge, "How will the War affect Business," *Rydge's: The Business Management Monthly* 12, 10 (1939), 743.

After an initial fall off, trade returned to normal. The Christmas of 1939 was particularly busy, indicating that the government's "business as usual" maxim had been adopted. However, as the frontline situation deteriorated over the coming years, the "business as usual" approach was abandoned. Prime Minister John Curtin's call for an "all-in" effort also required advertisers to revise their appeals.

The curtailment of consumption caused by restrictions and rationing did not bode well for manufacturers, retailers, or advertising agencies. While they accepted the necessity of such measures, they also moved to protect their interests. Of the three industries, the advertising industry was the most vulnerable and it consequently drew attention to its wartime functions.[6] Adman Hugh Berry thus highlighted the importance of a stable economy and argued that the advertising industry was needed "to protect the structure of the nation's vast and miscellaneous industries."[7]

Austerity became the watchword of the homefront's "all-in" effort. The famed "Squander Bug" advertisements thus equated hedonistic consumption with the enemy. Non-government institutions propagated the same line. The *Australian Women's Weekly*, for example, resurrected thriftiness "as a womanly trait."[8] Commercial advertising consequently stood alone in promoting consumption. It struggled in this climate. In March 1942, things came to a head when Curtin asserted that advertisers were "probably more responsible than anyone else for the impression that we don't seriously mean an all-in war."[9]

Following Curtin's rebuke, adman Frank Goldberg defended advertising. Rejecting the "out-dated theory that advertising is ... simply a business measure to create sales," he claimed, "Advertising today is ... concerned with the all-important task of *moulding public opinion*."[10] While this final

---

[6] Robert Crawford, "Nothing to Sell? Australia's Advertising Industry at War, 1939–1945," *War and Society* 20, 1 (2002): 99–124.

[7] Hugh Berry, "A Discipline to Habit," *Rydge's: The Business Management Monthly* 15, 6 (1942): 341.

[8] Andrée Wright, "The Australian Women's Weekly Depression and the War Years: Romance and Reality," *Refractory Girl* 3 (1973): 11.

[9] Statement by Prime Minister Curtin, 9 March 1942, "War 1939 Control of Advertising During War," A 1608/1:G21/1/2, National Archives of Australia, Canberra.

[10] Frank Goldberg, "Advertising Must Carry On," *Rydge's: The Business Management Monthly* 15, 5 (1942): 275.

comment referred to the industry's government work, it was equally applicable to the industry's attempts to keep consumer desires alive. Maintaining such desires whilst avoiding the critics' ire demanded a delicate balancing act. Wartime advertisements therefore highlighted the advertiser's wartime service before inviting consumers to consume their wares (when they became available). Some ingeniously identified consumption as an act of thrift. Advertising observer Henry Ferguson thus applauded Kiwi polish for deftly pointing out that it "not only polishes but preserves, prolonging the life of … shoes."[11]

As the war continued, other advertisers fuelled consumer desires by looking to the future. A 1943 advertisement for steel tube manufacturer Stewarts and Lloyds illustrates the optimistic appeals that were now being deployed. In 1939, it explained, "None of us wanted the future we then saw ahead. But we faced it … Once again we are looking ahead."[12] A modern city represents this vision—combining art, science and technology. This trend was not lost on contemporaries. In April 1944, Ferguson observed that "Implicit in many advertisements last month was the promise of scientific progress after the war."[13] However, as victory neared, it became clear that these dreams would not be realised any time soon. The manufacturing, retailing and advertising industries understood that this transitional period would be critical to their long-term aspirations. If their dreams of a consumer boom were to be realised, they needed to offer simpler and more attainable dreams.

Haven of happiness

Headed, "Home is where the Heart is," a 1945 advertisement for Maples furniture stores featured the advertisers' new symbol for the imminent post-war age—the home.[14] Another furniture retailer went even further, identifying it as "the source of human achievement," a "refuge in times of stress," and "the jewel of civilisation."[15] Advertisements "peeping" into the post-war home and espousing the merits of home ownership had been steadily growing since 1943, and, by 1945, they had become *de rigueur*. "There can be few topics more timely than that of homes for the people," noted Ferguson in August 1945, "And when the interest in this subject is

[11] *Newspaper News*, August 1942, 6.
[12] *Bulletin*, November 24, 1943, 28.
[13] *Newspaper News*, April 1944, 8.
[14] *Argus*, October 5, 1945, 5.
[15] *Sydney Morning Herald*, June 11, 1945, 5.

FIGURE 3.1 Dreaming of the future. An advertisement inserted by the National Gas Association of Australia. *Australian Women's Weekly*, 27 April 1946. Image courtesy of the State Library of Victoria.

neatly capitalised by advertisers, a ready-made audience eagerly gives it attention."[16] By the time Figure 3.1 appeared in 1946 Australian consumers had become well acquainted with the dream on offer and were champing at the bit to realise it.

While the suburban image had become ubiquitous, it nevertheless remained the stuff of dreams. A 1944 advertisement for war savings bonds sponsored by Cane-ite insulation explained that "there's no reason why you shouldn't plan, and prepare, and save, for the home you're going to have when peace has followed the victory."[17] The accompanying illustration featured a large modern house that few could afford even twenty years later. Such images reinforced consumer desires and, with them, the resolve to win the war. Although the size and opulence of these imagined homes decreased as peacetime neared, they remained fantasies. Ferguson thus observed that "the great majority of home seekers will have to be satisfied with something infinitely more modest" than the advertisers' depictions.[18]

In 1944, the Commonwealth Housing Commission reported that Australia was facing a severe housing shortage.[19] By 1946, this shortage was already acute. Rydge thus used his editorial column to call for manufacturers to resume peacetime production. "What is the use of banked-up purchasing power if there is nothing to buy?" he asked: "There is only one way to get rid of the housing shortage and the thousand other scarcities—the legacy of the wasteful war years—and that is to build houses and to produce goods."[20] Tired of waiting for these dreams to materialise, many Australians took matters into their own hands. The commercial sector glowingly described these owner-builders as the "people of the hour."[21] In addition to embracing consumption, owner-builders would be locked into a spiralling consumerist vortex. Completing the dream home required more than just tools and materials. *Home Beautiful*, *Australian Home and Garden*, and *Australian Homemaker* all

---

[16] *Newspaper News*, August 1945, 10.
[17] *Bulletin*, January 19, 1944, 16.
[18] *Newspaper News*, August 1945, 10.
[19] Alastair Greig, *The Stuff Dreams Are Made Of: Housing Provision in Australia, 1945–1960* (Melbourne: Melbourne University Press, 1995), 31–3.
[20] Norman Bede Rydge, "Produce and Prosper," *Rydge's: The Business Management Monthly* 19, 11 (1946): 985.
[21] *Newspaper News*, September 1946, 9.

provided readers with a steady stream of instructions, hints and sales advice.

The frustrated owner-builder was also identified as a political force. For Robert Menzies and his newly formed Liberal Party, the housing shortage became an opportune election issue. During the 1946 campaign, they sought to channel these consumer frustrations into anti-Labor sentiment. Advertisements thus highlighted the unfulfilled dreams of home ownership and accused the government of denying Australians what they had fought for.[22] This ability to politicise the non-political, writes Judith Brett, was one of Menzies' most successful strategies.[23] The same could be said about the preparedness of the manufacturers, retailers and advertising agencies to commercialise the non-commercial: peace now meant consumption.

A return to normal or the start of a new age?

Looking ahead, the manufacturing, retail, and advertising industries asked whether they were returning to normality or standing on the cusp of a new age. While there were frequent references to returning to pre-war levels of production, distribution, and consumption, most felt that the current climate and the immediate future were both unique. G.L. Wood, for example, rejected the claim that the Australia's manufacturing sector would be reverting to the "good old days:"

> The problem is not merely one of going 'into reverse', because the capital sunk in war-time plants will be kept alive as far as possible for a variety of reasons … Financially and technically it is forward rather than backward gear changes that are called for.[24]

Implicit in Wood's comments is the fear of reliving the economic strains that followed the First World War. These bitter memories informed the advertising industry's wartime activities. As *Newspaper News* noted, wartime advertisers had deliberately worked to keep their "brands and trade marks in the consciousness of buyers, so that the tragic disasters

---

[22] See *Bulletin*, May 8, 1946, 6; June 12, 1946, 5.
[23] Judith Brett, *Robert Menzies' Forgotten People* (Sydney: Sun Australia, 1993), 56.
[24] G.L. Wood, "Prospects for Australian Manufacturers," in *On Marketing*, The Institute of Industrial Management (Melbourne: Ware Publishing, 1946), 7–8.

following the first World War should not be repeated in renewed public forgetfulness."[25]

The ongoing need to keep brand names in the fore of the consumer's mind demonstrated how little conditions had actually changed in the wake of the war. The *Monthly Summary of Australian Conditions* thus warned that the wartime dreams were still a long way away:

> It is now twelve months since the fighting ended … To those who imagined that this country was fighting for some ill-defined Utopia and that success in arms would at once bring a golden age of plenty, the immediate consequences of victory must appear disappointing.[26]

While the report reminded Australians that they were better fed and clothed than consumers elsewhere in the world, the frustrations remained. "There are no homes for returning servicemen, food is still rationed, clothing is still couponed," Rydge fumed, adding, "One cannot buy furniture, carpets, and even the essentials which go to make a home unless one takes a very poor selection at a very high, and sometimes prohibitive, cost."[27]

Frustrations about the unfulfilled expectations also fuelled anxieties. A key concern was the economy and the possibility of another depression. Rydge had flagged the issue in May 1945 and had also urged the government to take active steps to prevent unemployment in the face of demobilisation.[28] Although it soon became apparent that there was a shortage of workers not jobs, fears of an imminent depression lingered. Such fears, as H.G. Magaard observed, stemmed from past experiences:

> World War II has been over for three years and, like a condemned man on the gallows waiting for the trap door to open, many business men have been waiting for the post-war depression. Most of them have no other

---

[25] *Newspaper News*, August 1946, 18.

[26] "Twelve Months of Reconversion," September 10, 1946, in *Monthly Summary of Australian Conditions* (Melbourne: National Bank of Australasia Limited, 1927–1972), 3.

[27] Norman Bede Rydge, "The Atmosphere of Frustration," *Rydge's: The Business Management Monthly* 19, 6 (1946): 505.

[28] Norman Bede Rydge, "Let Us Slip into Peace Gradually," *Rydge's: The Business Management Monthly* 18, 5 (1945): 331.

> reason to expect it than the fact than it happened after 1918. They say this one is already overdue.[29]

While the optimists claimed that there could be no depression when consumers still lacked basic goods and services, the absence of a depression only enhanced the pessimists' anxieties. Both sides, however, remained wary of the government and how it would deal with the economy.

The government's wartime controls over Australia's manufacturing, retail and advertising industries had been accepted as part of the war effort. However, these industries were now uncomfortable with this arrangement. When Japan surrendered, the advertising industry also celebrated the news that "wartime restrictions on advertising have been lifted, and there is now nothing to stop any advertiser from maintaining the goodwill of his 'brand' name with the public."[30] This excitement evaporated when it became clear that the government would continue to monitor advertising expenditure. Basil Orr, president of the Australian Association of National Advertisers (AANA), claimed that this was an unnecessary imposition on the economy and a curtailment of civil liberties.[31] Such comments tacitly reveal further concerns about a Labor government and its socialist platform. Labor's moves to nationalise the banking industry, for example, did not bode well. Ideology, however, ran second to the more pragmatic question of price controlling.

Price control had been implemented during wartime as a means of ensuring that all Australians had equal access to the limited supply of goods. However, many now called for an end to these measures. Writing for *Rydge's* in November 1946, an exasperated "G.L." asked "How long do we have to put up with 'government planning' ... Must we carry the impoverishment process with 'absentee management' of business and industry by a government bureaucracy to the limit it has reached in Europe and Asia?"[32] In his review of the events of 1947, Rydge glumly observed that price controls would still "be with us for an indefinite period as

---

[29] H.G. Magaard, "Must There Be a Depression?," *Rydge's: The Business Management Monthly* 21, 10 (1948): 981.
[30] *Newspaper News*, September 1945, 17.
[31] *Newspaper News*, March 1946, 10.
[32] "G.L.," "Here is Proof," *Rydge's: The Business Management Monthly* 19, 10 (1946): 884.

indicated by the approaching referendum [on bank nationalisation]."[33] But, in October 1948, the advertising industry proudly announced that it was free from price control restrictions. *Newspaper News* noted that the announcement had "come at a very opportune time," as the increases "in the cost of paper, in wages, and in general expenses coupled with the shorter working week has been sorely felt and an increase in advertising costs is stated to be unavoidable in many cases."[34] Other industries were less fortunate and their calls for the abandonment of price control duly increased. In 1949, the former wartime Chief Investigation Officer of Canberra Prices Branch, M.S. Ruddock, questioned the ongoing necessity of this measure:

> But are we any better off now? It would appear that we are. Complete chaos of the price level all the time would surely have been worse than what actually happened ... But we are still not well off, and the position could deteriorate.[35]

Ruddock also drew attention to the ways the laws were being flouted, claiming that "it serves to show how the community is now failing to support a system which it believes to be outmoded and in many instances unjust."[36]

Manufacturers, retailers, and advertising agencies were also concerned about the implementation of the 40-hour week. Some had initially feared that decreased work hours meant a decreased pay packet.[37] Subsequent criticisms contended that the reduced rate of production caused further delays in consumption.[38] The inflated costs of goods—caused by both scarcity and exploitative businesses—were similarly identified as yet another impediment to consumption.[39] If consumption levels were to improve, these industries not only needed to overcome each of the aforementioned obstacles, they would also have to expand on their own

---

[33] Norman Bede Rydge, "1947 in Retrospect," *Rydge's: The Business Management Monthly* 20, 12 (1947): 1090.
[34] *Newspaper News*, October 1948, 1.
[35] M.S. Ruddock, "'Value' Price Control," *Rydge's: The Business Management Monthly* 22, 4 (1949): 357.
[36] Ruddock, "'Value' Price Control,", 357–8.
[37] John Byrnes, "Overcoming Today's Retail Problems," *Rydge's: The Business Management Monthly* 19, 10 (1946): 992.
[38] Ruddock, "'Value' Price Control," 357.
[39] "R.W.," "Saving—For What?," *Rydge's: The Business Management Monthly* 22, 4 (1949): 340.

wartime strategies and develop new ones for meeting the current conditions.

Facing the consumer

In 1942, Frank Goldberg had declared that the role of the post-war advertising industry would be to "educate the masses as to the best means of meeting the exigencies of this period of re-adjustment. Propaganda of the right nature will avert much of the confusion which would otherwise arise."[40] Five years later, concerns about the consumer's capacity to discard thriftiness were still being raised. Writing in *Manufacturing and Management*, Keith Pullman identified wartime habits as an impediment to growth:

> During the war period, consumers were forced to buy any brands available … and many became used to going without … Consumers became used to making things last longer, and this habit may continue. If it does, the first real budget must show this or additional advertising expenditure to influence a return to pre-war expenditure on the product.[41]

However, if the advertising industry was to stimulate further consumption, it needed to get its own house in order; the industry could not falter now. Orr thus told fellow members of the AANA in 1946 that it "would be fatal foolishness to relax our efforts," adding: "As national advertisers we should seek not only to preserve our existing markets, but to reach out for an expanding future market in Australia."[42]

Concerns about consumer behaviour and consumption patterns were exacerbated by the knowledge that the current conditions were in flux, albeit undergoing a gradual rather than a sudden change. Knowing that the current situation was only temporary, Rydge feared that consumers were not the only ones who had forgotten how to behave when trade returned to normal:

> The art of pleasing the public, the art of producing goods at low competitive prices, the art of salesmanship have been lost. Inefficiency, waste, extravagance, can today exist in an organisation and pass by almost

---

[40] Goldberg, "Advertising Must Carry On," 275.

[41] Keith Pullman, "Estimating Post-War Sales," *Manufacturing and Management* 1, 8 (1947): 319.

[42] *Newspaper News*, March 1946, 3.

unnoticed. Anyone who has goods can sell them at a profit. Today is the honeymoon of a seller's market.[43]

Seizing the opportunity, market researchers argued that they could help navigate advertisers through the present uncharted waters. Sylvia Ashby of the Ashby Research Services claimed that advertisers now "want to know the extent to which the public has or has not remembered their brand names."[44] The question on everyone's lips, however, was how long could the honeymoon of the seller's market last?

From a buyer's market to a seller's market

Since 1945, manufacturers, retailers, and advertising agencies had expressed concerns about the state of the market. E.A. Jones of Vacuum Oil typified these views:

> [N]o one can afford to be complacent, and think the present strong demand for domestic commodities will last indefinitely, for the day will come when consumers' personal stocks and reserves are satisfactorily re-built, when merchants' and resellers' shelves are once again filled, and then business will find its normal level.[45]

While the seller's market spanning the 1940s ensured that sales remained strong, it was a false economy and one that did not offer any great profits. A buyer's market would mean that manufacturers, retailers, and advertising agencies would have to work harder to attract their share of the market, but the potential financial returns were much higher.

By mid-1946, a growing number of consumer goods were in fact finding their way to the consumer. Although shortages were being experienced in the areas of "clothing, footwear, soft furnishings and speciality food lines," the *Monthly Summary of Australian Conditions* nevertheless found that a "wider range of articles, such as furniture, radios and electrical appliances, many types of hardware and sporting goods, has appeared in increased quantities in the shops."[46] The prevailing view,

---

[43] Norman Bede Rydge, "The Honeymoon of a Seller's Market," *Rydge's: The Business Management Monthly* 21, 6 (1948): 529.
[44] *Newspaper News*, March 1947, 5.
[45] E.A. Jones, "Facts, Not Guesses in Marketing," in *On Marketing*, The Institute of Industrial Management (Melbourne: Ware Publishing, 1946), 25.
[46] "Twelve Months of Reconversion," 10 September 1946, 4.

however, was that this was too little and too slow. Two years later, the buyer's market was still being discussed in the future tense. Eric Avery of GM Shell thus drew attention to "the inevitability of a buyer's market," adding that "elements of a buyer's market are already with us in certain directions, and the interval which may elapse before it is more completely with us may not be very long for a variety of further products."[47]

Press outlets sought to convince advertisers that they were perfectly poised to capitalise on this inevitable shift. Throughout the late 1940s, the *Daily Telegraph*'s campaign in *Newspaper News* told potential advertisers that the "Age of Accumulation" had arrived and that it was the perfect medium to reach them:

> People under 36 do most buying ... These are the people ... the families ... in the Age of Accumulation ... 66% of the sales of 47 of the most popular everyday commodities were made to people under the age of 36. After 36 buying slows up ... Our readers are the heavy spenders ... Go straight to them ... influence them ... educate them in the use of your product ... *sell* to them in the *Daily Telegraph*.[48]

While the "Age of Accumulation" campaign had initially run just prior to the outbreak of war, its reappearance throughout the second half of the decade suggests that it was now tapping into different sentiments. The idea of educating consumers played on the industry's own fears that it might have lost touch over the past few years.

By 1948, it was becoming clearer that the seller's market would be ending sooner rather than later. While many problems remained, it was stressed that they were not permanent and that each day brought the keenly anticipated consumer age closer:

> [D]ecentralisation ... will cause new consumer centres to be established. Again, the contemplated increase in the population by migration will provide a larger market ... Housing activity will soon reach a peak and then decline; this will have an influence on the demand for a very wide range of products ... Shortage of domestics, a war-born condition, has brought a greater potential market for mechanical appliances in the home

[47] Eric Avery, "Spring Cleaning the Selling Organisation," in *Meeting the Buyer's Market: Proceedings of the Sixth Australian One-Day Top Management Conference* (Institute of Industrial Management: Melbourne, 1948), 36.
[48] *Newspaper News*, July, 1946, 16–17.

> … Managers cannot long delay taking action on the formulation of a sales policy to meet the conditions that will be ruling in a year or two.[49]

The growing number of immigrants arriving in Australia was further complemented by the baby boom. "The number of families is increasing … many of the new families have been living with parents and sharing homes. Consider the fillip to demand when these people move into their own homes," enthused Rydge. Not only would this stimulate further manufacturing, he pointed out that:

> Our hospitals will have larger clinics; there will be a greater demand for medicine and medical treatment … More people will sleep on more mattresses between more sheets and under more blankets every night and each morning more will rise to take their stand beside the wheels of industry. This is healthy growth.[50]

Admen such as Coleman were equally aware of this baby boom and the opportunities it promised. "Babies are one of the most important factors in building a market," he observed, before adding somewhat bluntly, "If all else fails, an appeal to maternal and paternal instinct will take care of a lot of selling."[51] The industry's images certainly confirmed this point. Smiling families with a number of children and an ever-present baby were common images in post-war advertisements.[52] Such developments augured well. Although the impending buyer's market was as tantalising as it was frustrating, the future nevertheless looked to be in good shape.

Conclusion

Looking back on the immediate post-war period, adman John Bryden-Brown recalled that: "In the years 1945 to 1952 practically anything made

---

[49] "Future Marketing Plans Need Formulating Now," *Manufacturing and Management* 3, 1 (1948): 1.

[50] Norman Bede Rydge, "Babies Mean Business," *Rydge's: The Business Management Monthly* 21, 3 (1948): 217.

[51] Lloyd Ring Coleman, "The Potential of the Home Market," in *Meeting the Buyer's Market: Proceedings of the Sixth Australian One-Day Top Management Conference* (Melbourne: Institute of Industrial Management, 1948), 65.

[52] Robert Crawford, "Selling a Nation: Depictions of Australian National Identity in Press Advertisements 1900–1969," (PhD diss., Monash University, 2002), Chapter 8.

of metal, painted and fitted with an electric motor, was easily sold."[53] The seller's market, it seems, continued into the 1950s—a point confirmed by McLeod.[54] However, the new decade arrived with some discernible changes. Menzies had been elected into power on the back of Cold War rhetoric. Vehemently opposed to Labor's bank nationalisation and petrol rationing, Menzies celebrated the sanctity of the home and the "Australian way of life." The latter concept, as Richard White notes, was implicitly tied "to the image of Australia as a sophisticated, urban, industrialised, consumer society" that also "suited the needs of an Australian manufacturing sector which was increasingly aligning itself with the United States."[55] The Korean conflict symbolised this emergent relationship. In addition to enhancing the Australian–American alliance, the freezing climate in Korea also proved to be a financial windfall for Australia's wool industry. Locally, the baby boom and the influx of immigrants generated a growing list of needs (and desires). To this end, the future looked good.

Signs of improvement were also discernible in other parts of the economy. *Newspaper News* gleefully reported that the healthy advertising statistics for the financial year ending June 1950 had revealed that "the losses which followed the outbreak of hostilities towards the end of 1939, and further declines due to newsprint rationing and restrictions during the post war period, have been largely offset."[56] Contributors to *Rydge's* similarly suggested that the seller's honeymoon was ending. In 1950, J.S. Cockshaw, the managing director of the Robert Reid & Co. stores, announced that the future had arrived for the apparel business:

> Today, we are in a buyer's market. The entire position has changed ... When goods are short, the emphasis is on production. But now, the emphasis has changed to distribution. Today, the salesman has returned to his important place in the Australian economy.[57]

---

[53] John Bryden-Brown, "The Way Advertising works Today (Part 1)," *Rydge's: The Business Management Monthly* 32, 3 (1959): 215.
[54] McLeod, *Abundance*, 2.
[55] Richard White, *Inventing Australia: Images and Identity 1688–1980* (Sydney: Allen & Unwin, 1982), 161–2.
[56] *Newspaper News*, September 1950, 1.
[57] J.S. Cockshaw, "How Robert Reid Ltd Approach the Salesman's Market," *Rydge's: The Business Management Monthly* 23, 9 (1950): 914.

It had been a long wait. While it had been keenly anticipated, the golden age that that manufacturers, retailers and advertising agencies had constantly promised was never guaranteed. Restrictions and shortages, government controls, and the deep-seated fears of an imminent depression had all threatened to derail these industries' dreams of unfettered consumption. Yet these insecurities would prove to be a worthy motivator, pushing them to sell themselves even harder. And, after almost a decade of constant promises, their efforts were finally paying off. The buyer's market had arrived, but the desire to consume showed no signs of abating. In selling themselves and their brands to the consumer, it seems that the nation's advertisers had also succeeded in selling the culture of consumption to the nation.

CHAPTER FOUR

"THE 24-HOUR WOMAN": FEMINISM AND THE POLITICS OF CONSUMPTION IN 1980S AUSTRALIA

NATASHA CAMPO

In 1980, *Cleo* magazine ran a series of advertisements for a new cosmetic. A succession of images features a young, attractive woman with the caption, "24 hours in the life of Fresh Lash Mascara." We see her beating a friend at tennis, swimming laps in a pool and, after a day of revelry, relaxing with a glass of wine. "I feel on top of the world after 10 laps and my Fresh Lash still looks terrific," she says; even "way past midnight my Fresh Lash has stayed on all day, all night".[1] The message here is clear: in the decade following the advent of second-wave feminism in Australia, women were free to live their lives, on their own terms, 24 hours a day.

In response to feminists such as Germaine Greer, who encouraged women to "recapture [their] own will" and "explore their own desires,"[2] many of the popular images of women in the 1980s showed them actively engaging in various activities unencumbered by domestic responsibilities. Indeed, "Fresh Lash Mascara" was just one product of the many consumer industries that, keen to capitalise on the changes wrought in women's lives by feminism, re-presented and re-packaged feminism's message. In doing so, they brought into being a new subject position: the "24-Hour Woman." Liberated from the constraining expectations of marriage and motherhood, and freed from female "conditioning," the 24-Hour Woman was constantly "on the go," engaging in all life's pleasures and zipping between her different roles with efficiency and ease. Like other representations of femininity, this new identity was a figure of aspiration, but in reality it was a position only available to those who could purchase the right products.

---

[1] *Cleo*, April 1982, 65.

[2] Germaine Greer, *The Female Eunuch* (London: Paladin, 1971), 323.

Advertisements played explicitly on the idea of empowerment through consumption, and women were encouraged to consume as a means of expressing the financial and emotional independence feminism had won for them.

The figure of 24-Hour Woman spoke to wider social changes during the 1980s too. During that decade, Australia underwent a period of rapid social, political and economic transformation, particularly following the election of Bob Hawke's Labor government in 1983. In the wake of the electoral disaster of 1975, when Labor Prime Minister Gough Whitlam was dismissed by the Governor General, the Hawke government asserted that it would seek "to lay the ghost of Whitlam's reputation for economic mismanagement" as it tried to "pursue a commitment to social reform."[3] The government came to power on a largely conventional social democratic Labor platform, but quickly adopted a policy that came to be known as "economic rationalism," where fiscal efficiency became paramount.[4]

In this new economically competitive climate, wealth was flaunted and a new "class" of urban professionals emerged, embodying what seemed to be a new national ethos. It was in the 1980s that the term "yuppies" was coined to describe the ascendancy of the new generation of "young, upwardly mobile, urban professionals." Aged between 25 and 35, yuppies had a tertiary education and worked in middle to upper management positions. Significantly, they had disposable incomes and were willing to spend them, particularly on luxury goods, travel, health and fitness. Yuppies were defined by their "lifestyle" and "conspicuous consumption" and expressed themselves, and their success, as much through their carefully chosen brand names and leisure activities, as by their mode of employment.[5]

---

[3] Geoffrey Bolton, *The Oxford History of Australia, Volume 5: The Middle Way 1942–1995* (Melbourne: Oxford University Press, 1996), 276; Patricia Grimshaw, Marilyn Lake, Anne McGrath and Marian Quartly, *Creating a Nation: 1788–1990* (Melbourne: McPhee Gribble, 1996), 308.

[4] See Susan Ryan, *Catching the Waves: Life In and Out of Politics* (Melbourne: Harper Collins, 1999), 248–52.

[5] Greg Bailey, *Mythologies of Change and Certainty in Late 20th Century Australia* (Melbourne: Australian Scholarly Publishing, 2000), 184; Glenda Korporall, "Corporate America Discovers Youthfully Aggressive Yuppies," *Australian Financial Review,* October 19, 1984, 44. Elisabeth Whynhausen, "Yuppies—Origin of the Species," *Sydney Morning Herald*, October 4, 1986, 42.

In many ways, the 24-Hour Woman was a female version of the yuppie. Already primed to market to this "New Class," advertisers and publishers recognised women's desire to step out of their traditional roles and embrace the signifiers of success, and they developed a range of new products accordingly.[6] The1980s woman was faced with seemingly unlimited possibilities in the new context of equality, opportunity and affluence, and the implication was that she would take on a number of the various roles on offer, whether business woman, sexy mistress, fit athlete or party girl. Being busy and on the go (in more than one activity), while remaining sexually alluring throughout, consequently became a marker of modern youthful femininity and a sign of women's liberation.

Of course, it was not feminists who narrated this new story about Australian womanhood. Getting women into the workforce and winning for them the right to engage in all aspects of public life had been major feminist goals shared by most women's groups in the 1970s. And, in many ways, they had been successful. By the mid-1980s, many feminist demands, such as equal pay, federally funded childcare, and sex-discrimination and affirmative action legislation, had been met.[7] While feminists of all persuasions certainly celebrated their success, there was always an implicit understanding that these reforms alone would not

---

[6] Myra McDonald, *Representing Women: Myths of Femininity in the Popular Media* (London: Edward Arnold, 1995), 90.

[7] See Lyndall Ryan, "Feminism and the Federal Bureaucracy 1972–1983," in *Playing the State: Australian Feminist Interventions*, ed. Sophie Watson (Sydney: Allen & Unwin, 1990), 71–84; Marian Simms, "The Australian Feminist Experience," in *Australian Women: Feminist Perspectives*, ed. Norma Grieve and Patricia Grimshaw (Melbourne: Oxford University Press, 1981), 227–39; Sarah Dowse, "The Women's Movement's Fandango with the State: The Movement's Role in Public Policy since 1972," in *Women, Social Welfare and the State in Australia*, ed. Cora Baldock and Bettina Cass (Sydney: George Allen and Unwin, 1983), 205; Marian Sawer and Marian Simms, *A Woman's Place: Women and Politics in Australia* (Sydney: George Allen and Unwin, 1984); Marian Sawer, "Women: The Long March through the Institutions," in *From Fraser to Hawke: Australian Public Policy in the 1980s*, ed. Brian Head and Allan Patience (Melbourne: Longman Cheshire, 1989), 43; Marian Sawer, *Sisters in Suits: Women and Public Policy in Australia* (Sydney: Allen & Unwin, 1990), 10–11; Marilyn Lake, *Getting Equal: The History of Australian Feminism* (Sydney: Allen and Unwin, 1999), 264–5; Susan Ryan and Troy Bramston, *The Hawke Government: A Critical Retrospective* (Melbourne: Pluto Press, 2003), 202; Susan Magarey, "The Sex Discrimination Act 1984," *Australian Feminist Law Journal* 20 (2004): 127–33.

redress women's inequality in the public sphere. As it had emerged from the socialist movement (the New Left), 1970s Australian feminist theory was well aware of the limits of productive work as the means to liberation.[8] The goal of much feminist activism in this era was therefore the overthrow of capitalism and its replacement with a socialist society where men and women would share in productive and reproductive labour. It was the "sexual division of labour," and its attendant structures—the workplace and the home—that were identified as the problem, the cause of women's oppression.[9] Thus women's integration into the workplace on men's terms would never be the answer. Although socialist feminism eventually lost its discursive hold in Australian feminist debates, these ideas were still asserted through calls for paid maternity leave and a reduction of the standard working week—key feminist platforms throughout the 1980s and 90s.[10]

The success of these legislative reforms, however, did lead the Australian women's movement to privilege women's employment and integration into the public sphere over its original goals, namely the

---

[8] Women's Liberationists in Australia drew on the work of Marxist feminist historians such as Juliet Mitchell, *Women's Estate* (London: Penguin, 1971); Sheila Rowbotham, *Woman's Consciousness, Man's World* (London: Penguin, 1973); Kate Millet, *Sexual Politics* (London: Virago, 1972).

[8] Greer, *The Female Eunuch*; Lake, *Getting Equal*, 228; Anne Summers, *Ducks on the Pond: An Autobiography 1945–1976* (Melbourne: Viking/Penguin, 1999). See also Anne Coombs, *Sex and Anarchy: The Life and Death of the Sydney Push* (Melbourne: Viking, 1996).

[9] See also Ann Curthoys, *For and Against Feminism* (Sydney: George Allen and Unwin, 1988); Patricia Grimshaw, "Only the Chains Have Changed," in *Staining the Wattle: A People's History of Australia since 1788,* ed. Verity Burgmann and Jenny Lee (Melbourne: McPhee Gribble, 1988), 66–88; Ann Curthoys, "Doing it for Themselves: The Contemporary Women's Movement," in *Gender Relations in Australia: Domination and Negotiation*, ed. Kay Saunders and Raymond Evans (Sydney: Harcourt Brace Jovanovich, 1992), 425–7; Ann Curthoys, "Australian Feminism since 1970," in *Australian Women: Contemporary Feminist Thought*, ed. Norma Grieve and Ailsa Burns (Melbourne: Oxford University Press, 1994), 14–28; Gisela Kaplan, *A Meagre Harvest: The Woman's Movement 1950s–1990s* (Sydney: Allen & Unwin, 1996); Katy Reade, "Struggling to Be Heard: Tensions between Different Voices in the Australian Women's Liberation Movement in the 1970s and 1980s," in *Contemporary Australian Feminism*, ed. Kate Pritchard Hughes (Melbourne: Longman Chesire, 1994), 198–222; Lake, *Getting Equal.*

[10] See Marilyn Lake, "A Question of Time," in *Moving Left: The Future of Socialism in Australia,* ed. David McKnight (Sydney: Pluto Press, 1986), 135; Kaye Hargreaves, *Women at Work* (Melbourne: Penguin Books, 1982).

abolition of sex roles and the restructuring of society. In the effort to translate feminist ideas into government policy, feminist practice lost some of its original critique and many women were caught by the "catch-22" of feminism. As many forged careers as public servants, lobbyists, politicians and corporate executives, they became "more integrally part of a male-defined world and less able to resist it."[11] The new brand of feminism to emerge after the flourish of Women's Liberation had a distinctly liberal vision; the goal reverted from liberation to equality with men. The ensuing focus therefore concerned the rewards of the workplace and success in the public sphere.

It was these aspects of feminism that were taken up by the popular media, most significantly by women's magazines, which glorified success in the workplace and in the public sphere through the figure of the 24-Hour Woman. This figure represented these developments in the popular media and thereby turned the challenge of women's increased employment and freedom into an attractive and appealing narrative. However, the more revolutionary aspects of the feminist critique were forgotten in this process.

Both *Cleo* and *Cosmopolitan* magazines played an integral role in cultivating the image of the 24-Hour Woman. Australian Consolidated Press had founded *Cleo* in 1972 after losing the deal to Fairfax to run the Australian edition of *Cosmopolitan*. Ita Buttrose, an ambitious young journalist, was appointed *Cleo*'s inaugural editor. The magazine was an instant success, and within five years it had grown to be the fifth largest selling magazine in Australia. *Cleo* was directed at the new female type Buttrose called "the progressive woman": young and middle-class, who wanted more than marriage and motherhood but found Women's Liberation "too aggressive."[12] *Cosmopolitan* magazine was also aimed at the "modern woman." Originally founded as a general interest periodical, it was revamped in 1965 as a magazine devoted to the interests of the young career woman. Under the direction of Helen Gurley Brown, the American author of the best-selling book, *Sex and the Single Girl*, it became hugely successful. Launched in Australia in 1973, it, like *Cleo*, had an ambivalent relationship to the women's movement. *Cosmopolitan*

---

[11] Hazel Moir, "Comment on 'Women in the Australian Labour Force'," in *Unfinished Business: Social Justice for Women in Australia*, ed. Dorothy H. Broom (Sydney: George Allen and Unwin, 1984), 97.

[12] Ita Buttrose, *A Passionate Life* (Melbourne: Viking, 1998), 4; *Cleo*, November 1972, 4.

represented feminism as a success and encouraged young women to celebrate their success through their purchasing power.[13]

The most important sphere of activity for the new 24-Hour Woman, a female embodiment of the "yuppie," was consumption. Feature articles in women's magazines, which admonished women, in the face of feminism's successes, to "take control of their lives," also recommended that they buy products as a means of their self-creation.[14] Advertisements emphasised the idea of empowerment through consumption. As Hilary Radner has commented, they promised "to transform looks into accomplishments through consumerism."[15] Max Factor cosmetics, for instance, ran an advertising campaign for their "Colorfast" range, which promised women the means to live a busy life. Colorfast cosmetics, women were told, would last all through the day, because who "has time for touch-ups after lunch," indeed, "who has time for lunch?"[16] It also promised to work on into the evening, allowing consumers to "dance all night" without the need to reapply. Moreover, it sought to induce confidence, energy and stamina because, if "you can keep pace without fading, why shouldn't your lipstick?"[17]

Although these advertisements were playing on the old-fashioned idea of women as vain and self-obsessed, they were also acknowledging women's new desire to be active and to perform in more than one guise—something both feminism and economic independence had promised them. Being a successful woman in the 1980s meant leading a "hectic" and "frantic" life, where an individual woman could act in an astonishing number of roles in a single day or night. We also see an explicit engagement with the yuppie ethos—fulfilment and success through overwork, wealth and consumption.

---

[13] Oliver Whitehorne, *'Cosmo Woman': The World of Women's Magazines* (Worcestershire: Crescent Moon, 1997), 3.

[14] "All About You: Dare to Be the Woman You've Secretly Longed to Be," *Cleo*, September 1980, 92–6.

[15] Hilary Radner, *Shopping Around: Feminine Culture and the Pursuit of Pleasure* (London/New York: Routledge, 1995), 56.

[16] *Australian Women's Weekly*, March 24, 1982, 24–5.

[17] *Australian Women's Weekly*, March 24, 1982, 24–5.

Of course, advertisers had long appealed to women through their role as objects of heterosexual desire.[18] What was different about these new constructions in the 1980s, however, was that advertisers courted women as members of a new generation of self-consciously liberated women. They were invited to consume, not just as a means to sexual attractiveness, but as a way to enable their multifaceted, energetic and active lives. Shopping was no longer "the recreational activity of the bored housewife who must incarnate her husband's wealth and success." It became, rather, the means through which a woman externalised her self-worth as "properly her own."[19]

The idea of empowerment achieved through endless activity was perhaps best expressed by advertisements for car companies marketing specially designed vehicles to yuppies and, by implication, the 24-Hour Woman. Thanks to feminism, she now had a larger disposable income and needed a stylish car that could accommodate her many personas and busy lifestyle.[20]

In a special promotion in *Cleo*, Ford turned its attention to "today's woman" who "knows she can have it all … good looks, sheer class, winning spirit" and, of course, "style." Ford Laser, the advertisement continued, was perfect for "zipping around the city or heading for the beach … where ever your busy lifestyle leads."[21] The image showed a young, glamorous woman leaning against her car and staring into the distance, perhaps imagining the endless possibilities her new life (with her Laser) held. Similarly, Toyota told women its new "Spirit Hatch" was "Specifically designed for busy women who've more to pack into their week than ever before;" it offered "just the sort of reliability you need at the start of a demanding week."[22]

---

[18] Jill Matthews, *Good and Mad Women: The Historical Construction of Femininity in Twentieth Century Australia* (Sydney: George Allen and Unwin, 1984); Marilyn Lake, "Female Desires: The Meaning of World War Two," in *Gender and War: Australians at War in the Twentieth Century,* ed. Joy Damousi and Marilyn Lake (Melbourne: Cambridge University Press, 1995), 60–80; Susan Sheridan, ed., *Who Was that Woman? The Australian Women's Weekly in the Post War Years* (Sydney: UNSW Press, 2002).
[19] Radner, *Shopping Around*, 64.
[20] A. Kennedy, "Fun Cars Will Miss Yuppies," *Sydney Morning Herald*, December 5, 1987, 44; Christopher De Fraga, "Luxury Wheels May Be a Thing of the Past," *Sydney Morning Herald*, April 19, 1990, 6.
[21] *Cleo*, November 1983, 75.
[22] *Cleo*, November 1987, 28–33.

These advertisements were particularly significant because cars were traditionally a consumer item associated with men that often promised them the freedom and power of masculinity.[23] The fact that car companies were marketing to women suggests the dramatic change in ideas about femininity precipitated by feminism. By encouraging women to pursue financial independence and physical freedom, feminists had inadvertently created a new market for consumer industries to target: 24-Hour Women, who needed their own cars to lead independent, fulfilling and glamorous lives.

Cars were necessary to enable "today's women" mobility. Travel was another important element in this new round of endless activity and consumption. The 24-Hour Woman was encouraged to spend her money and enjoy her independence, power and career success, not just through buying a car but in exotic and luxurious escapes. Travel sections in women's magazines recognised the new market of the lone female traveller. Advertisers in particular gratified women's desire for adventure through the use of the language of the "exotic."[24] Women did not even have to actually travel to experience adventure; they could consume it through their use of cosmetics, perfume and fashion.

Cleo regularly photographed their fashion features in "exotic" locations, for instance Fiji, Sumatra or Cape Town, where out-of-the-ordinary locations and peoples defined the freedom and independence of the modern (white) woman.[25] Cosmetics companies had long indulged this reverie[26] and, in the 1980s, explicitly used the discourse of the exotic to advertise their wares. Women could adorn themselves with Revlon's "China Reds" and experience the "magic and mystery of the Orient."[27] Or they could use Elizabeth Arden's "Primitives," which spoke "of lost civilizations and ancient cultures,"[28] while Madame Gres perfume allowed

---

[23] Diane Barthel, "When Men Put on Appearances," in *Men, Masculinity and the Media,* ed. Steve Craig (Newbury Park CA: Sage, 1992), 144–5; Joanne Finkelstein, *Slaves of Chic: An A–X of Consumer Pleasures* (Melbourne: Minerva, 1994), 27–32.

[24] Wendy Chapkis, *Beauty Secrets: Women and the Politics of Appearance* (Boston: Southend Press, 1986).

[25] "Fashion Safari," *Cleo* September 1981, 50–74; "Island Idyll," *Cleo,* August 1981, 90; "On the White Trail in Western Sumatra," *Cleo*, January 1981, 36.

[26] Lake, "Female Desires," 60–80.

[27] *Cleo*, April 1980, 28–9.

[28] *Cleo*, September 1982, 62–3.

women to be "seduced by the oriental mystique" of India.[29] Through purchasing these exotic products, the 24-Hour Woman could experience adventure and the allure of the "Oriental" vicariously. The non-western world functioned here as the source of sensuality, adventure and exoticism, thereby constituting femininity itself as Anglo/European. The reader (and the 24-Hour Woman with her) is thus assumed to be "white."[30]

Sex was more important than travel and consumption for the self-fulfilment of the 24-Hour Woman. The 24-Hour Woman was not only sexually active, she was sexually *pro-active*, the pursuer rather than the pursued. As in Britain and the US, 1970s feminism in Australia departed from earlier feminist platforms by claiming the right for women to be sexually active on the same terms as men.[31] Moreover, like the yuppie, the 24-Woman was usually single and had no desire for marriage or motherhood. There was simply too much fun to be had being free. Women's magazines in the 1980s regularly engaged with the idea that women could now enjoy sex too—whether they were in or out of relationships. Readers were encouraged to explore their sexual desires as part of their liberation: to embrace the position of sexual subject. Buttrose saw it as *Cleo*'s task to inform women about their sexuality and their bodies, including how to pleasure themselves.[32] *Cleo* magazine was groundbreaking for its inclusion of a male centrefold in recognition of women's right to "the gaze," and there was strong encouragement to sexual exploration.[33] However, there was always an implicit caution

[29] *Cleo*, May 1982, 87.

[30] Barbara Brook, "Femininity and Culture: Some Notes on the Gendering of Women in Australia," in *Contemporary Australian Feminism Two*, ed. Kate Pritchard Hughes (Melbourne: Longman Cheshire, 1997), 121–2.

[31] Zelda D'Aprano, for instance, spoke about her friends buying each other dildos. Zelda D'Aprano, *Zelda* (Melbourne: Spinifex, 1995). See also Summers, *Ducks on the Pond*; Boston Women's Health Collective, *Our Bodies, Our Selves* (New York: Simon and Schuster, 1972); Curthoys, "Doing It for Themselves".

[32] "Editorial," *Cleo*, November 1982, 10; Buttrose, *A Passionate Life*; Interview with Ita Buttrose, Sydney, July 22, 2004.

[33] Centrefolds ran from 1972 to 1985, when new editor Lisa Wilkinson decided that equal objectification did not equal equality: Lisa Wilkinson, "Editorial," *Cleo*, June 1985, 11; Jenny Cullen, "Tails, Taut and Terrific: The Newest Erogenous Zone," *Cleo*, March 1981, 76–8; Priscilla Flood, "In the Flesh: What Women Love best about Men's Bodies Part by Part," *Cleo*, September 1981, 32–6; Bettina Arndt, "Love, Sex and the Australian Woman: Sealed Section," *Cleo,* September 1985, 131–7; Tara Barker, "Tasteful Pornography: Would You Buy It?," *Cleo*, June 1989, 113–17, 206.

against wanton promiscuity. Women should feel free to express their sexual desire, but not at the expense of their own safety or autonomy; they should always feel in control and use protection.[34]

Advertisements invited the 24-Hour Woman to use her purchasing power to buy the means to sexual liberation and fulfilment. An advertisement for Kayser Kapers—women's underwear—for instance, showed three women, clad only in their "Kapers," straddling a semi-naked man, one actually riding him like a horse, while another looks on, obviously amused. The three women stare at the viewer confidently yet playfully, making it obvious who the sexual aggressors are. The woman looking on wears glasses and a suit jacket—markers of a professional woman—over her naked torso. She is no sex object; she is a liberated woman, a sex subject and totally in control.[35] An advertisement for Clairol hair products similarly positioned the 24-Hour Woman in control: "Change your hairstyle as often as you change your mind … Now you can have one style for breakfast with Bob. Another style for lunch with Leonard. Yet another for dinner with Dave." This is an explicit invitation for women to explore and purchase their potential for sexual promiscuity—an incitement to endless sexual activity that is no longer confined to love or marriage.[36]

The 24-Hour Woman was encouraged to consume in order to enhance the sexuality of her male partner, too, just as men had always bought sexy lingerie for women. An advertisement for Jockey underwear, for instance, had the caption "if a woman dresses for a man, why can't a man dress for a woman." It showed a male model—clad only in Jockeys—his muscular, hairless torso rippling in the spotlight, being watched by a similarly scantily clad woman, who is clearly appreciative of his form.[37] More telling was a 1985 advertisement for Speedos: three blonde-haired, suntanned young women lean on their surfboards admiring the shapely behind of a blonde-haired man who dashes past them into the surf. The

[34] Wendy McCarthy, the then chairperson of the Australian Federation of Family Planning and an active member of the Women's Electoral Lobby, was the resident health adviser at *Cleo* in the early 1980s. In this capacity, she often warned readers of the dangers of sexually transmitted diseases and unwanted pregnancies, while at the same time encouraging women to explore their sexuality.

[35] *Cleo*, November 1982, 39.

[36] *Cleo*, December 1984, 21–2.

[37] *Cleo*, November 1982, 226–7.

caption reads "playing him at his own game."[38] This advertisement signifies a clear shift in sexual relations: women could be voyeurs too.

Although it has been argued that these images are regressive and that positive and powerful representations of women's sexuality were heavily outnumbered by those that continued to depict them as sex objects, others have argued that images must be analysed through a consideration of the cultural context in which they are received.[39] It could be argued that these images *were* empowering, showing, as they did, women being sexually assertive rather than passive. Either way, their existence is important in signifying an important shift in the meaning of femininity. Women could be sexual agents, too, without fear of condemnation. To be sexually liberated meant being empowered.

Another important area in which 24-Hour Women were encouraged to consume was physical fitness. Indeed, for women of the 1980s, there was an explicit connection drawn between their physical strength and their "empowerment," which, again, was a matter of consumption. While the fitness craze of the 1980s also affected men, exercise had increased significance for women because vigorous physical activity symbolised their desire to break away from ideas of feminine passivity and weakness, and gave the impression of strength, power and control.[40] Throughout the 1980s in Australia, as in America, depictions of the "new body beautiful"—the strong yet feminine body—could be found everywhere, in newspapers, magazines, movies and television, and connections were soon made between this new ideal shape and feminism: liberated women desired strong bodies to mirror their inner strength.[41]

For the first time, muscles for women were "sexy"[42] and female body builders were hailed as the embodiment of this new ideal form.[43] Here,

---

[38] *Cleo*, November 1985, 34–5.

[39] See, for instance, Rosemary Betterton, ed., *Looking On: Images of Femininity in the Visual Arts and Media* (London: Pandora, 1987); Catherine Lumby, *Bad Girls: The Media, Sex and Feminism in the 90s* (Sydney: Allen & Unwin, 1997).

[40] For instance: "The Sporting Woman: Every Bit as Good as He Is!," *Cleo*, February 1981, 83–8; Anne Woodham, "Competition Is the Game and We're all Players," *Cleo*, August 1981, 136–40.

[41] "Fit for '83'," *Sydney Morning Herald,* January 9, 1983, Tempo section, 109; Lynda Gray, "The New Body Beautiful," *Sydney Morning Herald*, July 3, 1983, Tempo section, 130.

[42] Cullen, "Tails, Taut and Terrific."

"bodily discipline" produced "empowered" rather than "docile" bodies.[44] While the ideal female body in the 1980s—slender and appealing to the male gaze—was constructed to be "looked at," it was also physically strong; working out became "an assertion of control."[45] However, it remained imperative that women retain their femininity. Ultra-fit yet beautiful Hollywood heroines such as Bo Derek and Jane Fonda were thus celebrated for their embodiment of the new ideals of female beauty and power.

This connection between physical exercise and liberation was demonstrated by a number of advertisements that recognised the new demands on women, which required special products. A now infamous advertisement for "Carefree" tampons, for instance, showed a young woman windsurfing, with the slogan "Total freedom? Why settle for less?" Women had come "a long way" from the old days when having a period meant being "unwell," it said. Menstruation need not impact on women's lives at all, either in pursuing their careers or in leading active lives.[46] An advertisement for Tampax engaged with the same ideas, informing its viewers that these tampons were "for active women, for busy

---

[43] See Susan Butler, "Revising Femininity: Review of *Lady,* Photographs of Lisa Lyon by Robert Mapplethorpe," in *Looking On*, ed. Betterton, 120–6; Susan Price-Root, "Lisa Lyon—Superbody," *Cleo*, August 1980, 90–9; Terence Man, "Women Muscle In," *Australian Women's Weekly*, September 1988, 77–9.

[44] Diana Goldsmith, "Women Working Out" (Honours diss., La Trobe University, 1996); Sandra Dworkin, "'Holding Back': Negotiating a Glass Ceiling on Women's Muscular Strength," in *The Politics of Women's Bodies: Sexuality, Appearance and Behaviour*, ed. Rosemary Weitz (New York: Oxford University Press, 2003), 240–56.

[45] Radner, 45. See Susan Bordo, "The Body and the Reproduction of Femininity: A Feminist Appropriation of Foucault," in *Gender/Body/Knowledge*, ed. Alison Jagger and Susan Bordo (New Brunswick: Rutgers University Press, 1989), 13–34; Susan Bordo, "Material Girl: The Effacements of Postmodern Culture," in *The Madonna Connection: Representational Politics, Subcultural Identities and Cultural Theory*, ed. Cathy Schwichtenberg (Sydney: Allen & Unwin, 1993), 265—91; Susan Bordo, *Unbearable Weight: Feminism, Western Culture and the Body* (Berkley: University of California Press, 1993); Susan Bordo, "Feminism, Foucault and the Politics of the Body," in *Up Against Foucault: Explorations of Some Tensions between Foucault and Feminism*, ed. Caroline Ramazanaglu (London/New York, Routledge, 1993), 179–202; Susan J. Douglas, *Where the Girls Are: Growing up Female with the Mass Media* (London: Penguin, 1995); Susan Bordo, *The Hidden Life of Images from Plato to OJ* (Berkeley: University of California Press, 1997).

[46] *Cleo*, July 1984, 20.

women; for times when you find yourself somewhere a tampon simply couldn't be changed." Here, we see a blonde-haired, youthful woman in her office, on a date, and skiing the slopes. She is not only a career woman and a lover, she is also an active woman who does not let her femininity or menstruation impact on her active life. She could be feminine and successful in a man's world, but only with the help of Tampax.[47] "Women's Mega vitamins" were similarly aimed at the woman whose "hectic daily activities" and "frantic social life" caused her "to neglect her diet." The subject of this advertisement is also shown in different settings: in a leotard; at work; playing tennis with a friend; in her new car; in a pair of sexy bathers; and in an evening dress.[48] In each advertisement, the depicted women are strong, liberated, active, and very busy.

Women of the 1980s were encouraged to take up physical exercise (and purchase the attendant products), not only to improve their heterosexual attractiveness but also to give them the energy they needed to perform these multiple roles. Being sexy no longer meant being a sex object. Sex appeal was constructed as a by-product of women's self-confidence and personal power and the fact that, because of feminism, they were more in touch with their own bodies than ever before.[49] However, while it was suggested that the new body beautiful was available to all women who were willing to work hard, it was in fact restricted to women of particular race, class, size and age. The ideal "look" was more often than not that of a young, white-skinned, blonde-haired, slender and middle-class woman. Supermodel Elle McPherson, for instance, was quickly labelled "the Great Aussie Body" of the decade, ostensibly because she made feminine strength "sexy," but also because she presented a normative image of Australian womanhood.[50]

Despite the oft-repeated idea that a fit, healthy body was all that was required to become "today's woman," 24-Hour Women had to dress their active bodies, too. The fashion industry recognised a lucrative new market, and designers created clothes with the 24-Hour Woman in mind. Young designer Felicity Rulikowski, for instance, told *Cleo* how she designed comfortable clothes for the typical 28-year-old woman, who was "very busy, going straight from work out to dinner" and needed clothes that

---

[47] *Cleo*, June 1980, 195

[48] *Cleo*, May 1988, 16.

[49] Nikki Barrowclough, "What Makes Us Sexy Now: The New Allure," *Cleo*, July 1984, 32–4.

[50] Helen Hawkes, "The Great Aussie Body," *Cleo*, October 1988, 88–93.

could take her through "a lot of different phases in the day".[51] Similarly, magazines and newspapers contained regular fashion spreads that boasted that their clothes could take women from nine to five (and longer), with a few accessories and alterations.[52] A 1988 article in *Cleo* entitled "Desktop makeover" thus gave active women step-by-step advice (by way of illustrations) about how they could go from "daytime cool to after dark sizzle in 20 minutes."[53]

Moreover, a whole new line of fashion—sportswear—was created in recognition of the fact of women's physical liberation.[54] Adidas, for instance, created its first line of women's shoes.[55] And gym wear—leggings, leotards and lycra—became a fashion statement, allowing women to display their fit, sexy and powerful bodies inside and outside the gym.[56] Fashion photography also made greater use of the active sportswoman motif with fashion feature spreads often containing images of women in sportswear running along the beach or playing sport (albeit in revealing and impractical clothing).

As well as encouraging consumption, the figure of the 24-Hour Woman offered a discursive framework in which some women of the 1980s made sense of and spoke about their lives. In this new story, femininity was conceptualised as the ability to lead an active and multifaceted life, and many women responded to this appealing narrative. From 1980 to 1985, *Cleo* featured a special section called "Active Women" that profiled a different woman each week. These women were finding empowerment in their bodily fitness and ability to command their active lifestyles. Sue Roberts was one such example. A schoolteacher and champion weight lifter, she explained to *Cleo* how she was up at 4.45am on weekdays to train before work.[57] Similarly, Liz Wilder was presented

---

[51] Andrea Jones, "Woman with Style: The Very Fashionable Felicity Rulikowski," *Cleo*, July 1988, 122–5.
[52] Narelle Simpson & Susie Pitts, "Working Class: How to Get It," *Cosmopolitan*, March 1989, 128–9.
[53] Deborah Thomas, "Desktop Makeover," *Cleo*, December, 1988, 164–7.
[54] "The Urge to 'Get Physical' Boosts Sales of Leotards," *Australian Financial Review*, April 29, 1983, 24; Claudia Gray, "Swimwear for those who Want to Swim," *Sydney Morning Herald*, September 30, 1986, 3.
[55] *Cleo*, November 1983, 26–7.
[56] Janet Brown, "Let's Get Physical and in Style," *Age*, July 27, 1983, 19; "Fit for 83," *Sydney Morning Herald*, January 9, 1983, 109.
[57] Kim Douglas, "Active Woman: Sue Roberts," *Cleo*, March 1981, 90–3.

as a singer who thought nothing of "putting in a 14 hour day," reporting how she spent her spare time riding, jogging or skating through Sydney's Centennial Park.[58] Then there was Pamela Clarke, a Sydney model, who ran, swam, danced, acted, did yoga, and taught jazz ballet and fitness classes, as well as studying at university.[59] Nina Gare, an educational officer, was venerated for her ability to work full time and still find the time to row competitively. She trained for three hours a day, starting at 5.30am, and told *Cleo* that "when your body feels good you seem to be able to do a lot more … when I'm fit and I look better too."[60] Similarly, Georgina Stroud, a freelance designer, told *Cleo* how she worked and exercised everyday and never took a day off because she was "terrified" of appearing lazy.[61] Such stories contained new narratives about women's lives. In the decade following the advent of feminism, women, like men, were encouraged to work hard, play hard and work out rigorously, and were assured through images and stories such as these that happiness, success and a sense of personal fulfilment would be their reward.

In this new narrative of femininity, 24-Hour Women, with their increased purchasing power and economic independence, could indeed do anything—anything, that is, except have a baby. Indeed, a notable absence from the 24-Hour Woman's repertoire was motherhood. Having children was treated as an optional extra, something one might consider later in life. There were echoes of some strands of the feminist critique in the argument that having children was the cause of women's oppression and a hindrance to leading an active life. Motherhood did not quite fit with a glamorous, empowering and liberated lifestyle.[62] And babies, one *Cosmopolitan* correspondent wrote, were "not … compatible with strong, strident ambition."[63] They undermined one's financial independence, wrote another, and, said a third, they could spell the death of romance.[64] Some

[58] Sue Wendt, "Active Woman: Liz Wilder: Singer and Sportswoman," *Cleo*, November 1980, 140–2.

[59] "Active Woman: Pamela Clarke," *Cleo*, January 1982, 123.

[60] Shelley Gare, "Nina: Committed to the Discipline of Rowing," *Cleo*, June 1980, 98–101.

[61] Justine Johnson, "Georgina Stroud: Designing a Winning Career," *Cleo*, April 1986, 140–3.

[62] Paula Goodyer, "Are You Brave enough NOT to Have a Baby?," *Cleo*, September 1984, 96–101.

[63] Penny Vincenzi, "Aim for Your own High," *Cosmopolitan*, January, 1983, 47–9.

[64] Brenda Maddox, "Hard-Hitting Advice on Marriage," *Cosmopolitan*, January, 1983, 62–4; Susan Lapinski, "Hello Baby, Goodbye Liberated Marriage," *Cleo*, April 1985, 72–5.

writers from women's magazines in the 1980s recommended childlessness, while others encouraged women to delay motherhood until they had established their careers.[65]

Acknowledging that some women actually desired children, a few authors warned of the inconvenience to come: expectant mothers were advised to ensure their pregnancy and childbirth had a minimal impact on their relationships and career—by wearing normal instead of maternity clothes, working right up to their due date, never appearing tired or overworked, and by getting their "old bodies back as soon as possible" after childbirth.[66] Actual images of pregnant women were rarely seen, however, and, in comparison to the onslaught of images depicting women enjoying every other activity, their absence is notable.

The 24-Hour Woman was a figure of aspiration and desire. The majority of women in 1980s Australia led rather less glamorous lives. The Sex Discrimination and Affirmative Action Acts did improve women's employment opportunities, but allowing a few women into male-dominated occupations scarcely disrupted the deeply institutionalised sexism of the workplace and the tenacity and persistence of the sexual division of labour in both the public and private spheres. Throughout this decade, women continued to suffer discrimination on the basis of race, class and sexual orientation as well as gender—complex factors not effectively redressed by the new legislation and rarely discussed in the popular media, but continually discussed by academic feminists and those working inside politics.[67]

Throughout the 1980s, Australian women also formed the largest group of welfare beneficiaries and were thus the hardest hit by cutbacks to

---

[65] Vicki Linder, "Saying No to Motherhood," *Cleo*, September 1987, 154–8; Elaine Robertson, "Leave Me Alone, I Don't Want to Have a Baby," *Cosmopolitan*, January 1990, 67–8; Paula Dranov, "Having Your Baby when You're Older," *Cosmopolitan*, July 1983, 105–9; Paula Goodyer, "Is There a Right Age to Have Babies?," *Cleo*, July 1980, 60–3.

[66] Paula Goodyer, "Work and Pregnancy: Making the Best of Both Worlds," *Cleo*, October 1983, 108–10; Margot Paul, "Life after Pregnancy: Coping with the New-Parent Blues," *Cleo*, October 1983, 63–6.

[67] See: "Women's Jobs: Going, Going Gone," *Girl's Own* 7 (1982): 11; "Editorial," *Hecate* 9, 1 and 2 (1983): 4–6; "Editorial," *Hecate* 10, 1 (1984): 4–6; "Editorial," *Refractory Girl* 27 (1984): 1; Josefa Sobeski, "Tipping the Economic Balance," *Refractory Girl* 27 (1984): 30–3.

welfare spending under the government's economic reform agenda.[68] Moreover, it was women who lost out in industrial deregulation. The abolition of tariff protection led to the closure of the textile factories that had been important employers of women, particularly migrant and working-class women.[69] By reinforcing the "ideology of the family wage," the government's much-celebrated "Accord" further segregated women into second-rate labour.[70] In addition, the unemployment rate, particularly amongst young girls, who lacked the technological skills demanded by many of the new jobs, remained at around 20 per cent for most of the decade.[71]

However, despite the fact that the story of the 24-Hour Woman did not reflect the reality of most women's lives, many women found in this construction a narrative by which they could make meaning of their experiences and aspirations. Profiles of real women were important in giving substance to advertising images, and numerous younger women spoke about their lives in these terms. Women could identify with this discourse of multiple roles in a hectic life and the figure of the 24-Hour Woman became a compelling representation of and for 1980s women.

Importantly, the 24-Hour Woman contributed to a re-formulation of the very meaning of feminism in the popular media, and this has had a profound influence on how young women—those who had not participated personally in the women's movement in the 1970s and early 1980s—have remembered it. The recent assertions about the failures of "having it all" feminism espoused by journalists such as Virginia Haussegger, Miranda Devine and Cathy Sherry, who blame feminism for creating a generation of "childless-but-not-by-choice" women and "harried

---

[68] Linda Carruthers, Margaret Penson and Danny Blackman, "Women and the Crisis," *Scarlet Woman* 16 (1993): 3–7; Rosemary Pringle and Anne Game, "From Here to Fraternity: Women and the Hawke Government," *Scarlet Woman* 17 (1983): 5–11; "Editorial," *Scarlet Woman* 25 (1988–1989): 1.

[69] Grimshaw et. al., *Creating a Nation*, 310.

[70] Barbara Preston, "Women and the Accord," *Down to Business: A Melbourne Socialist Feminist Conference, Newsletter* 3 (1983): [unpaginated].

[70] See Natasha Campo, "'Childless But Not By Choice' or '24-hour Women Having it All'? Remembering Australian Feminism," *Lilith: A Feminist History Journal* 13 (2004), 106–16; "Rethinking Feminism: A Review Essay," *Lilith: A Feminist History Journal* 14 (2005), 105–113; Natasha Campo, *From Superwomen to Domestic Goddesses: The Rise and Fall of Feminism* (Bern: Peter Lang, 2009).

[71] "Women's Jobs: Going, Going Gone," 11.

working mothers," demonstrate how influential this representation of feminism has been.[72]

This singular representation of feminism, however, necessarily elided the diversity and complexity of the feminist movement and its aims and aspirations. It was not feminists who derided motherhood and encouraged women to find total fulfilment in the workplace and through consumerism. Nor was it feminists who promised women that "having it all"—children and a career—would be effortless and easy. Rather, in the 1980s, collective knowledge about feminism was shaped by consumerism, advertising and other global discourses in the popular media, where feminist achievement and aspiration came to be embodied in the figure of 24-Hour Woman. Sadly, the particularities of an Australian form of feminism, committed to collective goals such as subsidised childcare and the introduction of family-friendly hours in flexible workplaces, have been all but forgotten.

[72] Virginia Haussegger, "The sins of our feminist mothers," *Age*, July 26, 2002, 15; Virginia Haussegger, "Great theory, but feminism's left us in a fix," *Sydney Morning Herald*, April 24, 2003, 13; Miranda Devine, "Why women can't beat the biological clock," *Sydney Morning Herald*, August 9, 2001, 12; Miranda Devine, "Yes sister, choose what you want," *Sydney Morning Herald*, 1 July 2003, 11; Cathy Sherry, "Taking pressure off women means allowing baby to come first," *Sydney Morning Herald*, February 26, 2002, 15; Cathy Sherry, "Pay on need not status," *Sydney Morning Herald*, December 10, 2002, 11; Cathy Sherry, "Wanted, part-time work for wasted women's skills," *Sunday Age*, May 4, 2003, 19.

PART II:

BUYING

CHAPTER FIVE

THE HOUSEWIVES' ASSOCIATIONS 1915–1950: AUSTRALIA'S FIRST CONSUMER ORGANISATIONS

JUDITH SMART

When the Housewives' Association of Victoria announced the cessation of operations in March 1991, a report in the Melbourne *Herald* described it as "Victoria's oldest consumer-watch institution and fighter for women's rights."[1] Indeed, until the formation of the Australasian Consumers' Association in 1959, the Housewives' Associations were the only dedicated consumer-interest organisations in the nation. Furthermore, there were no consumer-protection authorities, the state of Victoria being the first to legislate for a Consumers' Protection Council in 1964. Since 1995, there has also been a national government-funded body, the Australian Competition and Consumer Commission, which succeeded the Australian Trade Practices Commission established in 1974.[2] Government recognition of the issue is thus less than half a century old, and most of the enforcement agencies are products of the last 25 years. Yet neither the Australian Consumers' Association (ACA), now operating as Choice, nor the government has acknowledged the Housewives' Associations as predecessor consumer-interest representatives. This chapter aims to redress that omission.

By 1940–41, the Housewives' Associations' membership stood at 115,000. Given that the population of Australia at this time was about 7 million, this was a remarkable figure. In relative terms it far exceeded

---

[1] *Herald*, March 10, 1991.

[2] Australian Competition and Consumer Commission, http://www.accc.gov.au/content/index.phtml/itemId/142.

ACA-Choice's current membership of 200,000 out of a population of 21 million.[3] Nevertheless, while it is clear that the Housewives' Associations were focused on representing the consumer from their inception, we should be wary of attributing to them the same concepts of consumer interest, rights, protection and surveillance that characterise the current government regulatory bodies and ACA-Choice. This chapter is therefore equally interested in examining how the Housewives' Associations understood the consumer from the 1920s through to 1950. The limitations of the Associations that emerge from this analysis, and also, paradoxically, their impressive breadth of compass and sense of mission, provide insights into some of the reasons for their eventual demise from the 1970s in a changed socio-economic environment.

The first Housewives' Association was established in Victoria in 1915. New South Wales (NSW) followed suit in early 1918, South Australia and Western Australia in the mid-1920s, and, after a couple of false starts, the Australian Capital Territory, Tasmania and Queensland in the 1930s. A national organisation, the Federated Associations of Australian Housewives (FAAH), was mooted in 1923 and the first national conference occurred in 1926, though not all states were represented until 1934.[4] As the largest and most stable state Associations before 1950 were in Victoria and South Australia, the discussion here will largely refer to them and to the federal body.

Although the term "consumer" was used from the outset, with the central objective of the original Housewives' Co-operative Association of Victoria defined as "to encourage co-operative buying and marketing of produce direct from the producer to the consumer,"[5] the name chosen for the organisation is revealing. The person the organisers always had in mind as the archetypal consumer was female, married and a full-time

---

[3] *Housewife* (Victoria), July 1940, 2–3, 17; July 1941, 10–11. The membership is said to have peaked at about 175,000 in the late 1960s—see *Modern Housewife* (Queensland), December 1968, 3.

[4] FAAH Minutes, May 7 and 10, 1926, FAAH Minute Books 1926–38, Housewives' Association of Victoria (HAV) Records, MS13340, Box 4, State Library of Victoria (SLV); "A Brief Chronology of the Housewives' Association of Victoria" (probably by Eleanor Glencross, c. 1927), Brookes Papers, MS 1924/38/51–67, National Library of Australia (NLA); *Housewife* (Victoria), November 1934, 18.

[5] *Housewife* (Victoria), September 1, 1915, 2–3.

housewife.[6] Though "co-operative" soon disappeared from the title, if not from the menu of Association activities in all states, the word "housewives" did not, and it remained the key signifier of their focus. Like their successor consumer organisations, they kept a watch on prices, but this was only part of a larger purpose that included consumer protection and co-operation, education and example, duty and responsibility, and representation and power. These were modern objectives, but underpinning them was a notion of moral economy premised on the pre-modern concept of a just price. It also embraced a conviction of feminine moral superiority. While this gendered understanding has all but disappeared and the moral element has diminished in mainstream consumer organisation, there remains a thread of continuity with the Housewives' Associations in the ongoing focus on reporting and regulation, with its implied assumption that exploitation of the buying public is incompatible with a fair society. Amanda McLeod's chapter in this collection deals with the emergence of this kind of consumer policy framework in Victoria. My concern, however, is with the earlier conception of consumer interest and need embodied in the Housewives' Associations.

The consumer as housewife

While the term "housewife" is of Middle-English provenance, the figure of the modern, full-time professional housewife was a social construction of late 19th-century capitalist economies.[7] Louise Tilly and Joan Scott have argued that industrialisation and its shifting of production out of the home increasingly emphasised the role of the wife and mother as consumer rather than producer. Rising average incomes, a growing middle class, the increasing availability of mass-produced household goods, suburbanisation and a more complex social and bureaucratic environment to negotiate all served to sharpen the distinction between male and female familial tasks in early 20th-century Australia. Wives became more exclusively concerned with child-rearing and household management, and men with

---

[6] On the gendering of household purchase as a woman's "duty," see also Kim Humphery, *Shelf Life: Supermarkets and the Changing Cultures of Consumption* (Cambridge: Cambridge University Press, 1998), 29.

[7] Ann Oakley, *Housewife* (London: Penguin, 1976), Chapters. 2 and 3; Louise A. Tilly and Joan W. Scott, *Women, Work and the Family* (London & New York: Methuen, 1987).

"breadwinning."[8] Other factors explaining the emergence of the professional housewife before the First World War include compulsory education, which kept children dependent and at home longer, and the propagation and application of the principles of science and efficiency to budgeting and buying, food preparation and cooking, cleaning, infant care and the raising of children. Kerreen Reiger and Meredith Foley have explained this process in the Australian context,[9] and contemporary census data confirms that full-time unpaid housework was the norm for married women, only 6.1 per cent of whom went out to work in 1911, dropping to 4.4 per cent by 1921; even as late as 1947 the figure was only 8.6 per cent.[10] Contemporary workplace doctrines of management and the cult of expertise entered the home via the medical profession, growing numbers of women's organisations, a new breed of scientific social reformers, and school programs in domestic science. New expectations about standards of home management required the scientisation of domestic tasks, including expenditure, and the reinvention of the home as a workplace different in kind and purpose from the cottage industry model of preindustrial times. Interestingly, *The Shorter Oxford English Dictionary*, first published in 1933, includes in its definition of "housewife:" "A woman who manages her household with skill and thrift, a domestic economist."

Central to this new understanding was the housewife's economic role as the spender rather than the earner of the household's income.

---

[8] Desley Deacon, "Political Arithmetic: The Nineteenth-Century Australian Census and the Construction of the Dependent Woman," *Signs: Journal of Women in Culture and Society* 11, 1 (1985): 27–47; Nancy Folbre, "The Unproductive Housewife: Her Evolution in Nineteenth-Century Economic Thought," *Signs: Journal of Women in Culture and Society* 16, 3 (1991): 463–85; Joanna Bourke, "Housewifery in Working-Class England: 1860–1914," *Past & Present* 143 (1994): 167–98; Judy Giles, "A Home of One's Own: Women and Domesticity in England 1918–1950," *Women's Studies International Forum* 16, 3 (1993): 239–53; On 'breadwinning' and gender in the Australian context, see Patricia Grimshaw, Marilyn Lake, Ann McGrath and Marian Quartly, *Creating a Nation 1788–1980* (Melbourne: McPhee Gribble, 1993), 200–01.

[9] Kerreen Reiger, *The Disenchantment of the Home: Modernizing the Australian Family 1880–1940* (Melbourne: Oxford University Press, 1985); Meredith Foley, "The Women's Movement in New South Wales and Victoria 1918–1938" (PhD diss., University of Sydney, 1985).

[10] Katy Richmond, "The Workforce Participation of Married Women in Australia," in *Social Change in Australia*, ed. Don Edgar (Melbourne: Cheshire, 1974), 268.

Housewives were "the buyers of the community,"[11] and Association leaders saw their mobilisation as a means of creating a mass organisation of women that eschewed class loyalty in favour of the economic interests common to all their sex. But they would exercise their power responsibly. As "one of the biggest influences in the community,"[12] they would be a force "For the good that we can do," which became the motto of the Victorian and federal Associations. Their undertaking was thus represented as both patriotic and ethical, and they were urged as "women who had worked so splendidly side by side during the war years to work together now for the State and country."[13] This purpose was counterposed to the overwhelmingly masculine, selfish and adversarial economic contests between capital and labour, and was asserted to be just as important in its "economic contribution to the State." As such, it should be recognised institutionally by the creation of a Chamber of Consumers or, even better, by a Chamber of Housekeeping, "which would deal necessarily with questions of consumption."[14] The Housewives' Associations' understanding of the consumer was thus subsumed in the identity and interest of the housewife, portrayed as the model ethical citizen.

Co-operation and protection

The Housewives' Associations' conceptualisation of their primary task in representing the interest of consumers fluctuated, and they adopted different approaches over time, sometimes simultaneously and sometimes intermittently.[15] Their sense of purpose also varied from state to state; Victoria for example gave more attention to co-operativist work than South Australia or NSW, though such activity subsided in Victoria too during the 1930s. It would be accurate, however, to describe an early and continuing imperative of all the Associations as consumer co-operation and protection. What did they understand this to mean?

Marilyn Lake has noted that the history of Australian feminism can be divided into "five overlapping phases," the first of which was protective. In explaining the early importance of protection, Lake emphasises

---

[11] *Housewife* (SA), March 1930, 21; *Housewife* (Victoria), December 5, 1929, 1.
[12] *Housewife* (SA), October 1929, 7.
[13] *Housewife* (SA), May 1930, 22.
[14] *Housewife* (SA), September 1932, 10–12.
[15] On ideological influences and overall world view, see Judith Smart, "The Politics of Consumption: The Housewives' Associations in Southeastern Australia before 1950," *Journal of Women's History* 18, 3 (2006): 13–39.

women's recognition of their vulnerability to men, and hence the focus of feminists on liquor law reform and prevention of sexual exploitation.[16] The early history of the Housewives' Associations indicates a parallel concern with protection from economic exploitation. Given the origins of many early Housewives' Association leaders in philanthropy, protection of the disadvantaged as a duty of benevolence can be seen as a key factor in their thinking. The early inspiration for the Victorian Housewives' Association—according to their own foundation legends—came from Anglican deaconess, Sister Eva Hurst, who, in 1912, called together a small group of women in North Carlton, a poor inner suburb of Melbourne, in order to form an organisation pledged to "serve the interests of the woman in the home, especially the woman of limited means."[17] Similarly, when the organisation finally came into being in mid-1915, the middle-class leaders again stressed the needs of working-class women; the bureaus would be established in the "thickly populated," "democratic" suburbs where groups of the most needy consumers could buy directly from producers at reasonable prices, thus avoiding the middle man.[18] When it became clear that the Association's starting capital was insufficient and that working-class women were not flocking to the bureaus, most of the leaders lost interest, and co-operation only revived with a new group of organisers and a serious shortage of sugar in 1920.[19]

In the ensuing decade, the protective focus became less obviously class based. A common and more egalitarian gender identity assuming priority among the leaders, who now saw the possibilities of this "wholesome mixture" of women "of all classes and creeds" for generating a mass movement capable of revolutionising the "ordinary channels of trade."[20] The groundswell of support—as many as 75,000 joined up during 1920 and 1921—led not only to the revival of suburban distribution depots for

---

[16] Marilyn Lake, "A History of Feminism in Australia," in *Australian Feminism: A Companion*, ed. Barbara Caine (Melbourne: Oxford University Press, 1998), 133–6.

[17] May Maxwell, "History of the Housewives' Association," *Housewife* (Victoria), June 1937, 26.

[18] "Housewives Co-operative Association," Brookes Papers, MS1924/38/9–14, NLA.

[19] Return for the year 1916 as a registered co-operative society, Housewives' Association of Victoria, 1924/38/26, and Ivy Brookes to Madam Chairwoman, April 5, 1916, both in Brookes Papers, NLA; Minutes of executive 1915–16, HAV Records, MS13340, Box 4, SLV. For an explanation of the sugar issue, see Judith Smart, "The Politics of the Small Purse: The Mobilization of Housewives in Inter-war Australia," *International Labor and Working Class History* 77, 1 (2010): 48–68.

[20] *Argus*, February 2, 1921.

fruit and now sugar,[21] but also to support for many elements of the contemporary feminist different-but-equal agenda. Having become convinced, for example, that "it was impossible to expect the men members to see the point of view of the housewife struggling to make her budget balance," the leaders urged the "need for a few sensible women in Parliament."[22] They thus agitated first for the right of women to stand for parliament (where, as in Victoria, it did not already exist), and then gave support to women candidates, especially independents, when they did so. It was assumed they would represent a distinctive female interest rather than the class-based interests that characterised male representation. The leading figures in the Victorian and South Australian Associations, Eleanor Glencross and Agnes Goode, entered the fray in the late 1920s and early 1930s.[23] In both states, too, the gender focus saw the leaders in the 1930s working to extend organisation to women in rural towns, to the ire of the Country Party and the Country Women's Associations.[24] But the co-operative enthusiasm that had initially inspired these political ambitions was subject to considerable ebb and flow. It died out altogether in late 1920s NSW, while in Victoria it experienced a brief but brilliant revival under the controversial leadership of Delia Russell in 1929 before collapsing when she was expelled and the deepening of the Depression caused suspension of so much economic activity.[25] Protection of the housewives' interest increasingly focused on defensive measures such as thrift, protesting against unreasonable prices, and identifying and agitating against the forces responsible for consumer exploitation. Government intervention in the marketing of primary produce fell into this category and came under increasing attack alongside profiteers and strikers.

---

[21] The 75,000 claim was made retrospectively by president Alice Thomas in the *Age*, April 2, 1930; *Argus*, February 2, 1921, refers to 65 suburban and 30 rural branches.

[22] *Housewife* (SA), April 1931, 4, and June 1931, 4, 11; *Argus*, July 15, 1921.

[23] Suzanne Edgar, "Goode, Agnes Knight," in *Australian Dictionary of* Biography (*ADB*) 9 (Melbourne: Melbourne University Press, 1983), 47, also at http://adbonline.anu.edu.au/biogs/A090045b.htm; Meredith Foley, "Eleanor Glencross," *ADB* 9, 27–8, also at http://adbonline.anu.edu.au/biogs/A090026b.htm.

[24] *Housewife* (SA), March 1930, 4; May 1930, 1;, October 1930, 3; January 1931, 20; and May 1932, 3; *Housewife* (Victoria), July 1937, 21; December 1937, 30; and June 1938, 3, 35.

[25] On Russell's expulsion, see Robert Oldfield, "The Early Years of the Housewives' Association of Victoria 1915–1930," (BA Hons diss., Monash University, 1989), 51–7; and Judith Smart, "A Mission to the Home: The Housewives' Association, the Woman's Christian Temperance Union and Protestant Christianity, 1920–40," *Australian Feminist Studies* 13 (1998): 215–34.

In this context, another understanding of protection as the economic pillar of what Paul Kelly has termed the "Australian settlement" is relevant. Comprising tariffs on imported manufactured goods and arbitration of wages, this dual protection of industry and workers was conceived as the means to ensure the survival of Australian manufactures and maintenance of the "fair and reasonable" standard of living for families that Justice Higgins had deemed essential to a just social order in his famous Harvester judgement of 1907.[26] The machinery of protection was greatly extended and systematised during the 1920s to minimise the impact of post-war foreign competition on the new and mostly otherwise unsustainable manufacturing industries that had arisen during the First World War.[27] The war had also seen rapid inflation and a significant decline in real wages, resulting thereafter in a greater sensitivity to the need for cost-of-living adjustments. In the 1920s, this interlocking system of protection meant that Australia's domestic price structure was maintained at artificially high levels at a time when export prices for Australia's primary products were moving sharply downward. By 1924, certain categories of primary producers were demanding the extension of protection, through bounties and embargoes, to guarantee their competitiveness in export markets and their profitability locally. The ensuing cry for "protection all round" became more strident with the emergence of the Country Party as a force in state and federal parliaments. From the Housewives' Associations' viewpoint, the term "protection all round" was misleading because it omitted from its compass a major interest group in the economy—consumers. In practice, it was also unjust because this group was given no protection against artificially raised home prices for essential foods, had only limited access to growers and producers and no possibility of purchasing cheaper imported goods.[28]

The Housewives' Associations, like most Australians, initially supported the principle of protection in the national economic interest, and agreed that essential secondary industries should be "encouraged by a carefully adjusted and generously administered tariff." But to safeguard

---

[26] Paul Kelly, *The End of Certainty* (Sydney: Allen & Unwin, 1992).

[27] See N.G. Butlin, A. Barnard and J.J. Pincus, *Government and Capitalism: Public and Private Choice in Twentieth Century Australia* (Sydney: George Allen and Unwin, 1982), 76. For a general overview, see Marnie Haig-Muir, "The Economy at War," in *Australia's War 1914–18*, ed. Joan Beaumont (Sydney: Allen and Unwin, 1995), 93–124.

[28] D.B. Copland and C.V. Janes, ed., *Australian Marketing Problems: A Book of Documents 1932–1937* (Sydney: Angus and Robertson, 1938), Introduction, x.

"the interests of the consumers as well as the manufacturers," the tariff also needed to be subject to a stringent set of criteria, including that the goods "be of guaranteed standard quality" and not used "to cover ineffective methods." To ensure this, they consistently argued "that a woman should be appointed on the Tariff Board."[29] However, protection of primary produce, especially foodstuffs, constituted a more direct threat to everyday household consumption. First sugar, then butter, received subsidies for export, enabling them to be sold cheaply abroad while domestic prices rose to pay for the cost of the bounties. Soon this two-price system saw quasi-monopolies granted to producers in a range of other export goods: cheese, dried fruits, canned fruits, meat, and, eventually, wheat.[30] The proliferation of state marketing boards in the1930s for an ever-increasing number of products with mainly local markets further reduced competition and the possibility of direct buying for household use, thus raising the cost of living in the wake of the Depression. As acquisition, grading, release and pricing mechanisms were assigned to these boards, the Housewives' Association leaders became increasingly opposed to the whole gamut of state regulatory measures and passed resolutions against "the growing tendency of Governments—State and Federal—to appoint Boards of Control for staple foods."[31] Their sense of purpose was now concentrated on the need to "protect the interest of the home against Government interference on the one hand and exploitation of the necessities of life by trade interests on the other."[32] Failing also to make headway in getting consumer representation on marketing boards, the Housewives' Associations had by the mid-30s come to believe that effective consumer protection was only possible in a state supporting open markets and competition between producers and traders.

While they achieved a symbolic victory in the defeat of a constitutional referendum aiming to restore the Commonwealth government's recently abrogated powers in relation to marketing in 1937, this did nothing to reduce the number of state boards, though it did provide some access to cheaper interstate food products.[33] Nevertheless, the Housewives' Associations continued the battle on the grounds of democracy, economy,

[29] *Argus*, June 11, 1925, 11; FAAH resolutions on tariff policy, 1926 Conference (Sydney), FAAH minute books, HAV Records, MS13340, Box 4, SLV.
[30] Butlin, Barnard and Pincus, *Government and Capitalism*, 86–7.
[31] FAAH resolutions, 1934 Conference (Melbourne), FAAH minute books, HAV Records, MS13340, Box 4, SLV. The resolution came from Victoria.
[32] *Housewife* (Victoria), November 1934, 1.
[33] On the referendum, see Smart, "The Politics of the Small Purse," 48–68.

gender equity and consumer protection, arguing instead for a "Food Control Council" "charged with the duties of watching prices and supplies of principal foodstuffs, advising the Government on food questions, examining complaints, and making public from time to time in periodical reports, important facts about food prices etc.," as well as having authority "to supersede all existing Boards dealing with primary produce."[34] The first part of this resolution virtually abandons the grassroots attempts to bring consumer and producer together in favour of the kind of consumer-watch functions that ACA-Choice would later assume.. Some government concessions in this direction occurred during the Second World War and the Director of Rationing also agreed to meet regularly with an advisory committee from the Housewives' Associations, but there was no replacement of boards.[35] The Associations, in looking for alternative ways to protect consumers, also stressed the material benefits of a discount-for-cash system, whereby local traders and retailers agreed to lower prices for paid-up members. In addition, they provided instruction programs through monthly lectures and *Housewife* articles on housework, childcare, labour-saving products, sewing, cooking and vegetable growing, as well as women's citizenship rights and responsibilities. The early nexus between co-operativism and protection thus gave way to a more pragmatic set of arrangements with existing small business enterprises and to provision of education. Though the latter can be seen as a step towards current consumer organisations' understanding of their purpose as information providers as well as lobbyists, the way the Housewives' Associations interpreted this function once again indicates a different vision.

Education

From its inception, the NSW Housewives' Association "endeavour[ed] to be an educational body, helping women to be more proficient in cookery, preserving and to understand food values and thus improve the health and wealth of the nation."[36] As in Victoria, the motives of the founders were clearly conceived in class and philanthropic terms, the middle-class leaders of the Sydney Association being excited by what a contemporary reporter in 1918 described as the "fine generosity of wishing to spread their knowledge and share with others the useful things they themselves

---

[34];HAV executive minutes, 5 July 1938, HAV Records, MS13340, Box 6, SLV; *Housewife* (Victoria), June 1942, 10.

[35] *Housewife* (Victoria), January 1943, 19, 20.

[36] Quoted from the *Housewife* (NSW), June 1934, 10.

have learned or invented." [37] The conservative women who took over the Victorian Housewives' Association after the collapse of co-operativism in 1916 turned their concern about the cost of living for working-class families to support for the "thrift campaign" of 1917, preaching the virtues of cheap cuts, meatless meals and fireless cookers.[38] Similarly, the *Sydney Morning Herald* reported of the NSW Association's first meetings that "economy is what this little gathering preaches;" demonstrations of fireless cookers were accompanied by instructions on "preserving fruit without sugar" and "cutting out" dresses to "eager … young girls and matrons—all eyes and ears to hear see and understand." The reporter imagined the keen working-class audience slipping away after the meeting "to the Markets [to] make some cheap purchases and go home with a basketful of bargains, as well as a head full of new economic ideas."[39]

The outbreak of violent demonstrations by working-class women over the cost of living and food shortages in Melbourne from August to October 1917 cast some doubt on the effectiveness of this approach. And the short sharp post-war economic downturn, combined with contemporary alarm about "profiteers" as well as "Bolsheviks," caused those who revived the Victorian Association in 1920–21 to revise their message and attitude to the thousands of ordinary women joining up to take advantage of the Association's exclusive access to supplies of sugar.[40] In addition to a resurgence of co-operativist activity, the formation of branches and the creation of a more participatory and democratic structure with regular meetings of branch representatives and election of state office bearers, this period saw the formulation of objectives without any paternalist references to education or training.[41] At this time, the NSW Association also began to

---

[37] *Sydney Morning Herald*, July 10, 1918, 8.

[38] See "A Brief Chronology."

[39] *Sydney Morning Herald*, July 10, 1918, 8.

[40] Judith Smart, "Feminists, Food and the Fair Price: The Cost of Living Demonstrations in Melbourne, August–September, 1917," *Labour History* 50 (1986): 113–31; *Ours*, July 1921; Humphrey McQueen, "Shoot the Bolshevik! Hang the Profiteer! Reconstructing Australian Capitalism, 1918–21," in *Essays in the Political Economy of Australian Capitalism,* vol. 2, ed. E.L. Wheelwright and Ken Buckley (Sydney: ANZ Book Co., 1978), 185–206.

[41] The objectives in the *Argus* report of what was misleadingly termed "the first annual meeting," held on 1 February 1921, were: "To advocate the equal status of women and adequate representation on all boards and tribunals dealing with the home and the cost of living; to encourage increased production and the manufacture of articles capable of being home-made; to advocate a standardised milk system, and municipal block distribution, and strict supervision of dairies; to

engage in some co-operative enterprise.[42] The focus in both states was the assertion of women's economic citizenship in a more egalitarian framework—an approach that confirms Lake's identification of independence and equality as the second and third stages of development of Australian feminism.[43] But there was no clear linear transition from one phase to another, and some elements of protection and paternalism persisted alongside the assertion of economic rights.

When the co-operative expansion of the early 1920s subsided, the educational function was reasserted, resulting in a split in NSW between the co-operators and the main organisation, which continued as the Housewives' Progressive Association and eschewed co-operative trading altogether.[44] Although co-operative enterprise briefly took off again in Victoria in 1929, it did not replace a growing program of education through lectures, demonstrations and articles in the Association's new journal by women from the medical, legal and other professions. President Delia Russell explicitly described one of the Association's purposes as "To advise, protect and guide housewives."[45] And, by the mid-1930s, the demonstrations, lectures and classes had become the Association's main attraction, together with discount-for-cash arrangements advertised through its "Pink Guide" to recommended retailers.[46] Activities and

---

advocate and promote open-air markets in every suburb for the sale of home products and articles of consumption and utility; to promote and support the establishment of a department of housing; to enable householders to build homes under easy conditions; to promote and establish cooperation among housewives; to oppose profiteering in every practical manner; to deal with manufacturers and producers for its members and branches, and to save commission and charges at present paid to middlemen; to provide facilities for social intercourse between members and their friends, and, if thought fit, to afford them the usual privileges, advantages, conveniences and accommodation of a club; to borrow money and to acquire real or personal property for the purpose of the association."

[42] "Early History of the Housewives Progressive Association of N.S.W.," *Housewife* (NSW), April 1934, 1, 30.

[43] Lake, "A History of Feminism in Australia," 134, 137–9.

[44] *Argus*, June 23, 1928, 26; Meredith Foley, "From 'Thrift' to 'Scientific Spending': The Sydney Housewives' Association between the Wars," *Sydney Gazette: Organ of the Sydney History Group* 6 (1984): 15–16; "Early History of the Housewives Progressive Association of N.S.W. continued," *Housewife* (NSW), June 1934, 10.

[45] *Housewife* (Victoria), November 1929, 4.

[46] The 'Pink Guide' was first published in 1934. See *Housewife* (Victoria), April 1934, 6.

viewpoints were advertised through regular radio broadcasts too. The objectives now explicitly included advice "on household matters which are for the betterment of home life" and education "in the use of labour-saving appliances and scientific home management."[47] The South Australian organisation also stressed education, its approach, as in Victoria, being largely didactic. In addition to the lectures, demonstrations, radio broadcasts, advice and instruction, there were essay and other competitions for members on subjects such as "A Well-balanced Dinner Menu" of three courses for six persons at one shilling per head. In explaining the criteria for assessing the entries, the judges noted: "It is necessary for housewives to understand food values so as to know which are best and most economical and so be sure that they are giving their families just what is needed."[48]

In one of the monthly lectures, members were told: "Every woman is potentially a house-wife or house-manager, with very important home duties," such duties obviously included knowing how and what to buy for a healthy home.[49] The annual South Australian Housewives' Weeks included the usual cooking, knitting, dressmaking, millinery and crochet competitions and lectures, but there were also visits to factories "to obtain knowledge of methods of production of articles in daily household use,"[50] as part of the stress on scientific spending.[51] By 1939, South Australia's president was hoping that "displays of locally-made goods will bring about a closer co-operation between housewives and producers of consumer goods." She organised demonstrations by companies such as Electrolux and Kelvinator Refrigeration, as well as an extended "Ideal Kitchen Exhibition" at which many firms providing "working demonstrations."[52]

Certainly such initiatives were greeted with enthusiasm, but the competitions and classes focusing on what could be made in the home also continued to grow in popularity.[53] In the war and immediate post-war years, production for military needs and consequent shortages meant that these activities, together with advice on vegetable growing and thrift in all aspects of life, remained important. It took the revitalisation of the

---

[47] *Housewife* (Victoria), December 1936, back cover.
[48] *Housewife* (SA), May 1929, 8; June 1929, 8; and September 1929, 10.
[49] *Housewife* (SA), March 1930, 11.
[50] *Housewife* (SA), June 1930, 2.
[51] Foley, "From 'Thrift' to 'Scientific Spending'," 16.
[52] *Housewife* (SA), July 1939, 7; August 1939, 19, 24; and October 1939, 7.
[53] *Housewife* (SA), August 1938, 20; and October 1939, 7.

economy in the 1950s to bring about the surge of expenditure on manufactured goods, especially household appliances, discussed by Tony Dingle in this collection, and attributed to the "younger housewives forming post-war households." This was to challenge the Housewives' Associations' underpinning raison d'être, for the consumer education they had provided was conceived of in terms of responsible citizenship and moral example over and above material acquisitiveness.

Responsibility and duty

In justifying their advice to members as for "the betterment of home life" and to "improve the health and wealth of the nation," the Housewives' Associations defined the role of responsible consumption as "trying to work in a wider and more national way … for the benefit of our homes, State and Nation."[54] In other words, the patriotic consumer-citizen had obligations and duties as well as rights.[55] These were inflected by gender and applied broadly. The Housewives' Associations' different-but-equal ideal of feminine citizenship was common to other contemporary women's organisations and, drawing on an essentialist view of women's nature, it advocated the elevation of public life through values seen as uniquely feminine. These included not only those special maternal and spiritual qualities that would "purify the political atmosphere" but also "an approach to economic matters that stressed exchange based on voluntary and mutually beneficial relationships rather than maximisation of profits."[56] Wartime Victorian and national president Cecilia Downing wrote, "while the organisation was the watchdog of the consumer, it was not out to get commodities at low prices at the cost of the producer, but wanted a fair deal for all."[57] Consumption was seen as socially nurturing, rather than confrontational or purely economic. As South Australia's president advised her members in 1930, consumption

> can never be divorced from the whole community. You live in the State, your means of livelihood is there. Therefore you are not a people apart …

---

[54] *Housewife* (NSW), June 1934, 10; *Housewife* (SA), June 1930, 27.

[55] In South Australian Adelaide Miethke's words, the qualifications of a housewife must include "realisation of the privileges and obligations of a citizen." *Housewife* (South Australia), June 1930, 34–5.

[56] *Housewife* (Victoria), October 1929, 4; Smart, "The Politics of Consumption," 28–9.

[57] *Housewife* (Victoria), December 1939, 7.

> and it is of little use for you to attempt to solely further your own interests at the expense of the whole community.[58]

The Victorian journal similarly pointed out that "the community after all is a collectivisation of thousands of homes."[59] Responsibility for its wellbeing applied to all spheres. South Australia's housewives were urged to buy South Australian goods first, Australian goods second and Empire goods third. At the more personal and local level, they were urged to "shop in your own district" and to consider the legitimate profit of the small trader, especially those that gave discount to the Association. They should not, for example, be tempted to buy wood at the cheapest price on offer but rather stick to the Association's preferred wood sellers: "Our merchants are loyal to the Association, and they have the right to expect the Association to be loyal to them."[60]

This was the Golden Rule in practice. For most women's organisations of the inter-war period, the concept of responsible citizenship was infused with a secularised Christian ethic stressing "the values of selfless service, probity, stewardship, responsibility and care for others, individual conscience and initiative, hard work, thrift, fair dealing, fidelity and … personal morality."[61] The Housewives' Association's attacks on restraint of trade and collusion tactics in certain industries were couched in moral as much as economic terms, and their own work was represented as primarily altruistic, "a sacred trust" accepted by the selfless wife and mother to look after "the physical, moral, social and spiritual care of the home."[62] Over time, their leaders recognised that this imperative, and the desire "to help set wrongs right," "to leave the world just a little better than they found it,"[63] was weakening. In 1946, for example, Mrs Downing worried that too many members were joining the Association for financial benefits rather than "For the good that we can do," adding, "It is more blessed to give than to receive."[64] Certainly materialist motivations were becoming more evident in the growth of consumerism during the 1950s

[58] *Housewife* (SA), July 1930, 1–2.
[59] *Housewife* (Victoria), January 1935, 7.
[60] *Housewife* (SA), June 1930, 27; April 1930, 43; March 1931, 28; May 1929, 10; and April 1933, 27.
[61] Smart, "A Mission to the Home," 217.
[62] *Housewife* (Victoria), December 1933, 19; April 1934, 15–16; February 1937, 25; and March 1936, 8.
[63] *Housewife* (Victoria), March 1936, 8; and March 1940, 5.
[64] *Housewife* (Victoria), July 1946, 2–4.

and 1960s, but, until then, the Housewives' Associations continued to preach responsible consumption as a means of improving the quality of life for all and solving many economic problems, including unemployment and wartime needs and shortages.[65]

During the Depression years, for example, South Australian housewives were reminded that local buying would help the "small trader who at present is having such a hard struggle to live."[66] If they "would make an honest attempt from to-day to consistently give preference to goods of local manufacture, the situation of our unemployed would be very materially eased," and, in the long run, this "would almost guarantee a prosperous future for our children."[67] In 1932, a new president similarly noted: "We have to remember that it is not only the economic welfare of our community that is affected by our actions, but also the social welfare."[68] For this reason, "a true Australian woman realises that a bargain is too dearly bought if it means unemployment to her husband or her son, or to her friends or neighbours."[69] The Victorian Association's message to housewives during the Second World War was that their patriotic duty of thrift, for "the production and proper conservation and use of food and other essential materials, provide[s] a sphere of national service quite as necessary as the discharge of guns, and this is where members of the Association can help."[70] A further "national duty," the president explained, was to spend the money saved on War Savings Certificates.[71] In supporting such appeals, the South Australian *Housewife* urged members to recognise their "real power for good in the community."[72] The word "power" was significant, for the concern to exercise consumption and citizenship responsibly was always underpinned by Housewives' Association leaders' belief that the power of numbers would ensure their views were heeded.

---

[65] Smart, "The Politics of Consumption," 29, 32.
[66] *Housewife* (SA), March 1930, 21.
[67] *Housewife* (SA), June 1930, 1, 8–9.
[68] *Housewife* (SA), August 1932, 14.
[69] *Housewife* (SA), June 1934, 14.
[70] *Housewife* (Victoria), March 1940, 2.
[71] *Housewife* (Victoria), April 1940, 19.
[72] *Housewife* (SA), August/September 1940, 7.

Representation and power

Where the claims of men to citizenship had been argued in terms of an individual contract with the state for rights and protection in exchange for service, their actual participatory power was based on organised economic interest, whether as workers or employers. Though women argued a parallel recognition as citizens through their maternal role, their access to power would also depend on an ability to wield economic weapons "for the purpose of guarding the interests of women in the home."[73] The Housewives' Associations represented consumption as just such a weapon. It was as essential to the functioning of the economic system as capital and labour, and therefore also subject to competitive organisation. All the state Associations' publications made frequent references to "the power of the purse" and controlling "the purchasing power of the nation."[74] It seemed the ideal basis for creating the feminist mass movement the leaders had in mind. The Victorian *Housewife* explained: "It is the day of organisation, and men and women who fail to link up with an organisation are likely to be left behind."[75]

Unlike working-class women whose political activity in defence of the immediate economic interests of their families was typically crisis instigated and ephemeral, the early middle-class leaders of the Housewives' Associations were familiar with organisation and public lobbying in other forums. Most were office bearers in the peak body for women, the National Council of Women (NCW), as well as being associated with political parties. The first president of the South Australian branch (1926), Agnes Goode, was an executive member of the NCW and belonged to the Liberal Federation. Eleanor Glencross and Cecilia Downing, who at various stages dominated the Victorian and federal organisations—and, in Glencross's case, the NSW branch too—held office in the NCW. Both had also belonged to the Australian Women's National League, which eventually became the Victorian Women's Section of Menzies' new Liberal Party in 1944. Glencross also worked for the Liberal Association of NSW and, in the 1930s, the women's section of the United Australia Party. But both Goode and Glencross gave priority to their feminism over party loyalty. Goode in 1926 stood for election as a representative of the Women's Non-Party Association. Glencross twice

[73] *Housewife* (Victoria), April 1938, 33.

[74] *Argus*, February 4, 1921, 9; *Housewife* (SA), June 1934, 14, 2; *Housewife* (NSW), November 1933, 20.

[75] *Housewife* (Victoria), April 1938, 33.

stood for parliament in Victoria in the 1920s without party endorsement because the male leaders were "strongly opposed to women taking their place in public life, except to work for them cheaply."[76] The South Australian Housewives could also boast one or two Labor Party stalwarts like Marie Skitch, who had been endorsed as a candidate for Thebarton in 1937 and became president of the state Housewives Association in 1940.[77]

Though some personal political ambition is evident in these women's activism, their work in the Housewives' Associations was, as "A Member" wrote, "entirely voluntary" without "thought of reward beyond the fact that living costs might be reduced."[78] They initiated and led boycotts, petitions and deputations while employing the forms of self-help already described. Examples of early boycott campaigns in Victoria saw children going to school shoeless and women appearing gloveless—"in three months the price of gloves had dropped again"—and the Association also claimed credit for a fall in the price of potatoes following a substitution campaign.[79] In 1921, Glencross explained that boycotts signified group power as well as achieving immediate outcomes. If members were loyal, they would show the politicians as well as the traders that they were "a force to be reckoned with."[80] Milder replacement schemes were occasionally recommended in all states (especially margarine for butter), and, at various times, the Associations asked women not to pay exorbitant prices for bread and instead to bake their own—lessons were conducted and cheap sources of yeast provided.[81] They also defended discount-for-cash arrangements against a determined onslaught from large retail interests until wartime price controls and rationing brought them to a halt in 1942.[82]

---

[76] Edgar, "Goode, Agnes Knight." On Glencross, see *Herald*, April 19 and 21, 1928, cited in Geoff Browne, "Eleanor Glencross and Ivy Weber: In and Out of Parliament," in *Double Time: Women in Victoria—150 Years*, ed. Marilyn Lake and Farley Kelly (Melbourne: Penguin, 1985), 347.

[77] Electoral Commission South Australia, "Electoral Development Time Line 1850–2000," http://www.ecsa.sa.gov.au/apps/uploadedFiles/news/93/electoral_development_timeline.pdf.

[78] *Housewife* (Victoria), March 1940, 5.

[79] *Argus*, December 4, 1919, 6; *Argus*, February 18,1921, 6.

[80] *Argus*, January 2, 1921, 9; *Housewife* (NSW), July 1934, 2.

[81] *Argus*, February 18, 1921, 6; *Housewife* (Victoria), December 1933, 9.

[82] *Housewife* (Victoria), October 1938, 4; August 1939, 2; October 1939, 8; April 1940, 17.

Occasionally, the influence of the leaders was recognised by appointment to boards and committees of enquiry—Glencross served on the royal commission into the high cost of living in 1923 and the Commonwealth Film Censorship Board from 1928, while other leaders were appointed to various state and Commonwealth prices and food control committees during the Second World War.[83] But, despite these concessions and occasional acknowledgements of their power, such as when Victorian Premier Albert Dunstan admitted "we were a powerful organisation," the leaders were increasingly frustrated by the failure of governments to recognise their interests and influence as equal to those of business and trade unions.[84] Dunstan's refusal early in the war to accede to the Association's request for representation on the Victorian prices control committee provoked president Cecilia Downing to ask "Are our methods so unspectacular?" and to admit "The rebuff has led to some self-examination." Appealing to members for suggestions to "secure more recognition of our community work," she could offer no new ideas herself apart from "doubling the membership" to produce the "necessary 'pull'. Force of numbers," she wrote, "is irresistible to the politician and the advertisers."[85]

Though there was some obvious truth to this claim, numbers were not the compelling factor the leaders had assumed. The Victorian Housewives' Association had nearly 80,000 members by this time but the power the leaders asserted in their rhetoric was not recognised by governments to the extent union and business peak organisations could expect as a matter of course. There were reasons for this that throw some light on the limitations of the Associations and help explain their fate after the 1960s.

Limitations and conclusions

The idea of consumption as the economic voice of women was a nice one but the actual problems of converting this to a mass movement with political impact comparable to that of business or labour were ultimately insuperable. For their numbers to have real effect, the Housewives' Associations needed to present a consistently unified economic position;

[83] Meredith Foley and Heather Radi, "Eleanor Glencross," in *200 Australian Women: A Redress Anthology*, ed. Heather Radi (Sydney: Women's Redress Press, 1988), 105–06; *Housewife* (Victoria), November 1939, 2; and February 1944, inside front cover.
[84] *Housewife* (Victoria), October 1939, 8.
[85] *Housewife* (Victoria), November 1939, 2.

in practice, however, there were unresolved tensions and contradictions. Consumption was not the sole defining economic interest of most members. While women could certainly come together with a common program of gendered concerns as homemakers and consumers, they also retained economic identities as wives and daughters and sisters of working-class men, employers and businessmen, or as members of regional communities. Some were themselves actually involved in the mainstream political parties that broadly represented these other economic interests. In this diversity there was always tension and occasional outright conflict of interest over issues such as strikes and the role of government in the economy. The Housewives' Associations attempted to contain dissent by insisting that they were "non-party and non-sectarian" but the leaders were unable to sustain this position consistently in relation to all issues relevant to the welfare of home and family that arose.[86] In 1928 and 1930, there were splits in the NSW and Victorian Associations, and, after Second World War, political tensions arising from the Cold War saw the emergence of the breakaway New Housewives' Associations in all three southeastern states. No longer able to pretend to neutrality during the 1950s, the continuing Associations lost much of their capacity to transcend political difference.[87] While membership climbed into the 1960s, the baby boomers' coming of age saw the end of generational renewal in the Associations and signalled their rapid demise.

In short, it appears that the Housewives' Associations had tried to do too much. The pattern of fluctuation in the Victorian Association's membership indicates women joined to gain access to goods in short supply, to obtain discounts, and to learn useful skills in dressmaking and millinery. While the political and citizenship education provided in lectures and the Associations' respective journals may have had an impact on members' attitudes and opinions and increased their knowledge, a gendered consumer identity is not evident in voting patterns and other measures of political behaviour. As Victoria's Premier Dunstan reminded the leaders in 1939, the Housewives' Associations had never actually put a woman into parliament.[88] The pragmatic approach of most women to

[86] Judith Smart, "'For the Good that We Can Do': Cecilia Downing and Feminist Christian Citizenship," *Australian Feminist Studies* 19 (1994): 51–3.
[87] Barbara Curthoys and Audrey McDonald, *More than a Hat and Glove Brigade: The Story of the Union of Australian Women* (Sydney: Bookpress, 2000), 1–5; Suzanne Fabian and Morag Loh, *Left-wing Ladies: The Union of Australian Women in Victoria, 1950–1998* (Melbourne: Hyland House, 2000), Chapter 1.
[88] *Housewife* (Victoria), October 1939, 8.

membership meant that, when the Association no longer provided the advantages and the type of consumer advice they required, their interest dissipated. Consumption turned into materialist consumerism during the 1950s and 1960s as the idea of the housewife's work as a calling and part of a uniquely feminine moral economy declined with the expansion of opportunities for paid work and the availability of labour-saving white goods for those who could pay. As consumption for domestic use also became less gender specific, and purchasing decisions on the larger more expensive items came to be made by men and women together, the Housewives' Associations lost the demographic constituency on which they had grown and, with it, their certainty of purpose and mission. The constituency of the new Australian Consumers' Association was a different one, and this may be the reason for the historical amnesia it has displayed towards the major contribution of its predecessor to the history of consumer organisation in this country.

CHAPTER SIX

LEGISLATING IN THE CONSUMER INTEREST: THE VICTORIAN CONSUMERS PROTECTION COUNCIL 1964–1970

AMANDA MCLEOD

In 2008, Consumer Affairs Victoria (CAV), Victoria's leading consumer protection agency, received more than 545,000 enquiries, resolved 10,972 investigations and recovered more than $5.7 million for consumers through dispute resolution and court orders. It spent $1.45 million funding community-based agencies to provide advocacy services and over $5 million on financial counselling services. It administers 47 Acts of parliament, oversees licensing and registration schemes, and regulates specific industries. Education, information and advice services form a major part of CAV's activities, many of which are directed at vulnerable and disadvantaged consumers.[1] The historical origin of CAV dates to the passage in 1964 of the Consumers Protection Act, which established the Consumers Protection Council (CPC). The purpose of this chapter is to trace the factors that gave rise to the first tentative steps by the Victorian government towards more effective and encompassing consumer protection policy.

Australia's pursuit of economic prosperity through mass production and consumption was firmly entrenched during the decades following the Second World War. In order to maintain growth, advertising and marketing increased exponentially as did the availability of credit to enable consumers to participate at adequate levels.[2] While commercial

---

[1] Consumer Affairs Victoria, *Annual Report 2007–2008* (Melbourne: Victorian Government Printer, 2008), II.

[2] Amanda McLeod. *Abundance: Buying and Selling in Postwar Australia* (Melbourne: Australian Scholarly Publishing, 2007); Robert Crawford, *But Wait, There's More* (Melbourne: Melbourne University Press, 2008).

interests pursued and promoted consumer sovereignty, hailing the "consumer as king," consumer power was tenuous, for material affluence and increased consumer choice had unwanted consequences and, in reality, the consumer was "a part-time and often incompetent sovereign."[3] Many consumer advocates and even some marketers concluded that some intervention was, in fact, needed to protect not only consumers but also the integrity of the market, healthy competition and reputable business from unethical and deceptive practices, even though defining what it meant proved to be complex and, at times, controversial.[4] David Bottomley, who would become the CPC's foundation chairman, summed up the marketing concept from his own point of view as a market researcher: "business serves itself best when it is best serving consumers."[5]

Formed in Sydney in 1959, the Australian Consumers' Association (ACA) emerged as the largest and most successful consumer-specific group in the post-war period. Calling for independent representation of consumers, the ACA believed that the key to protecting the consumer would be through providing information about products.[6] Although the ACA had done much to raise the consumer profile, by the mid-1960s it had become increasingly obvious to many that no amount of competition between businesses or information about products could solely or adequately protect consumers against deceptive practices.

By the 1960s, governments—somewhat belatedly—recognised the need to regulate consumption as part of the economy. The Victorian Liberal government did so by a continued reliance on British precedent for guidance, even as the consumer market took on more American characteristics. Drawing on recommendations made in the landmark Molony Report on Consumer Protection in the UK in 1962, the state of Victoria was the first Australian jurisdiction to take up the legislative challenge to redress the balance of power between buyers and sellers. Although the Victorian Liberal government expressed a commitment to

---

[3] Antony A. Erswell, "A Study of Consumer Protection Organisations in Great Britain and Victoria with Special Emphasis on the Consumer Protection Council in Victoria," (Unpublished Report, 1969), 11.

[4] McLeod, *Abundance*, 257.

[5] David T. Bottomley, *Why Protect Consumers?* (Melbourne: Fabian Society, 1970), 38.

[6] McLeod, *Abundance*, 159; Amanda McLeod, "Quality Control: The Philosophical Origins of the Australian Consumers' Association," *Business History* 1, 50 (2008): 79–98.

consumers when it introduced the Consumers Protection Bill in 1964, the Labor Opposition attacked it for merely paying lip-service to their interests. The government made it clear that the Consumers Protection Council was not to be a law-making or enforcing body; nor would it be a product tester or handle consumer complaints.[7] Armed with only four vague functions, the Council nevertheless fought stridently to represent the interests of consumers. Regardless of the impediments placed before it, including insufficient funds, staff, investigatory and enforcement powers as well as overt political interference calculated to curb its independence, the Council immediately became a rallying point for consumers, who turned to it with a myriad of complaints about defective products and unreasonable sales practices.

Although Victoria was the first Australian jurisdiction to legislate in the consumer interest, this is not to suggest that consumers had no legal protection prior to this time. Rather, until the 1960s, consumer protection legislation was developed on an *ad hoc* basis and included laws relating to weights and measures, pure food, truth in advertising, restrictive trade practices and hire purchase.[8] In addition to legislative controls, the consumer interest was represented by voluntary organisations such as the Housewives' Association and, to a lesser degree, the Country Women's Association and trade unions.[9] As Judith Smart's chapter in this collection demonstrates, the Housewives' Association's interest in consumer protection and representation meant that it was the antecedent of the Australian Consumers' Association. However, unlike its predecessor, the ACA was not gender specific in its aims and its conceptualisation of consumer interest was less diffuse. The ACA's ability to maintain an ongoing watch on consumer-related issues (such as price or quality) and to report back on them similarly marked it out from the Housewives' Association.

---

[7] *Consumers Protection Act 1964.*

[8] Matthew Hilton, *Consumerism in 20th-Century Britain* (Cambridge: Cambridge University Press, 2003), 51.

[9] Judith Smart, "A Mission to the Home: The Housewives Association, the Woman's Christian Temperance Union and Protestant Christianity, 1920–1940'," *Australian Feminist Studies* 13, 28 (1998): 215–34.

In the interests of consumers

At the 1964 state election, both the Liberal and Australian Labor parties promised to appoint a body to "act directly in consumers' interests."[10] Even for some within the Victorian Liberal Party, including Rupert Hamer, the focus on caveat emptor was becoming outdated. Highlighting a major change in the consumer market, Hamer, at the beginning of the second reading debate, explained that the bill

> comes before Parliament at a time when modern life is becoming more and more complex, especially for the consumer. It is an age of pre-packed and pre-packaged goods of immense variety, and of various types of synthetic fabrics and products of all kinds, as well as complicated household gadgets of which only the expert really understands the true working … perhaps it could be said that the doctrine of caveat emptor is in some cases wearing a little thin.[11]

The British Committee on Consumer Protection (the Molony Committee), appointed by the Board of Trade in 1959 to investigate measures "desirable for the further protection of the consuming public," "came to be recognised as a watershed in the history of state consumerism."[12] Hamer, supporting the Victorian bill to establish a body directly along the lines of the British Council, explained that the consumer needed an "independent and forceful authority to speak and to act on his behalf."[13]

The Molony Committee had given the British Council clear terms of reference and explicitly outlined the areas in which it would not intervene. The British Consumer Council, writes Matthew Hilton, embodied a non-interventionist approach to consumer protection and was deliberately prevented from conducting product testing, handling consumer complaints and enforcing the law. Both the government and Molony imagined the Council "as a body which added to the information held about the market;

[10] Consumers Protection Council (CPC), Memo no. 3, September 10, 1965, Appendix 1.
[11] Consumers Protection Bill 1964 (CPB), Legislative Council (LC), November 17, 1964, 1480.
[12] Great Britain, *Final Report of the Committee on Consumer Protection* (hereafter cited as Molony Report) (London: HMSO, Cmnd. 1781, July 1962); Hilton, *Consumerism in 20th-Century Britain*, 226.
[13] CPB, LC, November 17, 1964, 1480.

what it was not was an organisation allowed to interfere in the actual workings of the market."[14]

Molony's recommendations were far from a radical approach to consumer protection. The intention was not to introduce an all-encompassing consumer law, nor to interfere with the structure of the existing laws.[15] Indeed, as Aubrey Diamond noted, the Molony Committee was "very, very careful to see that it cannot be criticised for going too far."[16] The Victorian Consumers Protection Council, it seemed, would go even less far than its British counterpart and would be less independent. However, despite the deliberately cautious approach, the formation of consumer councils represents a major shift in the regulation of consumption as part of the economy of industrial societies. While the shift was one of emphasis rather than a complete change in direction, it marked the beginning of a governmental approach to consumer policy. The shift, it is also important to note, was one from an *ad hoc* approach to single industries and concerns to a more integrated approach to the interests of consumers as a group.

The "consumer interest" was, of course, not transparent and easily defined, and the consumer "could mean everybody and yet nobody at the same time."[17] While Hamer told parliament that the consumer interest "means all of us,"[18] on the other side of politics, Jack Galbally stated that the consumer was not "some curious animal that goes out and just consumes things—he is us."[19] Stressing the extent of the problem and the challenges faced by those in government formulating policy, the *Age* newspaper referred to consumers as an "amorphous mass" who were the

> least organised and most vulnerable majority group in our competitive and acquisitive society. In these days of skilled marketing, persuasive advertising and easy credit, the consumer is often at a disadvantage, confused and misled by questionable practices, enticed to spend beyond his means, and uncertain of his rights. Even Governments, in arranging such matters as trading hours, are likely to be influenced more by the wishes of

---

[14] Hilton, *Consumerism in 20th-Century Britain*, 228.

[15] Molony Report, 7.

[16] Aubrey L. Diamond, "Molony Committee, Final Report of the Committee on Consumer Protection," *Modern Law Review* 26, 1 (1963): 66.

[17] Hilton, *Consumerism in 20th-Century Britain*, 51.

[18] CPB, LC, November 17, 1964, 1484.

[19] CPB, LC, December 3, 1964, 2161.

> powerful pressure groups than by the interests of the amorphous mass of consumers.[20]

While consumers were indeed an amorphous mass, the definition of consumer protection was, from the Molony Committee's point of view, also an amorphous conception that could not be defined. It was simply "a convenient label for a great variety of measures designed to safeguard and assist the shopper" and, as noted, the Committee did not consider the consumer in need of any specific or new legislation to protect his/her interests.

So, what did consumer protection, or protecting the interest of consumers for that matter, actually mean? In Victoria in 1964, it meant the formation of the Consumers Protection Council—a Council with vague functions and no powers. While the functions were based on the recommendations of the Molony Committee, the circumstances under which the Victorian body was created were strikingly different. Although the governments of Holland, Norway, Denmark and New Zealand had already introduced some form of consumer protection, Victoria's Liberal government looked to the UK because, as Hamer noted, its "conditions [were] very similar to our own."[21] Contrary to the Molony Committee's recommendation that a country's particular needs should be based on a thorough investigation of local conditions and circumstances, the Victorian government chose to follow the operations of the British Council without any such investigation. In line with the lead set by its British counterpart, the Victorian Council would not be a law-making or enforcing body, a product tester or a complaints-handling agency. It would also not be given any powers to compel witnesses to give evidence at hearings.

Because the ACA had already assumed a role as the nation's quality controllers, preventing the Council from undertaking product testing did not disadvantage Victorian consumers.[22] But, unlike the UK Consumer Council's cordial relationship with the Consumers' Association, the Victorian Council had no working relationship with the ACA. Indeed, the reaction by the ACA to the establishment of the CPC and the appointment

---

[20] "Protection for Consumers," editorial, *Age*, November 17, 1964, 2.
[21] CPB, LC, November 17, 1964, 1480.
[22] McLeod, "Quality Control," 79–98.

of David Bottomley as chairman was hostile.[23] The ACA's chairman, Roland Thorp, and his deputy, Henry Epstein, both refused to co-operate with anyone associated with business and, until Bottomley's departure, refused even to correspond with the Council.

Complaints handling, however, was neither provided for in, nor specifically excluded from, the Council's stated functions. While the British Consumer Council had no powers to investigate consumer complaints, British consumers were served in this respect by Citizen Advice Bureaus, which had been set up during the Second World War to provide a range of services to the public. Australian consumers, it seemed, would have no such avenue.

Toothless tigers and drowsy dingoes

To what extent was the Consumers Protection Act, which outlined vague functions for a Consumers Council and gave it no power, a serious attempt to protect consumers? In 1980, reflecting on the formation of the Council, Norm Geschke, who had been appointed the first director of consumer affairs in 1974, remarked that Vernon Wilcox, the responsible minister, had "wished the Council had not been born"—a sentiment shared by the majority of the Liberal Party at the time.[24] Andrew Lachowicz, who became the CEO of the Consumer Affairs Bureau in 1970, had been interviewed for the position of secretary of the CPC in 1964. On enquiring as to the prospects of promotion, he was told it "would be impossible to predict as nobody actually could say whether the Council would cease to exist in a few months time or whether it would develop as an on-going concern." Not surprisingly, he did not pursue his interest in the position.[25]

Clive Stoneham, Leader of the Labor Opposition, also complained that the bill was not a serious attempt to protect consumers but "just tossed in as a pre-election stunt."[26] However, while Wilcox and Premier Henry Bolte simply wanted the whole issue to disappear, some within the Liberal Party were more committed to consumer protection. Hamer, a member of

[23] McLeod, *Abundance*, 193; Erswell, "A Study of Consumer Protection Organisations," 60–1.
[24] Norman Geschke, "Note of Action," February 29, 1980, 1.
[25] He did, however, join the Consumer Affairs Bureau as Chief Executive Officer in late 1970 when it was clear that the whole issue of consumer affairs would not go away. Andrew Lachowicz, "Note of Action," February 29, 1980, 1.
[26] CPB, Legislative Assembly (LA), November 4, 1964, 1174.

the ACA and a subscriber to its journal, *Choice*, accepted the necessity and urgency of providing "a rallying point for the consumers": "It is thought that in these complicated days the ultimate purchaser—the consumer—needs more guidance and more help than he has ever had before."[27] But guidance and help in what form?

The *Age* reported during the debate on the Council's composition and powers that its future was "in the balance."[28] While all parties agreed that a Council to protect consumers was needed, they differed on its powers and the constitution under which it would operate. The *Age* agreed with the Opposition that the "Council would be 'toothless' without power to summon witnesses and documents." The government, however, refused to budge. Bolte told the Legislative Assembly that he would not accept the proposals of any political party to allow the Council to compel witnesses; he would rather the bill be defeated than compromise. Ultimately, the government did have the final say and the *Age* concluded that a Council of "an advisory rather than of an inquisitorial character, relying on publicity and persuasion rather than a law-enforcing authority" was better than nothing. "A moderate council may be more effective than a militant one; it is certainly better than no council at all," a sentiment echoed by Diamond in his analysis of the British Council, about which similar criticisms had been raised.[29]

Both the Country Party and the ALP continued to question the government's commitment to consumer protection. Jack Galbally, Labor MLC, warned that the idea that the proposed council was

> a sort of modern Robin Hood redressing the wrongs done to society and locked in mortal combat with the sheriff of modern business is altogether too masculine a role for this toothless body. If the Bill is passed, all the public will have will be a council shooting a pointless arrow with a broken bow.[30]

Archibald Todd, ALP MLC, exclaimed: "The proposed council will be a paper tiger, and the Bill is worthless and fit only for the incinerator."[31]

---

[27] CPB, LC, November 17, 1964, 1480.

[28] "Consumers' Council Worth a Trial,", *Age*, December 8, 1964, 2.

[29] Diamond, "Molony Committee," 75.

[30] CPB, LC, December 3, 1964, 2160; *Sydney Morning Herald*, December 17, 1964, 2.

[31] CPB, LC, December 3, 1964, 2173.

William Divers, ALP MLA, thought the bill even worse: "it has not even the fearsome look of a toothless tiger but appears to be more like a drowsy dingo displaying dissolved dentures."[32] Likening the plight of consumers to that of Little Red Riding Hood faced with the Big Bad Wolf, Galbally explained: "Not a day passes when they are not faced with the wicked wolf in the jungle of modern society. There is a wolf lurking at every foot of the way."[33] But consumers did not just have the business community to contend with. Questioning the Premier's commitment to consumers, Galbally warned "we have the most unlovely physical specimen in Mr. Bolte as the wolf."[34]

Vague functions

Despite intense parliamentary wrangling, the functions of the Council as outlined in the 1964 Consumers Protection Act remained vague. Primarily the Council would:

> consider matters affecting the interests of consumers, inform itself of their problems, and consider, after consultation if necessary with other affected bodies, action to be taken to deal with problems and to safeguard the interests of consumers, as well as to make recommendations, if necessary.[35]

The problems associated with the vague functions outlined in the Act were numerous. Labor complained that: "The proposed council has virtually no powers and no functions—it will meet, discuss and present a report."[36] Despite being able to "investigate any matter affecting the interests of consumers referred to it by the Minister," the Council had no actual power to compel a witness to give evidence. It also lacked the independence to initiate its own enquiries into consumer problems. Although the Council made clear its recommendations to the government in its annual reports, the government was under no obligation to follow the Council's advice and, indeed, repeatedly ignored it. The Council's ability to act in the interests of consumers was further hampered by the government's deliberate disregard for some of the Molony Committee's most important recommendations. Furthermore, it was underfunded and prevented from

---

[32] CPB, LA, November 4, 1964, 1180.
[33] CPB, LC, December 3, 1964, 2160.
[34] CPB, LC, December 3, 1964, 2162.
[35] CPB, LA, October 6, 1964, 652.
[36] CPB, LC, December 3, 1964, 2160; *Sydney Morning Herald*, December 17, 1964, 2.

publishing an information bulletin and conducting research into consumer problems.[37]

In September 1965, some nine months after the passage of the Act, the Consumers Protection Council was finally appointed. Its limitations were immediately apparent, as an internal memo reveals: "As a Council, if we are going to stand up and carry out the obligations of our Act which require us to act in the interests of consumers, we have to have the means to act."[38] But it was the issue of consumer complaints that would be the most significant area into which the Council was thrust. Antony Erswell argues that "by not expressly forbidding 'the taking up of complaints on behalf of individual consumers,' it might be implied that the Government intended that the Consumers Protection Council should be able to receive complaints."[39] The *Sydney Morning Herald*, for example, assumed that that would be one of the Council's major roles, specifically stating it "will investigate complaints by the public about the advertising, design, marketing, packaging or labelling."[40] But Hamer had not intended this role for the Council because he had expressly told the parliament that the Government rejected

> any notion that the Consumers Protection Council should be a kind of forum for consumers' minor complaints about local retailers or particular products which might have been purchased. If that should happen, the Consumers Protection Council would become bogged down in a mass of detail and spend practically all of its time sorting out minor complaints, thus ceasing to concentrate on important issues.[41]

Hamer neglected to define the more important issues but, more significantly, he also neglected to acknowledge that British consumers had an alternative avenue already in place in the form of Citizen Advice Bureaus. Aggrieved Australian consumers, it seemed, would be given nowhere to go.

Lachowicz, the CEO of the Consumer Affairs Council from 1970, explained:

---

[37] Bottomley, *Why Protect Consumers?*, 17.
[38] Consumers Protection Council, "Notes for Consumers Protection Council," October 21, 1965, 3.
[39] Erswell, "A Study of Consumer Protection Organisations," 55.
[40] "Victoria's Watchdog for Housewives," *Sydney Morning Herald*, December 17, 1964, 2.
[41] CPB, LC, November 17, 1964, 1481.

> I was given to understand that nobody had given much consideration as to how the Consumers Protection Council was to function, and that it would depend on the Chairman as well as the Council members whether it would develop or lapse into dis-continuity.[42]

The Opposition had raised concerns that the "Council would be limited in its activities by being able only to investigate matters referred to it by the Minister," yet Wilcox stated that "the Council's activity to consult with manufacturers, retailers, and advertisers, relating to any matter affecting the interests of consumers will not be limited by reference to the Minister."[43] But, as Bottomley observed, "it was not made clear exactly in what way the Council could make recommendations without matters first having been referred to it by the Minister." The implication was that "the Council could suggest to the Minister what matters the Minister should direct the Council to enquire into."[44] Not surprisingly, he believed that this was not a very satisfactory state of affairs, one that was neither independent nor transparent.

It is uncertain why the Victorian Liberal government did not adequately define the functions of the Consumers Protection Council. Perhaps the Labor Opposition was correct in claiming its establishment was just an election stunt, with the Liberal government merely paying lip-service to the interests of consumers. Perhaps the Liberal Party hoped that the issue would go away, or perhaps there was too much internal division within the party to resolve the issue. On the other hand, there was little precedent to follow when it came to dealing with consumer-specific matters and formulating consumer policy. While Bolte warned that the Council was "on trial," Hamer had stressed that the Council was "somewhat experimental," suggesting that he was willing to accept change as time progressed rather than abolish it if it stepped out of line.[45] Change it did. Despite the government's intention that the Council not handle complaints, consumers themselves unexpectedly "took it over."[46] Complaints came in quickly during the CPC's first nine months, increasing dramatically from 353 to 1530 in 1967 and 2024 the following year. It was the influx of complaints that ensured the success of the

[42] Lachowicz, "Note of Action," 1.
[43] CPB, LA, November 4, 1964, 1196.
[44] David T. Bottomley, "Background to the Consumers Protection Council (Victoria)," September 9, 1965, 10.
[45] CPB, LC, November 17, 1964, 1484.
[46] Erswell, "A Study of Consumer Protection Organisations," 55.

Council, Erswell argues; without them, the "Council would probably have gone into limbo by now without having achieved anything significant."[47]

Independence and deceptive packaging

In addition to its lack of investigatory powers and undefined complaint handling capacity, the Council's proposed composition also raised concerns. The parliamentary debates reveal major sticking points between the Liberal, Country and Labor parties, highlighting competing philosophies in relation to who would best represent the consumer interest and the extent to which governments should intervene in the workings of the market (an issue that still consumes the consumer policy debate). Whether business interests could or even should represent the consumer interest was a matter of intense discussion. While everyone was a potential consumer representative because everyone was a consumer, almost all interest groups believed they knew consumers best so were in a better position to represent them. But it was commercial interests that posed the greatest concern, as Clyde Holding, ALP MLA, explained:

> Its title—Consumers Protection Council—implies that consumers need protection. If that is so, the question is: From what groups in the community do the consumers need protection? I should think all honourable members would be in agreement that consumers need protection from those manufacturing, retailing and advertising organizations, which, by a variety of high-pressure tactics and skills are ready to sell to the buying public goods that they cannot adequately use and at prices which, in many cases, they cannot afford.[48]

He made the ALP's position clear: "the Labor Party believe that the people who are likely to protect consumers' interests are consumers who do not have any other interests." Holding asked: "Is it not absurd that on a body called the Consumers Protection Council two groups which are to-day grossly exploiting the consumers are the first to be represented."[49] Along similar lines, Archibald Todd was also apprehensive about the Council's composition:

> Is the defendant given a say in the jury box when he is on trial? Why should the manufacturers and retailers be given a favoured position on this

[47] Erswell, "A Study of Consumer Protection Organisations," 55.
[48] CPB, LA, November 4, 1964, 1184.
[49] CPB, LA, November 4, 1964, 1185.

> council as against the great bulk of people who have no representation whatsoever?[50]

There was more to the Liberal government's reliance on British precedence than following tradition. The Victorian government pursued a conservative approach to consumer protection in order to appease members of its own party who feared that a consumer council would interfere in the market in the same way as the Federal Trade Commission in the United States. Hamer, treading a middle way between those within his own party who feared the Council would have too much power and those in the Labor Party who claimed it would have none at all, argued:

> This is not meant to be an inquisition or super-price control structure … [it is] to provide the means whereby their interests can be brought forcefully to the attention of Parliament. Other people have organizations looking after their interests … but as yet the consumer has not.[51]

After intense debate, the government finally appointed six persons to the Council—one each representing manufacturers and retailers, three (two of whom had to be women) representing consumers, and a chairman. Tim Ramsay, CMG, managing director of Kiwi Polish and former president of the Victorian Chamber of Manufacturers, and George McCowan, marketing director of G.J. Coles and former president of the Retail Traders' Association of Victoria, were both appointed to the Council. Although the two women appointed were publicised as being "housewives," their daily lives extended far beyond the domestic sphere. Dorothy Moss was a member of the Country Women's Association and the Women's Section of the Country Party of which she had been state president 1963–65. She was also the vice president of the Country Party's Federal Women's Council of Australia. Audrey Reader OBE, JP, was chairman of the House Committee for the Women's Liberal Club, a member of the Research Committee, Women's Section of the Liberal Party, and vice president of the National Council of Women of Victoria. John Waters JP, the Trades Hall Council representative, was a delegate to the Australian Council of Trade Unions and Trades Hall Council of Victoria. While Waters took a less active role, the other members of the CPC committed themselves to the important tasks afforded them. Both Ramsay and McCowan provided good insight into trade, but it was Reader and Moss, along with chairman Bottomley, who publicised the Council

---

[50] CPB, LC, December 3, 1964, 2173.
[51] CPB, LC, December 3, 1964, 2174.

and educated the public, sometimes giving up to three or four speeches per week each.[52]

The Council's most important member was the chairman, who would act as an independent mediator. It was assumed that the chair would be a member of the "consumer class" and that the Council's most powerful weapon would be his report to parliament, which was protected by parliamentary privilege.[53] The government insisted that it should "have a free hand in appointing consumer representation."[54] While all appointments to the Council were in a sense political appointments, Ivan Swinburne, Country Party MLC, argued that the government's control over appointments should not pose a conflict of interest because, as he noted, "we are all consumers."[55] But the government's control over appointments would not avoid all potential problems.

On hearing the government's announcement that it would establish a consumer council, market researcher David Bottomley approached his former boss, the head of advertising agency United Services Publicity, Major General Alfred Kemsley.[56] Nominated by the Australian Association of National Advertisers, Kemsley turned down the offer to become chairman, putting forward Bottomley as an appropriate alternative. For Bottomley, consumer protection could be a double-edged sword to fight "ill practices which cause consumers to suffer and which impair the reputation of reputable business."[57]

Initially, the loudest concerns as to the appointment of Bottomley came from the ACA, which referred to him as a "classical example of deceptive packaging. When opened up one finds that some of the protectors are the very ones from whom protection is needed."[58] He was, however, to become more of a problem for the Liberal Party. In the face of the potential conflicts, Bottomley was not what the government had expected—and certainly not what they had intended the chairman to be.

---

[52] Erswell, "A Study of Consumer Protection Organisations," 63, 65.
[53] CPB, LC, November 17, 1964, 1482; LC, December 3, 1964, 2170.
[54] CPB, LC, December 3, 1964, 2179.
[55] CPB, LC, December 3, 1964, 2164.
[56] David T. Bottomley, interview with author, Graduate House, University of Melbourne, May 8, 2008.
[57] Bottomley, *Why Protect Consumers?,* 3.
[58] *Choice*, October 1965, 18.

Bottomley, as a market researcher, had undertaken research for significant commercial interests such as Shell, Arnotts, Cadbury and Fosters. Believing that market researchers could best represent consumer interests because it was their job to understand them, Bottomley, the seemingly "accidental appointment," backfired on the government. As Erswell writes, perhaps "some of his business acquaintances thought that the government had appointment him because he seemed the quiet, retiring, backroom type, self-effacing and modest; not the sort to stir up trouble."[59] But, unknown to the Liberal Party, at the time of his appointment, he was also a member of the Labor Party and the Fabian Society and thus willing to accept more state intervention to regulate competition than many of his contemporaries and colleagues. In his view, the major role of consumer affairs as manifest in government was to act in the interests of both consumers and business—to facilitate the efficient workings of the market and to make a level playing field for both. Bottomley saw the Council as a middleman—a "go-between body" between consumers and business. The Consumers Protection Council would have a two-fold benefit, protecting the interests of both consumers and reputable business, as Bottomley explained:

> The consumer plays a very important part in our economy, yet it is appalling to see reports almost everyday detailing the chicanery and deceit which is used to dupe and defraud consumers of their money. The consumer who is defrauded is likely to retrench on his purchases, with the result that even the businessman who carries out his operations with integrity, is a victim.[60]

Bottomley was careful to point out that only certain sections of the business community posed concerns: "The Council has received sound support from reputable firms and business organizations and any criticism that has been launched against us has come from companies and business organizations whose ethics are questionable."[61] Bottomley reflected in 1970 that:

> Considering the enormous volume of business carried out by major stores and major manufacturing enterprises in Australia, hardly a complaint has been made to the Council about such groups. Major business enterprises

---

[59] Erswell, "A Study of Consumer Protection Organisations," 71.

[60] David T. Bottomley, "Food Stores: What Consumers Think" (Address by the Chairman of the Consumers Protection Council of Victoria, to the Glen Waverley Heights State School Mothers' Club, Melbourne, March 3, 1966), 2.

[61] Consumers Protection Council, *Annual Report* (1968), 3.

> know that they are in business to stay; have been in business a long time; believe in their reputation. They value customers' good-will and in their actions they often exceed legal requirements in meeting customer complaints.[62]

Hamer, too, shared Bottomley's view. "The great body of manufacturers and the great body of retailers are," he stated, "honourable, ethical people … just an anxious as anybody to cut out the unethical fringe practices which degrade their activities on the whole."[63] Consumer protection, therefore, was also in the interests of business.

There were some areas of commerce, however, that presented serious concerns. Generating increasing numbers of complaints in the Council's first few years, the house-cladding industry, for example, did not exemplify ethical salesmanship.[64] The major concern related to the deceptive practices of salesmen and actions of finance companies. As the 1967 annual report made clear, consumers were sometimes unaware that their contract with the cladding company had been taken over by the finance company, which offered no avenue for redress when things went wrong:

> A householder who has found faults in cladding (for which he may have paid up to $2000), or who finds he has been a victim of misrepresentation by a salesman, has no other redress than to take civil action for damages against the cladding company. He cannot suspend payment on the loan because the money borrowed is owed to the finance company.[65]

But, for the Council, it was not just a simple matter of dealing with the unethical finance companies. Bottomley, in a television interview with Barry Jones in August 1969, complained: "One started to wonder whom one exactly was working for, whether it was for the consumer or the Government."[66] Bottomley asked the government to conduct an "open inquiry into all aspects of the selling of house cladding in Victoria."[67] Refusing to comment on the concerns raised by Bottomley, John Rossiter, Minister for Labor and Industry, dismissed claims that a threat had been

---

62 Bottomley, *Why Protect Consumers?*, 38–9.
63 CPB, LC, December 3, 1964, 2174.
64 Consumers Protection Council, *Annual Report* (1967), 5.
65 Consumer Protection Council, *Annual Report* (1967), 7.
66 Erswell, "A Study of Consumer Protection Organisations," 69.
67 "Consumer Body May Get More Muscle," *Age*, August n.d., 1969, 3. (David Bottomley's private collection).

made to "bring political weight" against the Council. Bottomley also told the media that one finance company had a confidential Council document to which only the Council and government had held access.

The Council brought pressure to bear on finance providers and had dealt with one company in disputes involving more than $1 million. While the exact circumstances are unknown, "the industry probably sought to curb the Council by putting pressure on the Government. ... However, the Government took no action to implement the Council's concerns."[68] Despite the government's inaction, the Council was able to beat the rogue traders as the "bottom dropped out of the house cladding business largely as a direct result of the publicity given to it by the Council." Of all the complaints made to Consumer Affairs Victoria, house cladding is one of only a handful of commodities that now generates very little censure.

It was Bottomley, not the Council, who was sacrificed in the wake of this controversy. Despite making himself available for another term, he was not reappointed. But his sacking did not silence him. Instead of withdrawing from consumer affairs and returning quietly to commerce, Bottomley gave the new chairman, A.H. Hellstrom, six months to settle into his position before criticising the government's lack of commitment to the Council and consumer protection more generally. Bottomley's criticisms were as numerous as they were familiar:

> Failure to carry out the Council's recommendations and failure to give the Council adequate financial resources, and for obstructing the work of the Council by refusing to allow the Council to obtain regular legal assistance, to publish a magazine, employ a journalist on a part-time basis to help with publications, to spend money to publicize 'care-labelling' standards for clothes, to sample public opinion on such matters as shopping hours, and to inform the public about consumer protection in other countries.[69]

Conclusion: consumerism's coming of age

In 1970, after much criticism, the Liberal government abolished the Consumers Protection Council and the 1964 Act and established a Consumers Affairs Council and Consumers Affairs Bureau. In a deliberate attempt to limit the power of the Council, the government split its advisory

---

[68] Erswell, "A Study of Consumer Protection Organisations," 70; see also Consumers Protection Council, *Annual Report* (1967), 5-9.
[69] Erswell, "A Study of Consumer Protection Organisations," 69.

and complaints-handling functions. In the same year, the Consumers' Association of Victoria set itself up as a watchdog of the Victorian government's consumer policy and complained that neither consumer groups nor consumers themselves had been consulted, arguing that, "if consumers had been given a 'free choice,' they may have preferred the old model."[70] Its concern was that the new agency was even less independent because consumers would be forced to make complaints to the Consumer Affairs Bureau, which would be overseen by the Department of Labour and Industry—"another case of misleading packaging."[71] Not surprisingly, Bottomley was to be found at the centre of the Consumers' Association of Victoria's activism in this area.[72]

Despite the criticisms it received and the impediments placed in its way, the Consumers Protection Council had succeeded in promoting the consumer interest for three reasons. First, Council members were committed to promoting the consumer interest and serving individual consumers. Second, the Council's vague functions allowed it to become a powerful force to be reckoned with. And, finally, because consumers had nowhere else to go, the Council became a rallying point and complaints came flooding in.

While Wilcox had wished the CPC had "never been born," he quickly resigned himself to the fact that he and his government "would have to put up with it."[73] Whether it should have the powers to investigate complaints and follow its own initiative independent from the government bureaucracy, or have an advisory function only, would be issues that continued to plague both the government and the department for years to come. In 1974, the Ministry of Consumer Affairs was established and a minister was finally appointed. The Ministry's foundation director, Norman Geschke, would also lobby the government throughout his tenure for more and clearer power to be bestowed on the director—an issue that continues to trouble CAV to the present day. But, before the Ministry was set up, business, too, had learnt to live with the CPC and also how to influence it.[74]

---

[70] Consumers' Association of Victoria, "Consumer Protection: 1970 Model," *Consumer Comment* 1, 1 (1970): 1; McLeod has examined the formation of the Consumers' Association of Victoria in detail—see McLeod, *Abundance*, 185–220.
[71] Consumers' Association of Victoria, "Consumer Protection," 2.
[72] McLeod, *Abundance*, 194.
[73] Geschke, "Note of Action", 1.
[74] Consumers Protection Council, *Annual Report* (1968), 3.

A number of the issues faced by the CPC remain perennial concerns for those involved in the development and implementation of consumer policy. The extent to which governments should intervene in the operations of the market increasingly became an issue over which consumer advocates (particularly within the bureaucracy), business groups and the government would continue to battle. The issue of independence from the bureaucracy would also continually raise concerns. Should the body acting on behalf of consumers have more than an advisory function, to what extent should it be independent of government, and to what extent should it represent consumer interests? As this chapter has shown, defining the interests of consumers and the ways they should be "represented" is far from straight forward.

The shift in emphasis from consumer "protection" to consumer "affairs" (in an attempt to deflect criticisms that protection was "anti-business") illustrates the contentious nature of consumer interest. The government's entry into the consumer field did not result in a generic consumer law to protect the rights of consumers. Until very recently, this has not been at the heart of Australian consumer policy debates. That there is no clear definition of the "consumer interest" remains a major problem for those who are concerned with protecting the consumer. As one senior CAV insider told me, how one approaches defining this term depends entirely on where one stands.

From 1970, the responsibility for consumer protection was split between an increasing number of public institutions, including the Small Claims Tribunal, Market Court, Residential Tenancies Tribunal, Motor Car Traders Committee and, finally, from 1981, an independent Ministry of Consumer Affairs.[75] As a mediator—a go-between—connecting consumers and business, Victorian government consumer policy since the formation of the CPC in 1964 has had to act in the interests of both consumers and business to facilitate the efficient workings of the market. If the object of consumer protection was to promote the interests of consumers—rather than to interfere in the overall workings of commerce—then CAV has made a significant contribution. It has certainly helped to achieve redress for thousands of Victorians.

While the Council's intended role was primarily to advise the minister, it became a strident consumer advocate, even if it was more concerned

---

[75] Consumer Affairs Council, *Annual Report* (1983), 25–6.

with promoting consumers' interests than enhancing their rights. Interest in the latter was, of course, not absent from the debate but cannot be said to have been the major influence driving the Liberal Party's formation of the Council. The major success of the Consumers Protection Council, like that of its British counterpart, was raising the consumer profile—making the legislature and the public more "consumer conscious."[76]

To a large extent, the Liberal Party's unwillingness to pursue a more strident approach to protecting the interests of consumers ensured the viability of the Consumers Protection Council. By paying lip-service to consumer protection in loosely following the guidelines set by the Molony Committee, the Victorian Liberal Party's foray into consumer affairs was more successful than the party's leaders had intended. In refusing to define the functions of the Council and assuming that the business interest was akin to the consumer interest, they failed to foresee the Consumers Protection Council's potential to become a strong consumer advocate — one that continued to grow in strength and responsibility.

Its purely advisory successor, the Consumer Affairs Council, was finally abolished in 1983 as the result of an enquiry into shop trading hours and amidst a major Labor government restructure of the Victorian Ministry of Consumer Affairs. Although the Council had concluded that loosening restrictions on trading hours was in the consumer interest, the view conflicted with Labor government policy and other, potentially more powerful, interests. The Council's desire to act independently ultimately led to its demise. The 1982 management review of the Ministry of Consumer Affairs found that the "Council's work extended beyond advising the Minister on Government policy to initiating and developing policy in a way that is inappropriate." It recommended that:

> The Consumer Affairs Council be replaced by a new body, the Victorian Consumer Affairs Committee. The Committee to be a Ministerial advisory

---

[76] The United States president had outlined his four consumer rights—the right to safety, to be informed, to choose and to be heard—in a speech to Congress, March 15, 1962 ("Special Message on Protecting the Consumer Interest"). These rights would be adopted by successive groups such as the International Organisation of Consumers Union and state organisations. During this early stage, the notion of rights was focused on the idea of "rational choice." Erswell, "A Study of Consumer Protection Organisations," 44; Bottomley, *Why Protect Consumers?,* 4–5; Hilton, *Consumerism in 20th-Century Britain,* 306.

> committee with clearly defined policy advice functions and a composition reflecting a broad range of consumer and trader interests.[77]

Was the Council's role to be a "go-between" between consumers and government by acting in an advisory capacity representing the consumer interest? Or was it to mediate between consumers and business as envisaged by the CPC in its early years? Ultimately, the Council's work "initiating and developing policy" was considered inappropriate, with governments of both political persuasions preferring to restrict its power to an advisory function and inhibiting its ability to independently protect the interests of consumers. Throughout the history of Consumer Affairs Victoria, the most appropriate way to protect and promote the consumer interest has proved to be one of constant negotiation, and this will continue to be so into the future.[78]

As the consumer interest attracted increasing attention during the 1950s and 1960s, consumers—as an economic group—were forcefully "put on the map." But, as Geschke reflected, it would be during the 1970s that the pursuit of the consumer interest would "come of age."[79] In the decades that followed, consumer affairs would become more political as powerful lobby groups continued to promote the consumer interest and continue to push for, and obtain, more resolute government intervention, principally through the Victorian Ministry of Consumer Affairs. But many of the issues that faced the Consumers Protection Council in its early years are the same as those that confront Consumer Affairs Victoria today. Securing independence from the bureaucracy and ensuring the consumer interest is not sidelined by other more powerful business and government interests are challenges that remain as formidable as they were in the 1960s and 1970s. Even though everyone is a consumer and everything is a potential consumer issue, that does not mean that attending to the consumer interest is simple and straightforward. Nor does it mean that the government interest is always in the consumer interest. As long as the consumer is with us, attending to the consumer interest will always be complex, controversial and contested.

---

[77] Public Service Board Review of the Ministry of Consumer Affairs, *Final Report*, December 1982; Consumer Affairs Council, *Annual Report*, (1983), 5.

[78] Amanda McLeod, *A Fair Deal: A History of Consumer Affairs Victoria* (Melbourne: Department of Justice, forthcoming 2009).

[79] Hilton, *Consumerism in 20th-Century Britain,* 336; Geschke, "Note of Action", 1.

CHAPTER SEVEN

INSIDE SUBURBAN "PERSIAN BAZAARS": THE RECEPTION OF REGIONAL SHOPPING CENTRES IN SYDNEY DURING THE 1960S

MATT BAILEY

Large, pre-planned ("regional") shopping centres began being developed in Australia in the late 1950s.[1] The first was opened at Chermside near Brisbane in May 1957. It was followed by Top Ryde in Sydney later the same year, and by Myer's massive Chadstone centre ten miles from Melbourne in 1960.[2] Shopping centre construction became a boom industry and the major form of new retail development in the country.[3] Department store companies and property developers scoured the suburbs of Australian cities for suitable sites on which to build.[4] In Sydney, Top Ryde was followed by Warringah Mall, Miranda Fair, Roselands and Bankstown Square—all of which were opened between April 1963 and September 1966. This chapter draws on newspaper reportage, trade journals, council records, industry promotion and secondary sources to explain the development of shopping centres in Australia. Evidence of their reception is provided by the written testimony of over 120

[1] Throughout this paper, "shopping centre" refers to regional shopping centres.
[2] Peter Spearritt, "Suburban Cathedrals: The Rise of the Drive-in Shopping Centre," in *The Cream Brick Frontier: Histories of Australian Suburbia*, ed. Graeme Davison, Tony Dingle and Seamus O'Hanlon (Melbourne: Monash Publications in History, 1995), 96–9.
[3] Editorial, *Retail Trader*, October 1962, 3.
[4] Peter Spearritt, "I Shop Therefore I Am," in *Suburban Dreaming: An Interdisciplinary Approach to Australian Cities*, ed. Louise C. Johnson (Geelong, Vic.: Deakin University Press, 1994), 134–5.

respondents to a survey on shopping centre usage conducted by the author in 2007 and 2008.[5]

Drive-in shopping centres were a response by retailers and developers to changes in cities' demographic geographies and consumption patterns. In the post-war period, the former were transformed through the mass distribution and usage of the motorcar, the latter by the increasing spending power of suburban populations.[6] The car enabled the spread of people from the city to the suburbs in greater density and numbers than ever before, eroding the inner-urban customer base of the great city department stores.[7] In the suburbs, strip-shopping precincts that had developed along the busiest roads near public transport hubs or at major intersections to capture passing trade frequently became clogged with traffic as a result of an ever-expanding suburban population.[8] This reduced their amenity and made it increasingly difficult to obtain parking near shops.[9] The *Retail Trader* commented that: "the last justification for this kind of shopping centre goes when the volume of traffic makes easy, free customer-parking in front of the shops impossible."[10]

By accommodating cars and separating them from pedestrian shoppers, shopping centres solved an infrastructure problem. But the major motivation for developers was the market potential of the suburbs. Shopping centres married consumption, convenience and comfort to appeal to suburban populations riding towards affluence on the back of bi-partisan government support for full employment, the consolidation of an

---

[5] Records are stored in the Department of Modern History, Macquarie University. Throughout this chapter, they are referred to as Oral History Record (OHR), followed by the chronologically ordered number of the record and the date.

[6] Beverley Kingston, *Basket, Bag and Trolley: A History of Shopping in Australia* (Melbourne: Oxford University Press, 1994), 94–6; Spearritt, "Suburban Cathedrals," 94.

[7] *Retail Trader*, August 1956, 19–28; "Summary of the 5th Annual Residential Retail Trader's Association Conference," *Retail Trader*, July 1958, 32.

[8] Graeme Davison, "From the Market to the Mall," Background Report to the Victorian Government's Department of Planning and Community Development, *Retail Policy Review*, December 2006, 14; B.A. Grace, quoted in *Australian Retailing*, April 1969, 6.

[9] T.W. Beed, "The Growth of Suburban Retailing in Sydney: A Preliminary Study of Some Factors Affecting the Form and Function of Suburban Shopping Centres," (PhD diss., University of Sydney, 1964), 95–8.

[10] *Retail Trader*, July 1959, 14. See also, Peter Yeomans, "Shopping Centre Renewal: Some Recommendations," *Retail Trader*, March 1964, 13.

industrial economy and manufacturing sector, and consistently high levels of economic growth. This saw a steady growth in real wages and discretionary income, the expansion of credit, growing numbers of women entering the paid workforce, a population boom, and young families looking to establish themselves with a home of their own, usually in a suburban environment.[11]

Centres were thus built to harness the post-war consumer wave and to offer the car-driving suburbanite a full range of shops, including supermarkets and department stores close to home, in the comfort of a self-contained, climate-controlled environment.[12] The separation of pedestrian and car traffic made shopping safer and more appealing. Retail tenants were selected to provide a full-range of services and products, and were organised in configurations that were thought to maximise sales.[13] Centralised management controlled all aspects of individual shops and created co-ordinated promotional activities.

Shopping centres positioned themselves as emblematic of a new consumption-centric, casual lifestyle.[14] The big city stores had required by convention that people dressed up when visiting them; a woman without her best hat and gloves in the city could feel quite intimidated and might even be patronised by salesgirls.[15] While all classes could visit the big city stores, special areas such as hair-dressing salons, restaurants and sometimes even art galleries were clearly designated for elite and account holding customers.[16] This is not to say that appearances were unimportant to suburban shoppers, but the fashions sold in, and said to be representative of, suburban shopping centres were "casual" and "comfortable." It was a retail model attuned to its time.[17]

---

[11] Greg Whitwell, *Making the Market: The Rise of Consumer Society* (Melbourne: McPhee Gribble, 1989), 16–26; Richard White, *Inventing Australia: Images and Identity 1688–1980* (Sydney: George Allen & Unwin, 1981), 164–5.

[12] Kim Humphery, *Shelf Life: Supermarkets and the Changing Cultures of Consumption* (Cambridge: Cambridge University Press, 1998), 115–17.

[13] James B. Douglas, "The Future of Regional Shopping Centres," *Retail Trader*, March 1958, 45–6.

[14] Spearritt, "I Shop Therefore I Am," 133.

[15] Kingston, *Basket, Bag and Trolley*, 80.

[16] Spearritt, "Suburban Cathedrals," 88.

[17] *Manly Daily*, April 4, 1963, 26 and 30; Kim Humphery, "A Stranger in Daimaru," *Meanjin* 53, 1 (1994): 85.

Top Ryde's advertising called on shoppers to "come as you are [and] shop in comfort," claiming the centre had a "gay, casual atmosphere, where you'll feel quite at home in your slacks or casual clothes."[18] An ad for Roselands told prospective customers that in the "luxurious shopping showplace ... all around you is beauty, brilliance and bounteous colour" in an atmosphere that is "relaxing, happy casual—contagious."[19] The invitation to casualness did not mean an abandonment of standards: in the 1960s, Roselands' Grace Bros store still employed floorwalkers who wore white carnations in their lapels.[20] But customers did not have to reciprocate by dressing to city levels. Shopping centres were designed to be the "city in the suburbs;" service and style supplied in a convenient and relaxed forum.[21]

The big welcome

In 1963, New South Wales Opposition Leader Bob Askin opened Warringah Mall, describing it as "a tribute to the prosperity of Australia."[22] Subsequent shopping centre openings were heralded with the same enthusiasm. When Premier Bob Heffron opened Miranda Fair in 1964, he declared that in his overseas trip the previous year he had not seen such an impressive shopping centre.[23] Not to be outdone, at the end of 1965, Askin, now premier, claimed that Roselands' "million dollar spread of merchandise … brings the city to the suburbs in a glittering way that must rival even the fabled Persian Bazaars."[24] A year later, he described Bankstown Square as "private enterprise at its best:" a monumental business achievement that would "help keep New South Wales as the leading State in Australia."[25]

---

[18] *Sydney Morning Herald*, November 12, 1957, 19.
[19] Roselands advertisement, *Torch*, October 6, 1965.
[20] Pauline, personal communication, April 20, 2006.
[21] "Shop with Ease at the Warringah Mall," advertisement, *Manly Daily*, April 4, 1963, 18; *St George and Sutherland Shire Leader* (Sutherland ed.), March 16, 1964, 4.
[22] *Manly Daily*, April 6, 1963, 1.
[23] *St. George and Sutherland Shire Leader* (Hurstville ed.), March 18, 1964, 5.
[24] Robert Askin, quoted in *Sydney Morning Herald,* October 12, 1965, cited in Lindsay Barrett, "Roselands or Everything under One Roof," *UTS Review*, 4, 2 (1998): 124.
[25] *Sydney Morning Herald,* September 21, 1966, Special Feature, 6; *Bankstown Observer*, September 21, 1966.

Local government was equally enthusiastic. Prior to Miranda Fair's construction, Sutherland Council had assured the Farmer–Myer group that they "could expect every co-operation from the Council,"[26] and afterwards publicly proclaimed the company's "fine spirit of cooperation."[27] Sutherland's Shire President congratulated Farmer–Myer on its "splendid choice" of site, marvelling at the "rock courage [taken] to spend £3.5 million on this wonderful development."[28] Similarly, Bankstown's Mayor was quoted on the front page of a local paper arguing that Lend Lease's Bankstown Square would bring in thousands of pounds of rate revenue and greatly assist in the "progress of Bankstown."[29] The city's town planner reported that the Square would significantly increase Bankstown's sphere of influence and its status as a district centre.[30]

Centre openings offered grand spectacles that filled the headlines of the local press, as bargains covered their inner pages.[31] The big shopping centres were said to herald a new way of life for suburban shoppers: a transformation of shopping from chore to pleasure.[32] For the first time in its history, the *St George Sutherland Shire Leader* published an additional edition to coincide with the opening of Miranda Fair, describing the occasion as a major event in Sutherland's "remarkable development." The Fair, it said, was a "landmark in progress" that would "help greatly in the successful expansion of the Shire."[33] It was described as "Australia's newest and most revolutionary regional shopping centre … excitingly ultra-modern in design … as modern as tomorrow."[34] At Roselands, the *Sun* declared that "the visitor's first reaction is to wonder … at the sort of courage that was needed to sink 6 million pounds into a spot by-passed by

---

[26] Sutherland Shire Council, Special General Committee Meeting, Minute No. 161, May 7, 1962.

[27] *St George and Sutherland Shire Leader* (Sutherland ed.), March 16, 1964, 4.

[28] *St. George and Sutherland Shire Leader* (Hurstville ed.), March 18, 1964, 5.

[29] *Bankstown Observer*, September 11, 1963, 1.

[30] "Report of the Town Planner to Bankstown Municipal Council," Item 455, Lend Lease Development Pty Ltd (P32/714/—/S267), August 6, 1963; *Bankstown Observer*, August 14, 1963, 1.

[31] *St George and Sutherland Shire Leader* (Sutherland ed.), March 16, 1964, 1.

[32] Barrett, "Roselands," 124.

[33] *St George and Sutherland Shire Leader* (Sutherland ed.), March 16, 1964, 1, 7.

[34] *St. George and Sutherland Shire Leader* (Hurstville ed.), Feb 5, 1964, 9. For the widespread application of revolutionary rhetoric, see, Megan Morris, "Things to Do with Shopping Centres," in *Grafts: Feminist Cultural Criticism*, ed. Susan Sheridan (New York: Verso, 1988), 209.

commerce." One could only respect the men who had this "necessary courage."[35]

Such press coverage was indicative of the widespread enthusiasm that brought huge crowds to spectacular openings of major centres: Bankstown Square pulled 100,000 people on its first day of trading, 70,000 the next.[36] Eager Sydneysiders came from nearby and afar—some even brought packed lunches to cut back on expenses.[37] A long trip by public transport was worth it, just "to see what the fuss was about."[38] Primary school students visiting Top Ryde shortly after its opening were given showbags: "What a hoot—and on a SCHOOL DAY!" wrote one erstwhile student fifty years later. "Benjamin's … had ESCALATORS! We only saw them when we went into the city in school holidays."[39]

Advertising and press reports of shopping centre openings emphasised the American expertise that imbued their designs. For people looking back at these openings, though, the words most often used are "exciting" and "modern."[40] In accounting for this difference, we might find that "American" is not as tightly entwined with progress and modernity as it was more than fifty years ago. Whether the terms have separated, or "modern" was always more than "American" for Australians, the shopping centre created a distinct and lasting impression of modernity's arrival in the suburbs. Shopping centres not only sold a modern consumer life, they embodied it. Their scale, the abundance of goods they had to offer, their marriage with the car, loud displays and endless promotion all celebrated the seemingly limitless economic prosperity of the post-war West.[41]

---

[35] Barrett, "Roselands," 126.
[36] *Sydney Morning Herald*, September 22, 1966, 4; and September 23, 1966, 6.
[37] Pamela, OHR no. 94, January/ February 2008; Stefania, OHR no. 87, January/ February 2008.
[38] Ray, OHR no. 55, January/ February 2007; Shonagh, OHR no. 32, January 2007.
[39] Carol, OHR no. 42, January 2007.
[40] Maire-Louise, OHR no. 33, January 2007; Judith, OHR no. 66, February/ March 2007; Meredith, OHR no. 71, February/ March 2007; Jan, OHR no. 36, January 2007; Margaret, OHR no. 44, January 2007; Jenny, OHR no. 45, January 2007; Robyn, OHR no. 47, January 2007. On the appeal of "the new" and shopping centres, see John Fiske, Bob Hodge and Graeme Turner, *Myths of Oz: Reading Australian Popular Culture* (Sydney: Allen & Unwin, 1987), 104–5.
[41] Barrett, "Roselands," 124.

Shopping for women

Western post-war economic prosperity had deeply gendered demarcations. Women had long been identified as the principal users of retail and the managers of domestic space.[42] In the post-war boom, this role continued and was given new meaning as the "housewife" became the manager of the post-war nuclear family's consumerist lifestyle.[43] She was targeted by shopping centre promotions, which claimed that their new public space allowed her to seamlessly mix her economic role with leisurely social interaction.[44] At Top Ryde, "the spacious traffic-free central mall" offered the housewife convenient and safe shopping "for both herself and her children."[45] Miranda Fair's architects had given "careful consideration to the needs of the women of Sutherland" during the design phase of the centre.[46] And Bankstown Square was promoted as "the Housewife's Square," where every day was "ladies day."[47]

Catering to the suburban home-building boom, homemaker stores and the homeware sections of department stores offered products and advice for housewives "seeking inspiration, ideas and know how."[48] To assist with their mothering responsibilities, shopping centres offered everything necessary for the comfort and sustenance of consumer society's next generation. Roselands claimed it was "the place to be if you're a lucky mother."[49] Cots, baby mattresses and clothing were the subject of frequent sales and a regular spotlight of advertising.[50] In 1970, Roselands held a "Bonny Bouncer contest" in which babies—separated into "novice" and "open" divisions—were placed in a Bonny Bouncer and "judged on creative ability, fluency of movement and general vitality." This was followed by a "baby crawling derby," conducted next to the centre's iconic Raindrop Fountain.[51]

---

[42] Humphery, *Shelf Life*, 5.
[43] Ann Game and Rosemary Pringle, "Sexuality and the Suburban Dream," in *Memories and Dreams: Reflections on Twentieth-Century Australia (Pastiche II)*, ed. Richard White and Penny Russell (Sydney: Allen & Unwin, 1997), 205.
[44] Barrett, "Roselands," 134; Spearritt, "I Shop Therefore I Am," 133.
[45] *Building, Lighting Engineering*, April 24, 1958, 42.
[46] *St George and Sutherland Shire Leader* (Sutherland ed.), March 16, 1964, 23.
[47] *Bankstown Observer*, September 21, 1966.
[48] A.J. Benjamin Supplement, *Daily Telegraph*, November 13, 1957, 31–45; *Torch*, October 13, 1965; *Manly Daily*, April 4, 1963, 26 and 30.
[49] *Bankstown Canterbury Torch*, September 9, 1970, 17.
[50] *St George and Sutherland Shire Leader* (Sutherland ed.), March 16, 1964, 10.
[51] *Bankstown Canterbury Torch*, September 9, 1970, 17.

Shopping centres, then, consciously and continually targeted women shoppers.[52] They offered (a limited) freedom, couched in the language of convenience and circumscribed by consumption—and it was not all marketers' hot air. Juggling young children and bags of shopping across multiple locations could be onerous, annoying and time consuming. The provision of one-stop shopping with parking close to shops was a great boon for many women and has been a key attraction since their inception.[53] This has not been universal. Indeed there were, and continue to be, complaints about the inconvenience of large centres, which can make the purchase of a few items a time-consuming activity. Early on, the demise of the grocery store, which had delivered and offered credit, was lamented by some women forced into unfamiliar and unwanted patterns of shopping.

Washing over these issues, shopping centre advertising emphasised convenience at every opportunity. Nowhere was this more evident than in their provision of child-care facilities. Where experts, media and governments dismissed regular child minding as an indulgence for undeserving mothers, shopping centres celebrated short-term, casual care as the freedom of opportunity for (shopping) women.[54] Warringah Mall's "Mini-Mall" was filled with toys, and included a nursery and an outdoor play area complete with seesaws, miniature houses and a racing track. Three nursing sisters in starched white uniforms looked after the children for a small fee whilst their mothers shopped.[55] Roselands went a step further with its TV Child Minder—the largest close circuit television system in Australia at the time. In an age before the public observance of small children had become taboo, monitors positioned around the centre allowed mothers to watch their children happily playing, sleeping and being looked after by Sister M. Johnston, "a triple certificate nurse, and mother of two," and her small cohort of "baby sitters."[56]

---

[52] Davison, "From the Market to the Mall," 20.

[53] Jan, OHR 36, January 2007; Jody, OHR 6, January 2007; Kate, OHR 19, January 2007; John Stevens, "Shopping Centres on the Attack," *Age*, July 18 1992, 2.

[54] On attitudes towards child-care, see, Deborah Brennan, *The Politics of Australian Childcare: Philanthropy to Feminism and Beyond* (Cambridge: Cambridge University Press, 1998), 52–9.

[55] Judy Judd, *It's Not Bricks and Mortar, It's People: A Tribute to Warringah Mall Shopping Centre's 25th Anniversary*, (n.p., c1988), 52.

[56] Canterbury Council (Campsie) Library Local Studies: "Explore Roselands," Grace Bros promotional brochure; Barrett, "Roselands," 127–8.

There were limitations to the child-care services; the free time they enabled was predicated on women remaining within a privately owned, largely internalised, consumer-oriented space. The big shopping centres, in this way, were an expression in the built environment of the cultural, social and economic role of the post-war housewife. Both role and building, however, contained contradictions. Even as women were publicly being defined as housewives, they were entering the workforce in increasing numbers; and, even as shopping centres were marketed towards the stay-at-home housewife, they offered women employment outside the domestic sphere.

Working in shops

Women's retail employment coincided with significant changes in the retail industry, particularly in the post-war period. Considerable deskilling had occurred with the advent of mass production, the innovation of self-service and the rise of marketing.[57] This saw a reduction in the status of retail jobs, even as women were entering the trade in growing numbers. They tended to fill lower range jobs, while management remained male dominated. As the supermarket chains spread through the suburbs during the 1950s and 60s, women signed up en masse as cashiers.[58] Shopping centres followed, congregating dozens of small and large shops that offered further and much-appreciated employment opportunities.[59] The relationship was symbiotic: working women increased disposable family income, further fuelling the consumption economy on which shopping centres were built.[60]

The creation of employment helped to embed shopping centres in their local communities.[61] At Miranda, the manager of the National Bank branch was a local, as was the child-care sister, and the operator of the newsagent. The latter individual was also the head of the local chamber of

---

[57] Ann Game and Rosemary Pringle, *Gender at Work* (Sydney: Allen & Unwin, 1983), 75–8.

[58] Game and Pringle, *Gender at Work*, 63; Humphery, *Shelf Life*, 106.

[59] Ros, OHR no. 14, January 2007; Sylvia, OHR no. 29, January 2007; Maire-Louise, OHR no. 33, January 2007.

[60] Spearritt, "I Shop Therefore I Am," 135.

[61] A number of survey respondents recognised shopping centre employment as an important contribution to their communities. These included: Ros, OHR no. 14, 14–20 January 2007; Sylvia, OHR no. 29, 21–27 January 2007; Maire-Louise, OHR no. 33, 21–27 January 2007.

commerce, a "chosen son" of the Shire's Liberal Party and, according to the *Leader*, the "unofficial mayor" of Miranda.[62] For the families and friends of employees, the shopping centre could become an integral element of their day-to-day lives. One former resident of Sutherland remembered that:

> My mother went to work in the centre for decades and this brought the centre into our family life as we felt, through my mother's dinner time stories, that we knew many of the shop owners and businesses ... Later, in high school, my best friend's parents also had a shop there so the whole centre was intertwined in my life.[63]

After growing up hearing the inside stories of shopping centres, kids might find themselves following their parents and working there too. After she left school, Lorne—one respondent to the survey on which this chapter is based—joined her mother, who worked in Grace Bros, Roselands: "I loved working with my mother," Lorne writes, and "had a great time getting to know people in Grace Bros. It was like a big family (not always happy though!) but everyone knew everyone else."[64] Lorne met her future husband, Ken, when he came in to make a payment on his $10 credit account. They were engaged in two months, married in four, and held their reception in Roseland's spectacular "Rose Room."[65] The shopping centre had provided parental income, a first job, a chance meeting that led to marriage, the venue for the couple's wedding reception, and many nostalgic visits over following years.

Retailers valued young workers like Lorne. Some industry literature suggested dressing them up in the latest fashions, creating live display models—walking examples of the culture and lifestyle up for sale.[66] Young people, for their part, saw good opportunities for local, part-time work,[67] and found jobs throughout retail organisations. Pauline, another survey respondent, joined the display department of Grace Bros, Roselands, after finishing art school as a teenager in the mid-60s. She

---

[62] *St George and Sutherland Shire Leader* (Sutherland Edition), 16 March 1964, 22–4.

[63] Maire-Louise, OHR no. 33, 21–27 January 2007.

[64] Lorne, personal communication, October 3, 2006.

[65] Ken, personal communication, December 4, 2006.

[66] "Promoting for the Teenage Market," *Retail Trader,* December 1963, 29–30.

[67] Lorne, personal communication, October 3, 2006; Ken, personal communication, December 4, 2006; Robert, OHR no. 11, January 2007.

recalls that it was an unusual occupation for a girl at the time, with most of her workmates being male and gay:

> I loved it and them, they treated me like a favoured child teaching me everything they knew from the 'hey day' of window dressing … at Mark Foys in Sydney. They … introduced me to a lot of things, 'completing' my education with ballet, films, food and fashion. I can remember going to see *Elvira Madigan* with 'Tilly' after he had taken me to the original Adam's Marble Bar. We sat and held hands and cried throughout the movie.[68]

Occasionally, Pauline and the display staff would run through the store with a naked mannequin, shrieking with laughter as they clutched at its crotch or breast. When the store manager commanded Tilly "to pull his finger out," he received a broken-off mannequin's finger in reply. One memorable night, Pauline helped sew her boss into a ball gown covered in thousands of tiny mirrors, before helping transport him—flat on his back, unable to bend, in a station wagon—over the Harbour Bridge, past a flabbergasted toll collector.[69] The city had come to the suburbs and taken the young suburban girl back to the city.

Hanging at the mall

Australian youth not only worked in shopping centres, they hung out, met friends, observed fashions and entertained themselves there.[70] Whilst some still found a trip to the city more exciting,[71] many others embraced the new world on their doorsteps. Ken recalls that, as a youth, he regarded Roselands as "like a magnet … the centre of the area."[72] For Robert, a high school student in the 1960s, it became:

> the central focus of my life and that of my friends … Each afternoon after school and every weekend was spent meeting up within Roselands to 'hang' with the guys of Punchbowl, Belmore and Narwee Boys and the girls of Wiley Park and Beverly Hills Girls … I met my first girl friend [there] and had my first kiss.[73]

---

[68] Pauline, personal communication, April 20, 2006.
[69] Pauline, personal communication, April 20, 2006.
[70] Beth, OHR no. 28, January 2007; Dianne, OHR no. 48, January 2007; Fiske, Hodge and Turner, *Myths of Oz*, 115.
[71] Deborah, OHR no. 18, January 2007.
[72] Ken, personal communication, December 4, 2006.
[73] Robert, OHR no. 11, January 2007.

Promotions featuring stars of popular culture helped set the scene. Miranda had only just opened when Col Joye and Little Pattie came in to sing and sign autographs at Farmers' record bar.[74] Teenagers gathered for fashion parades and rock shows at Westfield Burwood.[75] At Roselands, "the raindrop fountain was the focus:" crowds "would gather on the top (third) floor to view" celebrities below, such as Robert Vaughn from "The Man from UNCLE."[76] Johnny Farnham performed "Sadie the Cleaning Lady," and, when Tiny Tim sang, "Tip Toe through the Tulips," Pauline and her friends "stood near the stage and pelted him with plastic flowers."[77] Ronnie Burns came to Roselands in 1969 to perform his single "Age of Consent," causing, according to teen music magazine *Go-Set*, a "near riot." Photos depict security guards struggling to hold back female fans and Ronnie being dragged off stage (before centre management shouted him lunch in "the beautiful 'Viking' restaurant").[78]

Riots for rock stars singing about loving young girls aside, the close association of shopping centres with suburban values gave them a sense of respectability and safety for teenagers and young adults. For Lorne, Roseland's was preferred over the local milkbar, which "gave you a bad name!"[79] For Deborah, Westfield Burwood was a place to hang out where she could "avoid the punks and ruffians."[80] And, for Beth, Warringah Mall and, later, Lemon Grove at Chatswood provided "an excuse to go out legitimately" by herself—"after all it was SAFE to go to the shops."[81]

Australian retailers and marketers were aware of the enormous growth of the youth market. Almost half the population was under the age of twenty-five and had money coupled with a desire to spend it.[82] Stores were advised to take the lead in setting styles, with research suggesting that youth looked "to their favourite store for their fashion guidance."[83] This may have been wishful thinking by retailers hoping to dictate fashion to a market they did not truly understand, but Robert credits Roselands with

[74] *St George and Sutherland Shire Leader* (Sutherland ed.), March 16, 1964, 15.
[75] Maire-Louise, OHR no. 33, January 2007.
[76] Robert, OHR no. 11, January 2007.
[77] Pauline, personal communication, April 20, 2006.
[78] "Ronnie in Near Riot," *Go-Set*, January 29, 1969, 9.
[79] Lorne, personal communication, October 3, 2006.
[80] Deborah, OHR no. 18, January 2007.
[81] Beth, OHR no. 28, January 2007.
[82] *Australian Retailing*, April 1967, 18–9.
[83] "Promoting for the Teenage Market," 29–30.

introducing "fashion to my group … [because] trends were on show that would have been unknown to those outside the complex … Gary Darby's surf shop gave me the look I wanted."[84]

If consuming youth was welcomed, miscreant youth was feared. Youth "gangs" at times associated themselves with shopping centres: at Roselands the "Hairies" or "Surfs" faced off against the "Sharps" from Bankstown Square, who would arrive to intimidate the locals on their home turf.[85] Onlookers remember the Sharps "always bashing up kids (boys) with long hair."[86] For retailers, though, shoplifting was the major concern, and the industry literature was filled with warnings and advice on how to deal with it.[87] One journal declared that "the under-21 group … [was] on the greatest shoplifting spree in history."[88]

Lorne remembers that "shoplifting was rife at that time," and girls at her school would frequently talk about it and show off shoplifted items. Her husband also knew a lot of boys who would steal EPs and singles. Lorne tells the story of being unjustly accused of shoplifting herself, being grabbed by a store detective, taken to security and harangued by a "bully" of a manager: "The dickhead security manager told my father I was rude, and a juvenile delinquent … It was a horrendous experience and certainly just reinforced my point of view at that time about authority figures."[89]

Some local residents feared the concentration of teenagers that centres had brought so close to their homes. One man living next to Roselands claimed that his property was being used by a "hooligan element" as a getaway exit from security guards and demanded that a fence be built to protect his home.[90] Towards the end of the 1960s, other residents began complaining to Canterbury Council about youths holding night-time car races and noisy parties in and around Roselands. One local resident

---

[84] Robert, OHR no. 11, January 2007.
[85] Robert, OHR no. 11, January 2007.
[86] Lorne, personal communication, March 3, 2007.
[87] "Shop-lifting—$25m. a Year and Growing Rapidly," *Australian Retailing*, July 1967, 5–9.
[88] "Why do Young People Steal?," *Australian Retailing*, May 1968, 17–19. For the longer history of shoplifting, and the changing characterisations of shoplifters, see Kingston, *Basket, Bag and Trolley*, 69–76.
[89] Lorne, personal communication, March 3, 2007.
[90] Canterbury Council records index, "Roselands Shopping Centre," 2 (April 1968), 68/1763.

interviewed for this study recalled no drag races, but the number of complaints is hard to ignore.[91] Certainly this was the case for the local council, which forwarded a group of complaints to Roselands management requesting that a regular security patrol be provided to crack down on the troublemakers.

At other shopping centres, however, there were efforts to accommodate local youth culture. Ros, a teenager in the 1960s, recalls that "the [Warringah] Mall" was "a very big thing to people in my age group as we had something else to do on weekends apart from going to the beach and playing sport … We all loved going to the 'Mall' after the beach."[92] On the weekends, David Jones' two storey blank facade was used to show surfing movies, with local youth watching from the car park:

> The first time I saw *Endless Summer* was from the roof of my boyfriend's car, which was a VW… Imagine several hundred teenagers all sitting in the car park, which was an open-air style, either in or on top of their cars watching movies. Surfing movies of course, because we were all Northern Beaches kids who lived and breathed that stuff then.[93]

For Ros and teenagers like her, as well as their parents and other local residents, shopping centres transformed their suburbs. Centres were iconic of the abundance of the post-war good life. They provided a social space that was bursting with consumer energy: designed as a modern market, calling shoppers to buy with all the intensity the marketers of the time could muster. They were air-conditioned social and retail sites, with masses of goods on show for an increasingly affluent mainstream population. For political leaders, shopping centres signalled progress, promised growth and brought jobs—incentive enough to associate themselves with grand centre openings. For business, they were a triumph of capitalist efficiency, a contribution to the country and, over time, an immensely valuable investment.

This early celebration of shopping centres in Australia was not universal, nor did it last forever. The very success of shopping centres brought dramatic rental increases for their retail tenants and a vast power

[91] Brent, personal communication, January 17, 2007.
[92] Ros, OHR no. 14, January 2007.
[93] Ros, OHR no. 14, January 2007.

differential emerged between developers and small retailers.[94] There were complaints over the abuse of market power from the mid-1970s on, and legislation designed to curb it was created in all states through the 1980s and 1990s. Retailing in traditional shopping strips struggled to compete, losing anchor shops and services as well as shoppers. People lamented this change, even as they chose the efficiency of the shopping centre, and recognised its enormous advantages.

Popularity bred further success, with more major anchor stores, specialty shops and services attracted to the blossoming markets. While this increased the power of shopping centre developers, it also alienated some people; and continues to do so.[95] In the contemporary era, many are turned off by the homogeneity of countless replicated chains that now dominate the pedestrian causeways of the mega-mall.[96] Others, as they move into a different phase of life, simply find thorns where once there were roses, the convenience of the shopping centre having worn off.[97] In the 1960s, though, shopping centres were new, exciting and offered gilded avenues of consumerised freedom. People came to shop and meet up, spend time together, chat, browse, enjoy a meal, work, pass the time, and shop again. Mainstream Australia has been doing much the same things in shopping centres ever since.

---

[94] Peter Carkagis, *The Law of Retail Leasing in New South Wales* (Sydney: Prospect Publishing, 1997), 4.

[95] Frank, OHR no. 10, January 2007; Shairon, OHR no. 15, January 2007; Stephanie, OHR no. 25, January 2007.

[96] Jan, OHR no. 36, January 2007; Vanessa, OHR no. 83, January/ February 2008; Pamela, OHR no. 94, January/ February 2008.

[97] Gretchen, OHR no. 1, January 2007; Jody, OHR no. 6, January 2007.

CHAPTER EIGHT

A DRINK WHOSE TIME HAD FINALLY COME: WINE CONSUMPTION IN AUSTRALIA 1950–1980

DAVID DUNSTAN

An aspect of Australian consumer habits struck curiosity in French and other continental European visitors to Australia in the 19th century. Here was a continent blessed with the capacity to produce wine of virtually every type but showing little or no interest in drinking it. Edmond Marin La Meslée reflected in 1883 that "men and women of British antecedents do not suddenly lose their natural taste for their traditional national beverage."[1] This, he surmised, was beer. But, at this time, British tastes were beginning to change, following the Gladstone government's relaxation of duties imposed on light European table wines in the early 1860s and the freeing up of their sale to an urbanising middle class.[2] Yet, as late as 1943, the leaders of the Australian wine industry were still puzzling over how tea might be supplanted at the Australian dinner table with wine.[3] It was remarkable that Australia had a wine industry at all. Vignerons established their enterprises in advance of a market. Some were migrants from continental Europe who were transplanting the agricultural traditions of their homelands. "Colonial wine" was promoted from the middle decades of the 19th century in New South Wales, South Australia and Victoria. But it was only after 1886, when British restrictions on

[1] Edmond Marin La Meslée, *The New Australia*, translated by Russel Ward (Melbourne: Heinemann Educational, 1979), 34, first published as *L'Australie Nouvelle* (Paris: E. Plon, 1883).

[2] John Burnett, *Liquid Pleasures: A Social History of Drinks in Modern Britain* (London: Routledge, 1999), 149–51.

[3] *Wine and Spirit News & Australian Vigneron*, May 20, 1943, 5. See also Tony Dingle, "The Truly Magnificent Thirst," *Historical Studies* 19, 75 (1980): 244; and Ted Henzell, *Australian Agriculture: Its History and Challenges* (Melbourne: CSIRO Publishing, 2007), 271–3.

naturally higher alcohol-content Australian red wines were lifted, that an export trade developed. The industry gravitated to the warmer regions of Victoria and South Australia to specialise in the rich and naturally sweeter "Australian Burgundy" style of red wine, following that which the French had themselves developed for British and foreign markets with grapes from their own hot-climate vineyards as well as those in Algeria.[4] Why the British could be persuaded to drink Australian wine when Australians were reluctant to do so is perhaps best explained as a triumph of entrepreneurship by those, mainly British, merchants who marketed and sold an inexpensive but smartly packaged alcoholic beverage to a much larger urban-based middle-class population than Australia possessed at the time. The Frenchman and professional observer of the English, Max O'Rell—who predicted a future for the colonial product—observed with nice irony: "when all the other inhabitants of the globe are drinking it, perhaps the Australians may make up their minds to taste what it is like."[5]

The First World War restricted but did not altogether interrupt this trade, and, afterwards, grape growing became a focus of soldier settlement activity in the Australian Riverland districts. It was as a consequence of over-production that in 1924 the industry received bonus assistance from the Australian government to export this surplus in the form of sweet fortified wine and brandy. It received a further boost from the British government, with imperial preference granted to the trade the following year in recognition of Australia's role in the war effort.[6] A boom in exports in cheap fortified wines resulted. This ceased with the depredations of German U-boats in the 1939–45 war and restrictions on merchant shipping. The export bounty ceased in 1947 and Britain's consumers turned up their noses at the Australian product. France's vineyards and stocks had survived the hostilities, and the pre-war reputation of Australian wine as cheap and dependent on subsidies resurfaced. The collapse of the export trade to Britain during and after the war set the scene for a change in Australian consumer habits as attention was directed towards the domestic market. Alcoholic beverages of all

---

[4] David Dunstan, "A Sobering Experience: From 'Australian Burgundy' to 'Kanga Rouge': Australian Wine Battles on the London Market 1900 to 1981," *Australian Studies* 17, 2 (2002): 179–210.

[5] Max O'Rell, *John Bull & Co.: The Great Colonial Branches of the Firm: Canada, Australia, New Zealand and South Africa* (London: Frederick Warne, 1894), 159.

[6] H.E. Laffer, *The Wine Industry of Australia* (Adelaide: The Australian Wine Board, 1949), 75–81.

kinds were rationed during the war and were in short supply for years afterwards. Shortages of beer had meant that Australian wine, known contemptuously as "plonk," was by necessity the second choice of servicemen on leave and for those who entertained them. Sweet fortified wine—"fourpenny dark" and "madeira"—was the standard fare in wine saloons, where the elderly, the lonely and, undoubtedly, the alcoholic gathered. Wine saloons were vilified after the war when there were an estimated eighty of them in the Melbourne metropolitan area.[7] They did little harm and probably some good but temperance advocates, social reformers and modernisers generally swept them away. By the end of the 1950s, they had gone, their licences transferred or abolished, the properties turned to other purposes and their drinkers consigned to even less salubrious venues.

The interest in table wine gathered slowly in the 1950s and, in the late 60s, it took off. The industry, initially at least, was still geared to the production of fortified wine. But, within thirty years, this had changed and Australians had more than doubled their per capita consumption of wine of all types. It continued to climb, and the latest figures (2006–07) are 29.2 litres of wine per person annually.[8] For some time now, Australians have been among the highest consumers of wine in the English-speaking countries, though still well behind the Europeans, particularly the French, Italian and Spanish. The period from the 1960s was also when consumption of new manufactured goods and services showed a marked increase. Their sale and distribution coincided with population growth, increased wealth and leisure, and new demands for social activities such as entertaining and dining out. Wine now became more of a mass-produced commodity than it had been, with the trend markedly in favour of table wine. But what circumstances or attitudes had changed to alter Australian drinking habits?

The legacy of the past

In the 1950s, the main centres of the wine industry could be found in hinterland agricultural areas like the Barossa Valley, McLaren Vale, Clare and Coonawarra in South Australia, Rutherglen in Victoria and the Hunter

[7] *Herald*, April 12 and 14, 1947. See also Sidney J. Baker, *The Australian Language* (Melbourne: Sun Books, 1970[1945]), 226–7, for an irreverent discussion of vernacular wine terminology.
[8] Australian Bureau of Statistics Cat. 403.0.55.001 "Apparent Consumption of Alcohol."

Valley and Mudgee in New South Wales, together with the Swan Valley in Western Australia. Here table wine producers had "hung on," many of them since the 19th century. Many were family enterprises, mixed farms where wine was often not the most important part of the output. In 1955, the Current Affairs Bulletin, *Wine in Australia*, listed fourteen viticultural regions: South Australia (5), New South Wales (4), Victoria (4), Queensland (1) and Western Australia (1).[9] The hot, irrigated agricultural districts along the Murrumbidgee and Murray rivers, which had been suppliers of dried fruit (sultanas) and grapes for spirit distillation, now supported the spirit and fortified wine market that still constituted the bulk of sales to the public in the immediate post-war period. Larger companies with a national reach for their products included B. Seppelt & Sons, G. Gramp & Sons (Orlando), Thomas Hardy & Sons, Lindeman's Wines, McWilliams Wines Ltd, S. Smith & Sons (Yalumba) and Penfold's Wines. These had their origins as family companies, and a dynastic character still influenced their operation. All would experience the tensions of growth in the coming decades and some would give way to take-over pressures, assuming new corporate identities. Many smaller concerns would expand to become fully dedicated winemakers, or sell out at a profit to second-order businessmen and corporations diversifying. In 1955, Australians drank 6.1 litres of wine per head per year but twenty-five times that amount of beer. For every bottle of light table wine, they also consumed several bottles of sweet fortified wine, known either as Port or Sherry.[10] The Australian economy may have been poised on the edge of a great period of growth but its wine industry was moribund and many of the more individual, smaller producers were finding it harder to carry on.[11] The advantage to the consumer was that wine prices had risen comparatively little over the years, inflation notwithstanding. With exports stagnant, demand trending downwards and much surplus stock in bond, the industry could do little other than absorb increasing costs of production. Yet, already by 1956, the Australian Wine Board was able to claim that "sales of table wines are increasing and that greater interest is being shown in the consumption of wine with meals."[12]

---

[9] The Corowa–Rutherglen region was shared by NSW and Victoria. *Current Affairs Bulletin: Wine in Australia* 17, 5 (1955): 69.

[10] *Wine in Australia*, 73.

[11] *Wine in Australia,* 75–6.

[12] Australian Wine Board, cited in James Halliday, *A History of the Australian Wine Industry 1949–1994* (Adelaide: Australian Wine and Brandy Corporation in association with Winetitles, 1994), 17.

By the 1960s, Australia was becoming a more multicultural and sophisticated society as a result of post-war immigration and improved communications, but it was still Anglo-centric in its values and the overall composition of its population. Australians' embracing of wine was consistent with modernising trends, as well as a rising standard of living and exposure to international and other cultural influences. The wine industry was not a passive participant in this process. Indeed, many believe it led the way by adopting more scientific and technologically sophisticated techniques of production and adapting existing vineyard and production assets to make more palatable wines.[13] According to Ted Henzell, four main innovations underpinned the modernisation of Australian winemaking in the second half of the 20th century: mechanical refrigeration, stainless steel, superior yeasts and instrumented measurement.[14] Branded products were advertised and packaged more conveniently, and priced to suit changing tastes and new social situations. Production was better informed by science, and a new professional ethos was emerging. The identity of wine as a product possessing that special traditional mystique so revered in places like Spain, France and Italy was challenged in the "new world" Australian context. But the image-makers and merchandisers wanted to have it both ways. Wine was becoming a mass-production item but its producers—both large and small—had a vested interest in maintaining its image as a hand-crafted, elite and individual product. So, too, and perhaps more interestingly, did the consuming public. Devotees of wine needed to be seduced.

Wine's changing image

Initially, wine's social image was unflattering but so too were the images of its rivals, beer and spirits. Hotels were the main public outlets for drink, and the prevalence of "tied houses" meant the virtual monopoly of brewery interests. In the first half of the 20th century, the temperance movement fought the liquor industries with polls on prohibition, no-licence and licence reduction, and it remained politically strong, in the southern states especially. An unholy stalemate between the temperance interests and the breweries saw the sale and public consumption of liquor tightly controlled. Six o'clock closing of hotels had been introduced as a temporary wartime measure in 1915 in South Australia, Tasmania and

[13] Halliday, *History of the Australian Wine Industry 1949–1994*, 2, 13–23.
[14] Henzell, *Australian Agriculture*, 264, 267–9.

New South Wales and in 1916 in Victoria.[15] A referendum held in Victoria in 1956 to extend trading hours was lost, and it was not until 1966 that 10 o'clock closing was permitted. Similar restrictions in relation to the consumption of liquor at restaurants were relaxed in 1960. The licensing laws were progressively liberalised thereafter. But, initially at least, the breweries and hotels were no friends to the wine industry, whose leaders knew that they must make their way independently.[16]

At the beginning of the period in the 1950s, most Australian table and fortified wines were identified by generic descriptors, which, supposedly, indicated the classic styles to which they conformed. The glaring exception was "Burgundy." Rich, full and alcoholic styles of Australian dry red wine, made principally from Shiraz, had nothing in common with the subtle, fine-boned red wines made from Pinot Noir produced in the Burgundy district of France. Australian producers, like those in other parts of the new world, maintained generic descriptors—Champagne, Chablis, Hermitage, Moselle, Sherry and Port—as long as they could, notwithstanding opposition from the European Community, whose wine-producing place names had been appropriated. But the main thrust of marketing as producers came to bottle and label their own wines was to create brands.[17] Among the most successful popular white wines of the 1950s and 60s were Rinegolde, Hamilton's Ewell Moselle, Ben Ean Moselle, Barossa Pearl and Starwine. In certain instances, a company's products came to be recognised as synonymous with styles of wine: Penfold in premium red wine, Seppelt in sparkling wine, for example. Regional descriptors were also style and quality indicators, as in Europe, but without the subtle gradations that came with the various controlled labelling systems, and especially the French AOC (*appellation controlée*) regime. The Barossa Valley, Hunter Valley, Rutherglen and Coonawarra districts all attracted customer interest and loyalty, Coonawarra especially, because of its supposed limited territory and claim to really being a premium red wine region, akin to those of France.

Australia rejected the idea of industry or government–imposed regulations on labelling that would have meant more specific descriptions of wines as regards their origin and character. The larger companies that

---

[15] Walter Phillips, "'Six O'Clock Swill': The Introduction of Early Closing of Hotel Bars in Australia," *Historical Studies* 19, 75 (1980): 250–66.

[16] Halliday, *History of the Australian Wine Industry 1949–1994*, 5–6.

[17] John Beeston, *A Concise History of Australian Wine* (Sydney: Allen & Unwin, 2001), 190.

owned vineyards or sourced fruit from different regions blended their products, and sought to attract the consumer not so much by the wine's regional origins but by the company or brand name. In certain instances, a place or vineyard actually became a brand. Jacob's Creek, a place in South Australia, came to embrace nearly every commercial vineyard in south-eastern Australia, as its company, Orlando, sourced grapes to satisfy the national (and later the international) demand for this product. Grange and Dalwood provide examples of estate names retained as brand names. In the case of the historic Dalwood property, Penfold quit first the estate and then the Hunter Valley altogether but retained the name for commercial brand purposes.[18] The larger companies could afford newspaper, magazine and even television advertising to support their larger production, branded products. One of the most successful was the "you make us smile Dr Lindeman" campaign, with its repeated jingle and sepia-toned images of young women relaxing.[19] Women were a new market and responsive to clever strategies such as this one. Sociologists John Smart and John Wiggers concluded in their study of the white wine boom of the 1970s that "the massive increase in white wine sales is a direct outcome of the desirability of an alcoholic beverage which is acceptable to both sexes."[20] The social milieu was becoming more accommodating for women to drink in public settings like licensed restaurants and even hotels following the extension of licensing hours. In the 6 o'clock swill days, hotels had been almost exclusively masculine domains.[21]

The industry peak body, the Australian Wine Board, was only given the power to promote wine and brandy on the domestic market in 1954. An immigrant Welshman, Len Evans, played an important role when he became national promotions manager for the board in 1965. Evans had been the Sydney *Bulletin*'s wine columnist, "Cellarmaster," since 1962.

[18] Jaki Ilbery, "Vineyards and Vignerons of Australia," in *Australia and New Zealand Complete Book of Wine*, ed. Len Evans (Sydney: Paul Hamlyn, 1973), 47–9.

[19] Author Peter Carey claims to have created the jingle whilst working in advertising. See Peter Morley, "Information," photograph of Peter Carey, 1989, National Portrait Gallery, Canberra.

[20] John Smart and John Wiggers, *The White Wine Boom: A Sociological Interpretation* (Newcastle: Department of Sociology, University of Newcastle, 1981?), 5.

[21] Tanja Luckins, "'Time, Gentlemen Please': The End of Six O'Clock Closing and the 'Post-swill' Pub," in *Go! Melbourne in the Sixties*, ed. Seamus O'Hanlon and Tanja Luckins (Beaconsfield, Victoria: Melbourne Publishing Group, 2005), 174–87.

With assistants in three states, he enlisted journalists, industry colleagues and editors to publish on wine.[22] A compliant media now assisted the awareness of wine as a high-profile consumer product. Scarcely a newspaper or magazine of note lacked a dedicated scribe, and the association of wine with food and hospitality was made explicit. [23] With the wine show system incomprehensible to most consumers, and the industry's own indicators of quality uncertain and changing, a role was created for the new self-styled experts.

The evidence of public interest provided by the sheer number of books and published columns in newspapers—well in advance of equivalent advertising—suggests deeper forces were at work. Taking her cue from Pierre Bourdieu, Marion Demoissier has argued that taste is socially constructed and that in France, the exemplar of a traditional wine–producing and consuming society, the hierarchy of wines became identified with the social hierarchy.[24] In a society with few established boundaries of class, wine offered a strategy for Australians to differentiate themselves. The 1960s saw a plethora of convivial wine clubs, extending from the humblest suburban "Beefsteak and Burgundy" club through to elite French wine-worshipping fraternities. Many of these were promotions by shrewd businessmen such as Melbourne wine merchant Dan Murphy, who founded the Vintage Club in 1955; by 1977, it had 18,000 members.[25] At the Rothbury Estate Society's design award–winning winery headquarters in the Hunter Valley, members attended dinners and competed to achieve grades of palate excellence as green, red, or the especially coveted purple, ribbon holders. By 1981, it boasted a membership of 33,000.[26] The 1968 dinner of the Confrérie des Chevaliers du Tastevin was a black-tie affair attended by members of Australia's pastoral families, together with leaders of business, the public service and artistic communities, and the French consul and former prime minister Sir

[22] Jeremy Oliver, *Evans on Earth: The Story of Len Evans' Affair with Wine* (Melbourne: Lothian Publishing Company), 35–44.
[23] David Dunstan, "The Wine Press," *Meanjin* 61, 4 (2002): 34–43.
[24] Pierre Bourdieu, *Distinction: A Social Critique of the Judgment of Taste* (London: Routledge & Kegan Paul, 1984); Marion Demoissier, "Consuming Wine in France: The 'Wandering Drinker' and the Vin-anomie," in *Drinking Cultures*, ed. Thomas M. Wilson (Oxford: Berg, 2005), 131.
[25] *Vintage Club News* (Melbourne), October 1977.
[26] *Rothbury Pressings*, 53 (1981): 8.

Robert Menzies as guests of honour.[27] Wine had become a cultural object, a focus for companionship and conviviality, and knowledge of its varied discourses was now prized. Individuals honed their tasting skills, and elite wines such as Penfold's Grange Hermitage evoked reverence.

Wine appreciation partook of the same rituals and connoisseurship as in cultural circles. In an early example of niche marketing, David Wynn advertised his company's elite products from the Coonawarra region selectively in theatre and concert programs.[28] With his European background and shrewd understanding of cultural capital, the Sydney art dealer, Rudy Komon, assisted in the education of the Sydney nouveaux riches—"the barbarians," as he often called them. In addition to conducting his Woollahra Gallery, Komon was an extensive buyer of wine and chairman of wine judges at the Sydney Show.[29] But, although the emergence of a class of taste makers, publicists and experts was important in disseminating knowledge and encouraging curiosity, it does not by itself account for the rise in the popularity of wine in Australia. What other factors were at work?

Innovations in production

One view holds the increased consumption was driven by the industry's technological and scientific innovation. The abolition of the wine export bounty in 1947 was compensated for by increased government support for scientific research.[30] By 1955, Australian winemakers had solved problems of spoilage associated with the manufacture and storage of fortified wines. Fortified wines—sherry and port—still accounted for more than 80 per cent of the industry's production and sales, and, in the first decade of the period covered in this chapter, more fortified wine was consumed than table wine in Australia.[31] But, within ten or fifteen years, these wines would be in relative decline. The pre-war problems of the industry arising from bacterial spoilage provided some benefits in the long

[27] *Confrérie des chevaliers du tastevin (Australia): menu (1968)*, http://www.winelit.slsa.sa.gov.au/sip_sup/SP_Chevaliers_1968_02.htm (accessed August 10, 2009).
[28] David Wynn, personal communication.
[29] Lenore Nicklin, "Komon, Rudolph John (Rudy) (1908–1982)," *Australian Dictionary of Biography* (*ADB*) 17 (Melbourne: Melbourne University Press, 2007), 637–8; Records of the Rudy Komon Art Gallery, MS8327, National Library of Australia.
[30] Beeston, *A Concise History of Australian Wine*, 190–1.
[31] Halliday, *History of the Australian Wine Industry 1949–1994*, 4.

run by generating heightened understanding of issues of pH and acid adjustment to produce more stable and longer-living wines. The improvement of vineyards and the cultivation of new table wine varieties were other key factors. Although the drinking of any kind of table wine may have been a mark of distinction early in the period, as interest began to escalate it was the type of wine, its origins, or the maker, brand or variety that began to command attention in the consumer's mind. The inherent complexity of varietal and regional offerings presented (as they still do) extraordinary scope for connoisseurship and difference. Australian vignerons inherited an impressive array of vine stock from the 19th-century pioneers. Premium grape varieties were singled out for improving the quality of the wines produced. Riesling (originally Rhine Riesling), Semillon, Sauvignon Blanc, Pinot Noir and even "the workhorse" variety, Shiraz, attracted special attention. Wines made from Cabernet Sauvignon and Chardonnay brought higher prices in the 1970s and 80s respectively.

Penfold's Wines first refrigerated their red wine ferments in 1951, and Orlando introduced pressure fermentation (the precursor for them to cold fermentation) for its 1953 Barossa Riesling.[32] A pressure fermentation sparkling wine, Barossa Pearl, was planned by Orlando for the 1956 Olympic games in Melbourne but did not make it in time. However, the wine and others like it—white, sweet and slightly sparkling—proved a huge popular success. Later, refrigeration during fermentation and the use of stainless steel for storage were used to capture and hold the fresh fruit flavours and natural sweetness—so much so that, in time, inexpensive white wine became an acceptable substitute for beer.[33] A proper understanding of secondary (malo-lactic) fermentation permitted the making of superior red wines, most notably in the cooler region of Coonawarra. But the industry preferred, initially at least, to capitalise on its warm and hot climate locations rather than the potential quality advantage of the cooler areas. The truly cool, southern regions were pioneered, or re-established, by hobbyists and weekend professionals from the 1960s and 70s.[34] They reflected a new tourist interest in the Australian countryside as much as in wine and did not, initially, make a significant contribution to production.

But there were difficulties as well. The years following the red wine boom of the 1960s saw many quality wines stretched, and the influence of

---

[32] Henzell, *Australian Agriculture*, 267.
[33] Beeston, *A Concise History of Australian Wine*, 230.
[34] Beeston, *A Concise History of Australian Wine*, 214*ff*.

new plantings was all too apparent in many thin, flavourless and poorly made wines. The increase in consumer demand that accompanied the white wine boom in the 1970s prompted the agribusiness expansion of new irrigation vineyards in the Riverland districts of New South Wales, South Australia and Victoria, machine harvesting of grapes and extensive use of cool fermentation and storage technology, all of which made for the production of greatly increased commercial quantities of wine. Ben Ean Moselle was Australia's leading bottled white wine for many years and is a story in itself. The collapse of the market for dried fruit had meant that crops of sultanas such as Thompson's Seedless, which is not a recognised wine grape, could be turned to wine if the facilities existed. For the 1974 vintage, Lindeman constructed a vast wine-making plant at Karadoc near Mildura capable of processing the extensive production of the region and accommodating the spiralling demand for this and other products. As the public taste matured, the sultana vines were grafted over to better white wine varieties. Later, Karadoc accommodated the district Chardonnay grapes that helped make this variety a household word.

With a long lead time on investment and realisation, mistaking trends in consumer interest could be a costly business. Plantings were made that could have been disastrous but for the viticultural practice whereby whole vineyards could be grafted over to another variety, retaining the rootstock with the loss of only one year's crop. In this way, winegrowers were able to improve vine stocks and accommodate changing tastes. James Halliday has observed that the extent of land under vines in 1949 was almost identical with that in 1991—54,741 hectares as compared with 54,585 — but with a 300 per cent increase in production and many other differences. The grape varieties at the end of the period "bore little or no resemblance to those of 1949; the geographic origins had radically changed; and the techniques of growing, trellising, pruning and harvesting of the vines had been revolutionized."[35] But remarkable as the industry's capacity was to adapt and develop production to accommodate changing consumer tastes, it does not of itself explain why those changes occurred.

Possibly more important than the improvements in the manufacture of wine were improvements in packaging. Little of this can be attributed to the influence of the monopoly suppliers of glass bottles, Australian Consolidated Industries, which resisted the development of new bottle styles (different coloured glass, punted bottles, and the like) for longer

---

[35] Halliday, *History of the Australian Wine Industry 1949–1994*, 117.

than either reason or commerce dictated. The development of "flagons" (larger half-gallon glass containers containing roughly three bottles) was an important early step in getting wine into the home as something to be kept in the pantry or kitchen and had at parties or with meals. The managing director of S. Wynn & Co., David Wynn, reported six million of his company's distinctive glass Wynvale flagons in circulation throughout Australia in 1968.[36] Even more ubiquitous and successful was the flagon's successor, the plastic bag-in-the-box. This was an invention that many claimed but none truly owned. The promoters of the prototype in the early 1960s were a South Australian company, Angoves, although a British antecedent was used for cooking oil.[37] Various refinements had to be made to ensure the tap allowed no spoiling air into the bag. David Wynn acquired the product rights and brought the bag to national prominence just prior to his company selling out to a major brewer, Castlemaine Tooheys, in 1972.[38] Almost immediately, the bag-in-the-box—or "wine cask" as David Wynn had misleadingly christened it—was recognised for nondescript but enjoyable white and red wine. The box encouraged a multitude of sins, not the least of which was the amount of wine consumed, and it was easily disposed of, more convenient to use than bottles, and required no decanting of table wine. The bag had a degree of porosity, a short shelf life and no keeping potential. But this did not trouble the increasingly wine-thirsty public. The industry separated into two markets, bottle and box, with the latter quickly defined as a heavily advertised, cheap and fast-moving consumer good, lacking in sophistication. Yet availability and convenient packaging were initially a response to, more than a cause of, the growth in the popularity of wine. Demographic factors must also be considered to explain the origins of the new demand.

The migrant influence

Increased numbers of migrants from continental and especially from southern Europe arrived in the decades after 1945, and they are often held responsible for the increase in wine consumption, although research documenting a cause-and-effect relationship is not readily available. Italians were among the most visible of new migrant cohorts, in the 1950s and 60s especially, but Australia's Italian-born population in 1981 was

---

[36] *Herald,* April 27, 1968.

[37] *Australian Wine, Brewing and Spirit Review*, 25 (1965): 64; Information from Ian Hickinbotham held by the author.

[38] Beeston, *A Concise History of Australian Wine*, 234.

only 276,000 out of a population of 14.5 million, hardly sufficient to contribute greatly to the overall trend.[39] They made wine in their backyards from grapes grown either by themselves or purchased. The Melbourne *Herald* observed in 1966 that, if home winemaking were made illegal, 80 per cent of Italian migrants in Victoria would be outlaws.[40] We may never know the exact extent to which the new migrants drove commercial sales. We do know that many of them became involved in the wine and hospitality industries. None was more celebrated than the young German, Wolf Blass, who in 1960 was brought out by a Barossa co-operative winery, Kaiser Stuhl, to make sparkling wine but who initiated his own company and made a name for himself in red wine.[41] Previous generations of migrants had been active in the industry as well, including the de Bortoli family of Griffith or, even earlier, the merchant, Samuel Wynn, who arrived penniless from Poland just before World War 1.[42] Migrants of continental European origin—both before and after the 1939–45 war—worked in restaurants ("wine bars") and in liquor sales and distribution. J.C. "Jimmy" Watson of Watson's Wine Bar in Lygon Street, Carlton, was a symbolic and influential figure in the inner-city wine trade in Melbourne in the 1950s. He lacked a European name but his mother (Panelli) was Italian born, and Watson was related to a network of Melbourne owners of wine bars, restaurants and cafes, including the Denat, Virgona and Massoni families.[43] Networks of family capitalism may have been declining in the host society but this now became a major phenomenon among new immigrants and was particularly evident in the food, import, hospitality and drink industries.[44]

French and Italian restaurants, in the major cities especially, are often cited as having changed Australians' tastes and social habits along the

[39] R.J.B. Bosworth, "Post-War Italian Migration," in *The Australian People: An Encyclopedia of the Nation, its People and their Origins*, ed. James Jupp (Sydney: Angus & Robertson, 1988), 616.

[40] *Herald*, July 21,1966.

[41] Ian Hickinbotham, *Australian Plonky* (Adelaide: University of Adelaide Barr Smith Press, 2008), 83–4; Beeston, *A Concise History of Australian Wine*, 196.

[42] Allan Wynn, *The Fortunes of Samuel Wynn: Winemaker, Humanist, Zionist* (Melbourne: Cassell Australia, 1968), 17.

[43] David Dunstan, "Watson, James Calexte (1903–1962)," *ADB* 16 (Melbourne: Melbourne University Press, 2002), 503–04; Grania Poliness, *Jimmy Watson's Wine Bar* (Diamond Creek, Victoria: Grapevine, 1989), 13.

[44] Leon Glezer, "Business and Commerce," in *The Australian People*, ed. Jupp, 861–2.

European model.[45] In Melbourne, the public consumption of wine with meals preceded the extension of hotel trading hours in 1966, and Diane Kirkby has pointed to the 1960s as a key moment when dining out was moving from a bohemian and exotic experience to becoming "an expectation of normal routine." More migrants were involved in restaurants but "it was not immigration per se that changed Melbourne's dining out experience … they were not driving the changes."[46] Smart and Wiggers' 1981 view is comparable—that the migrant contribution to increased sales of wine "either through actual purchase or imitation, has been exaggerated."[47] Their influence in the host community was probably greater as industry facilitators and contributors to a general climate of enthusiasm about the public culture of wine, food and hospitality. But, as we have observed, women were probably a greater factor. It is evident that more studies are required. And, to the demographic changes underpinning the growth in consumption, we need to add changing policies in Australia towards the manufacturing and retail trades.

Restrictive trade practices, tax and the new era of retail laissez-faire

Until at least 1974, the liquor industry was riddled with restrictive trade practices, and this was especially evident in the wine trade. In addition to government restrictions on the manufacture, sale and distribution of the product, the industry fixed prices and punished any retailer who stepped out of line with regard to retail price maintenance. The big companies—Penfolds, Hardy's, Seppelt, Lindemans, Orlando, and McWilliams—controlled the market, limiting and fixing the prices of quality categories especially. There were ways around this. Wholesalers and retailers could develop "buyers'-own-brands," which firms like Rhinecastle and innovative merchants like Douglas Lamb in Sydney and Doug Crittenden and Dan Murphy in Melbourne did very successfully. This entailed retailers buying directly, in bulk usually, from producers, and putting their

---

[45] For example, Beeston, *Concise History of Australian Wine*, 191; Halliday, *History of the Australian Wine Industry 1949–1994,* 117.

[46] Diane Kirkby, "…In Love with a Café and What He Could Buy…? Commodity, Desire and the Transformation of Dining Out in 1960s Melbourne," in *Go! Melbourne in the* Sixties, ed. O'Hanlon and Luckins, 169.

[47] Smart and Wiggers, *The White Wine Boom*, 4.

own labels, often suggestive of the wine's origins, on the bottles.[48] Consumers could themselves visit the wineries and either buy directly or order in bulk to undertake home bottling. This involved a significant price—and sometimes quality—advantage on the marked-up, branded consumer products in the established retail outlets. Further changes occurred with the passage of the Trade Practices Act of 1974, which made resale price maintenance illegal and set in train the evolution of the highly competitive retail liquor trade, resulting in increased sales and reduced profit margins, all so beneficial to the consumer and ultimately the industry itself. The beer trade by contrast seemed to escape the new discount regimes. The retail revolution, accompanied by the growing sophistication of packaging, branding and advertising in the industry, was another factor in the popularisation of wine.[49]

A final contributing factor to the growing consumption of wine lies in changes to taxation schedules. The relative level of tax imposed on wine as opposed to spirits and beer has been neglected in many explanations of the rise in wine's popularity. Beer was Australians' preferred alcoholic beverage in the early 1950s and for some time afterwards. But, by the end of the 1970s, wine was gaining ground. In 1970–71, Australian beer consumption was an average 123.8 litres per head per annum. The equivalent figure for wine of all types was 8.5 litres. Both continued to rise steadily. The peak year for beer was 1974–75, when Australians drank 139.6 litres per head and wine consumption had gone up more than 30 per cent to 12.5 litres. The Commonwealth budget of that year, which increased the tax on beer but left wine untouched, meant that beer consumption went down, while that of wine continued to climb.[50] By the mid-1970s, white or red wine in the now popular wine "cask" had more than twice the percentage of alcohol by volume of beer but was cheaper. In the three years to 1984, it was estimated in a survey quoted by the *Australian* newspaper that beer consumption had fallen from 133 litres to 117 litres per head, a drop of 11 per cent. The same period saw three increases in excise tax, and Australian Associated Brewers executive director Hugh Bingham claimed the squeeze was so great that beer drinkers were turning to other alcoholic beverages. Of the $1.16 paid in

---

[48] Bill Schroder and Nikki Marks, "The Retailer-Driven UK Food Industry: Structure, Performance and Implications for Australia," *Australasian Agribusiness Review* 4, 2 (1966): 30–42.
[49] Beeston, *A Concise History of Australian Wine*, 190.
[50] Keith Dunstan, *The Amber Nectar: A Celebration of Beer and Brewing in Australia* (Melbourne: Viking O'Neil Penguin Books Australia, 1987), 147.

Victoria for a 750 ml bottle of beer, federal excise tax accounted for 49 cents and state tax 8 cents.[51] Wine was not only cheaper than beer but cheaper than lemonade or Coca Cola.[52]

Wine enjoyed its underdog status for much longer than it probably should have, owing to a belief that somehow it was a more benevolent and social form of alcoholic beverage, even positive in social and health terms. This could not so easily be said about beer and spirits. The wine industry's tendency to boom and bust, with consequent over-production, company failures and cutting of prices, meant discount bargains and considerable "cellaring" of wine purchased by consumers, often at less than the cost of production. With much of the growth of the industry in these years artificially stimulated by tax-subsidised plantings, take-overs fuelled by the enthusiasm of business executives bitten by the wine bug, and retirees and hobbyists attracted to the industry, the consequent fire sales saw many under-the-bed cellars and garage stores fully stocked. For the consumer, it was a golden age.

Conclusion

In just three decades, Australia had become a wine-drinking country. In little more than a generation, wine went from being a curiosity beverage and a marginalised "cottage" industry to being an integral part of the competitive consumer goods market.[53] Wine continues to occupy a large part of our waking consciousness as an adjunct to daily life and to public culture in the form of books, entertainments and tourist activity. It is a mainstay of both the hospitality and tourism industries in rural and regional Australia. It is now a major export industry again and contributes more than its fair share of tax revenue, although there is still a debate on how that tax should be applied. Wine consumers are generally more sophisticated, though enthusiasts still demand the detailed information and reviews that keep the professional wine pundits in business. Yet, although the industry has been transformed out of sight since the early days of the 1950s, many of the patterns and issues that became apparent in the succeeding two decades—the contrasts between the bulk and quality bottle markets, and between the big company and small and boutique producers,

[51] *Australian*, August 15, 1984.

[52] Halliday, *History of the Australian Wine Industry 1949–1994*, 45.

[53] Chris Quirk (Research Officer of the Australian Wine Board) quoted in Smart and Wiggers, *The White Wine Boom*, 2; Halliday, *History of the Australian Wine Industry 1949–1994*, 40.

for example—are still with us. Notwithstanding the changes that have occurred, patterns of consumption do not change overnight and, as we have seen, must be understood in the wider demographic, technological, economic and cultural contexts.

PART III:

EXCHANGING

CHAPTER NINE

GLORY BOXES: FEMALE DOMESTIC CONSUMPTION AND MATERIAL CULTURE IN AUSTRALIA, 1930–1960

MOYA MCFADZEAN

Introduction

The glory box, a deceptively simple symbol of Australian female marriage preparation, uncovers complex economic, sexual, consumer, and cultural meanings relating to the mid-20th century experiences of many Australian women. The glory box, encompassing the container, collections and cultural practices associated with the gathering of items for the marital home, was at its most visible during the decades from the 1930s to the1950s in Australia, a period of significant economic and social upheaval and change.[1] This temporal frame encompasses the 1930s Depression, the Second World War, unprecedented levels of migration and an acceleration of consumer activity. The study of the material culture and memories relating to glory boxes during these decades in Australia allows us to track a small but significant element of a whole range of socio-economic transformations relating to the evolution of 20th-century consumer culture. These include changes to notions of modernity, to women and work, and to sexuality and marriage; but they also point to the pervasiveness since the 19th century of the links between femininity, domesticity and consumption.[2] This chapter will focus on glory boxes as

[1] Other English-language terms include 'hope chest' and 'bottom drawer'.

[2] This chapter has been drawn from my doctoral thesis, which explores all of these complex themes in a cultural history of Australian glory boxes. Moya McFadzean, "Glory Boxes: Femininity, Domestic Consumption and Material Culture in Australia, 1930–1960" (PhD diss., University of Melbourne, 2009).

significant indicators of shifting consumer patterns in Australia, reflected in the changing ways women accumulated their premarital domestic property between 1930 and 1960.

Glory boxes provide an opportunity to explore the consumer experiences of unmarried women during the years before many of them embarked on a wedded domestic future. These experiences demonstrate the establishment of female domestic consumer practices long before women became household managers as wives and mothers. Working- and lower middle-class Australian-born women of British ancestry (still the dominant cultural group at this time) were the primary purveyors of glory box traditions between the 1930s and 1950s. The practices were also reinforced, adapted and even preserved by migrant women of many European cultures who arrived in Australia in unprecedented numbers after the Second World War. For many of these women, both local and overseas born, glory boxes represented a process of self-actualisation. They imagined their own future domestic spaces where they would fulfil roles as wives, mothers and domestic managers; in the collecting ritual, they moved through the "public" steps towards these roles, including the engagement party, the "kitchen tea" and the wedding itself. In the process, they progressed through their own stages of "becoming" as women, workers, consumers, wives, and citizens. For some women, however, dreams of marriage, or domestic happiness within marriage, were unrealised.

The oral testimony supporting this discussion reflects the glory-box experiences of around sixty mainly working-class women, including women from selected cultural backgrounds who migrated to Australia during the 1950s and early 1960s; the evidence also includes many informal anecdotes. These memories, as well as women's glory boxes and the collections they contained, reveal a number of complex dynamics relating to the material culture of consumption, including: the interplay between the handmade and the mass produced in terms of valuation; the influences of taste and tradition; the varied notions of desire that influenced definitions of essential and luxury items; and the impact of labour and wages on consumer activity. All of these factors relating to glory-box activities come together to enable an examination of the daily behaviours of these young single women in Australia between 1930 and 1960—behaviours informed by personal values that changed primarily in emphases rather than in fundamentals over these decades.

Women, glory boxes and post-industrial consumer culture

The impact of industrialisation on the accumulation of objects as commodities highlights the potential for glory boxes to be illustrative of both the process of industrialisation, and of commodification itself. The seeds of change that would influence the ways that women developed their glory boxes in Australia in the 1950s had been sown in the 18th and 19th centuries in industrialised England and North America, which were the key economic and cultural influences on Australian patterns of consumption.[3] The relevant primary consequences of western industrialisation include the evolution of the mass production of affordable domestic goods, the part played by women in linking domesticity with the consumption of those goods, and the broader roles women performed as both producers and consumers. Australia, following the example of England, North America and parts of western Europe, evolved as one of the world's most industrialised and consuming countries, and this would influence the nature of glory boxes in terms of the buying, selling and making of the goods they contained, as well as the shaping of their gendered character in particular ways.

These trends were also intimately connected to the 19th-century growth of a middle-class population that possessed an income above the basic requirements for survival, and desired to demonstrate its gentility through the material culture of modest luxury and leisure. Thanks to mass production, goods such as textiles, metals and furniture were less expensive, more available and, being made from cheaper materials, many were affordable even for the working poor.[4] Thus the changing nature of the production of domestic goods, the new ways in which they were sold and marketed, and the feminisation of the targeted consumer were processes in train in Australia during the decades prior to the Second World War, but they accelerated rapidly from the 1930s. This was evident in glory boxes and their contents, which featured in Australian newspapers and magazines of the 1930s and 1940s as highly marketable commodities. (See Figure 9.1) Advertisements in general were becoming more abundant and more targeted towards women as the principal domestic consumers,

---

[3] A useful overview of the evolution of consumerism in western Europe is provided in Don Slater, *Consumer Culture and Modernity* (Cambridge, Oxford & Massachusetts: Polity Press & Blackwell Publishers, 1997), 13, 15 and 18.

[4] Discussed in Linda Young, *Middle Class Culture in the Nineteenth Century: America, Australia and Britain* (Basingstoke, Hampshire & New York: Palgrave Macmillan, 2003), 159.

despite the Depression and wartime challenges that saw a lack of spending ability followed by a lack of things to buy.[5] Advertisers extolled the virtues of their sheets and pillowcases, guaranteeing their products would "add lustre to a 'glory box' you will treasure through a lifetime of happiness."[6] And they fuelled consumer desires by, as Robert Crawford puts it, the sale of "hopes and dreams" for a brighter consumer way of life in the future.[7] This delaying of gratification for a future married state was the very essence of the desire the glory box embodied as commodity.

Australian women who owned glory boxes were simultaneously producers and consumers, for they often themselves made the things that they later consumed, but they also consumed the produce of others (both the mass produced and the handmade), and they laboured to pay for the items they purchased.[8] As consumerism increased during the 1950s, so did its impact upon glory-box collections, gradually privileging the purchased and machine produced over the handmade. This trend is reflected in post-war glory boxes and supported by oral testimony. Nevertheless, the progression from production to consumption was not a straightforward or linear one, and glory boxes continued to contain a mix of both manufactured and handmade items, with the emphasis varying from box to box. Even within a thirty-year period, the shifts in production and consumption trends in Australia were making themselves felt in the way women filled their glory boxes—in terms of the items they sewed, how much they embroidered, and the extent to which these skills were nurtured and valued in public and private domains. Moreover, many post-1930s glory-box collectors in Australia (especially with the higher wages of the post-war period) now had a modest disposable income for glory-box purchases. Ruby, collecting during the 1950s, explained:

> We got paid once a fortnight at the telephone exchange and firstly it was straight into the State Savings Bank next door as soon as you got your wages, put your board money aside because that was for Mum and that would

---

[5] Argued by Beverley Kingston, *Basket, Bag and Trolley: A History of Shopping in Australia* (Melbourne: Oxford University Press, 1994), 66.

[6] Advertisement for Actil sheets, "Easter Brides," *Sun News Pictorial*, February 23, 1950, 18.

[7] Robert Crawford, *But Wait, There's More ... A History of Australian Advertising, 1900–2000* (Melbourne: Melbourne University Press, 2008), 124.

[8] Similar issues are explored by Ben Fine, *The World of Consumption: The Material and Cultural Revisited* (London & New York: Routledge, Second Edition, 2002), 83.

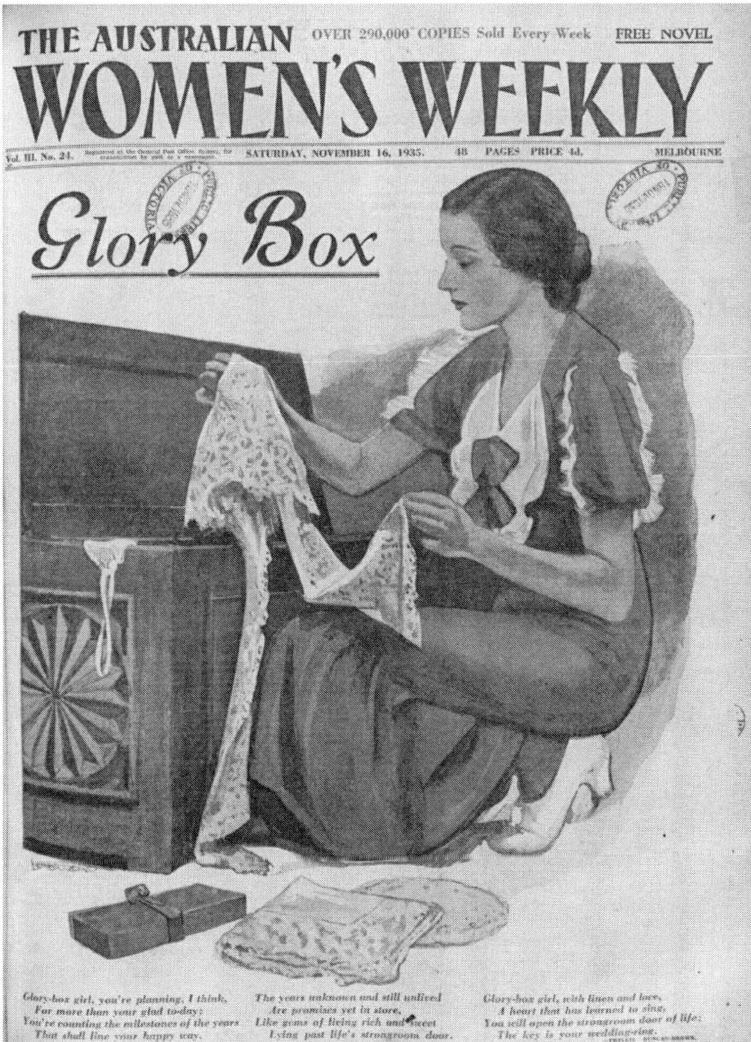

FIGURE 9.1 Glory-box girl prepares for the future. *Australian Women's Weekly,* 16 November 1935, front cover. Image courtesy of the State Library of Victoria.

> help the rest of the family as well, and then it was your lay-bys or whatever else you wanted to get.[9]

This process gave women who were working before marriage experience in consumption practices that they would continue after marriage. Consequently, glory boxes became a microcosm of industrial progression that saw domestic goods become increasingly affordable, abundant and feminised.

A matter of "need" and "want"

Within this evolving "democratic" environment of more goods available to more people, definitions of luxury and what might be considered as an essential item remained connected to a persistent Victorian morality and work ethic of frugality, caution and patience. It was an ethic that had important conscious and subconscious influences on women's acquisitive attitudes and practices in relation to glory boxes, particularly during the 1930s and 1940s. Hugh McKay has observed the social attitudes of Australians born during the 1920s and early 1930s who "embraced the so-called (Protestant, non-conformist) 'work ethic' with a vengeance … [having] seen what unemployment could do either to their own fathers or to relatives, friends and neighbours."[10]

These values were reflected in the very nature of glory-box collecting, which required planning, saving and the deferral of pleasure. Many domestic items that were once defined as "luxuries" became "decencies," and then "necessities."[11] They were designed to embellish a "civilised" domestic environment, including the kitchen, living room and bedroom, which were the key furnishing spaces for glory boxes. In fact, glory boxes can be seen as an act of "basic provisioning" by women as they accumulated portable property for married domestic life. Even the more "luxury" items, such as fine needlework, were the labour of the hand, while crystal and fine china were the result of rational selection and careful financial planning. Women talked about essentials in interviews but also articulated the process as an opportunity to acquire what they

[9] Interview with Ruby Kwijas, recorded by Moya McFadzean, Melbourne, 2003.

[10] Hugh McKay, *Generations: Baby Boomers, their Parents and their Children* (Sydney: Pan Macmillan Australia, 1997), 18.

[11] Progression outlined in Neil Brewer, John McKendrick and J.H. Plumb, *The Birth of a Consumer Society: The Commercialisation of Eighteenth-Century England* (Bloomington: Indiana University Press, 1982), 1.

might not have the means to buy later: the "nice things," such as nightwear for the wedding night, which were items of deferred desire rather than a requirement. As Gwenda, who was collecting during the 1940s, recalled:

> I guess it was an excuse to suddenly go out and buy nice underwear and actually let someone see it … Of course there would have been some impractical things that you bought, you couldn't not, but at the time you didn't think they were going to be impractical … It was a once in a lifetime [opportunity] to buy something frivolous and lacy that under normal circumstances you wouldn't bother.[12]

The "desire" that underpinned the planning, saving, selecting, storing and viewing of the objects, as well as their projection into their future domestic environment, meant that the process of collecting was as pleasurable as the actual use of the object itself. As Colin Campbell has argued, "the true focus of desire is less the object itself than the experience the consumer anticipates possessing it will bring."[13] Women filled their boxes with patience, thrift and pragmatism, and with an occasional dash of extravagance. They were consumers in a society that was increasingly looking to credit to satisfy acquisitive desires, but they were not aspiring to a world of instant gratification. They desired their portable property, and they took pleasure in its gradual accumulation. But they rarely wanted more than they could buy or make themselves, or receive as gifts. These collections were the work of time, taste and practicality. Pleasure was taken in their formulation and satisfaction garnered from them being the work of the collectors' own hands and pay packets. This sentiment is most evocatively expressed by Marjorie, collecting during the early 1950s, who reflected:

> I just loved gathering up my glory box, my collection … I totally enjoyed it. I saved and I used to be thinking about the home I might have one day, that's what it was for. It wasn't the thought of a glory box as such, it was more the homemaker part of it that I loved the thought of … I loved the thought of having a home … always loved looking at what I've got, and where I'd put it and what I'd use it for.[14]

---

[12] Interview with Gwenda Mutimer, recorded by Moya McFadzean, Melbourne, 2003.

[13] Colin Campbell, "Consuming Goods and the Good of Consuming," in *Consumer Society in American History: A Reader,* ed. Lawrence B. Glickman (Ithaca & London: Cornell University Press, 1999), 26.

[14] Interview with Marjorie Cope, recorded by Moya McFadzean, Melbourne, 2003.

Imagining the home

These assumptions about achieving a home of one's own were embedded in glory-box culture. Glory boxes contained objects to furnish the primary domestic living spaces (kitchen, living room and bedroom) over which women would assert their own taste, putting in place both handmade productions and purchased possessions. Deborah Chambers has observed that "the suburban lifestyle was not simply a response to the rising patterns of consumption of an expanding economy. It was also a material and cultural expression of the ideology of feminine domesticity: woman as homemaker."[15] Rarely acknowledged, however, is the fact that these expressions of material domesticity began for many young women between 1930 and 1960 with their glory boxes. The very act of collecting for a glory box, whether consciously or unconsciously, created and reinforced a certain female identity. Each time a woman bought a set of sheets, put a piece of crystal on lay-by or embroidered a supper cloth, she was furnishing her glory box in the present, and her marital home in the future with portable goods she (or relatives and friends) had made or acquired to fill a projected domestic space.

This engagement by women with things demonstrates how women constructed (and have had constructed for them) their femininity through objects, illustrating and extending an argument made by Emma Casey and Lydia Martens that women "use material culture to stimulate, enhance and enrich the everyday routines of the domestic sphere."[16] In this way, glory boxes and their varied contents provided a tangible means by which young women of modest means planned, saved for and aspired to influence their future domestic environment within a broad community of glory-box practitioners. As Daisy, who was collecting during the 1940s, reflected: "I didn't have much money, but I certainly had it in a glory box, with linen and stuff, I had plenty … [the box] is your start for your home … you're starting off with something and you're contributing."[17]

---

[15] Deborah Chambers, "A Stake in the Country: Women's Experiences of Suburban Development," in *Visions of Suburbia,* ed. Roger Silverstone (London and New York: Routledge, 1997), 87.

[16] Lydia Martens and Emma Casey, "Gender, Consumer Culture and Promises of Betterment in Late Modernity," in *Gender and Consumption: Domestic Cultures and the Commercialisation of Everyday Life,* ed. Emma Casey and Lydia Martens (Farnham, Surrey: Ashgate Publishing, 2007), 235.

[17] Interview with Daisy Chapman, recorded by Moya McFadzean, Melbourne, 2003.

In this way, glory boxes represent projections of spatial "becomings": kitchens, living rooms and bedrooms to be fitted out with the handmade and purchased material culture of imagined domestic spheres, drawn from memory, experience and desire. Thus the domestic environment was projected through consumerism, handcrafts and new notions of modernity. In this process of imagining future domestic spaces over which they would preside as wives, mothers and domestic managers, many women also progressed through their own process of "becoming" during these decades. This involved a series of sequential and overlapping identities: the single woman, the salaried worker, the shopper, the portable-property owner, the wife, and the Australian citizen (for migrant women). Glory boxes track this process of self-actualisation. Collecting took place at a time in women's lives when thoughts turned to separation from family, a degree of independence through work (especially if living away from home), and even differentiating themselves from their mothers. Glory boxes represented another life, independent from familial ties: a household of their own. It was a gradual evolution of self and identity, a process of individualisation within primarily domestic parameters.

Glory box as cultural commodity

Between the 1930s and the 1950s, glory boxes contained a mix of goods ultimately created or acquired for the Australian marriage market. They included the products of individual production such as needlecraft, which held intrinsic value as creative and memory objects. They also included gifts from mothers, grandmothers, aunts and girlfriends, inalienable objects attached to cross-generational memories. There were mass-produced items of kitchenware and household linen, which were purchased and therefore part of the commodity marketplace. And, for migrant women, there was the extra layer of meaning that all of these types of objects represented as portable property for the establishment of a home in a new country.

In fact, the contents of glory boxes were infused with multiple meanings and values. These included layers of personal and cultural meaning relating to an individual woman's family and place; an object could be connected to a gift-giver, a particular store or even the homeland from which it had been transported. For example, Josephine, who migrated to Australia from southern Italy with her family during the 1950s, remembered the sheets produced by her mother for the daughters' glory boxes: "I've still got two or three sheets that are actually made of hemp or flax … that were grown by her mother and grandmother and then they spun that by hand and then it was woven on the loom."[18] Objects also reflected the multiple values, such as fashion, tradition, availability and affordability, that were constructed and assigned by mothers, manufacturers, distributors, advertisers, and the women themselves. For instance, Melbourne women throughout the three decades fondly remembered Wests, where they bought quality imported British linen, and which was located in a city arcade on the corner of Swanston Street. One woman who was collecting during the 1930s recalled:

> As you walked down to the railway train you always went in to see what Wests had … They had fabulous imported stuff … If you were looking for cheaper things you went to Treadway's or Paynes but [Wests] was very good quality, the brands were good.[19]

Part of the power and complexity of glory boxes lies in the collective as well as individual nature of the objects, in the mix of production and consumption in the process of their acquisition, and in the layers of cultural values ascribed to them by society, by communities and by the women themselves.[20]

Thus seemingly ordinary objects of consumption can be extremely revealing, particularly when the meaning of one object is reliant on the meaning of another. In many respects, glory boxes were the embodiment of both the mundane and the intimate nature of collections of objects, of the personal choices involved in their acquisition, and of the way they were intended to be possessed and made to represent social conventions and personal identities. It was a two-way transfer of ascribed meaning between the creations and the creators of the world they inhabited. Women placed meanings on their glory boxes and the goods placed meanings on the women themselves. A mass-produced, impersonal item that was turned into a possession that belonged to someone could result in that person creating, as Grant McCracken has expressed it, "a personal 'world of goods' which reflected their own experience and concepts of self and

[18] Interview with Josephine Carey, recorded by Moya McFadzean, Melbourne, 2005.

[19] Interview with BS (request to remain anonymous), recorded by Moya McFadzean, Melbourne, 1992.

[20] See Mary Douglas and Baron Isherwood, *The World of Good: Towards an Anthropology of Consumption* (London & New York: Routledge, 1996 [1979]), ix.

world."[21] A glory box was indeed a "world of goods," containing objects of material and metaphorical, individual and collective significance.

Valuing the ordinary

Glory-box objects were often commonplace—mass-produced canisters, glassware, crockery and towels, as well as embroidered items in which the quality of the needlecraft varied but the patterns, colours and fabrics appeared over and over again. As purveyors of personal and domestic meanings, glory boxes provide a vehicle for analysing the symbols and personal relativities behind domestic objects. Domestic objects can have attached to them a significance that reveals their power beyond the ordinary and gives them a higher value because of their domestic nature, rather than in spite of it, so that, as Mihaly Csikszentmihalyi and Eugene Rochberg-Halton have observed, "the home contains the most special objects: those that were selected by the person to attend to regularly or to have close at hand, that create permanence in the intimate life of a person, and therefore that are most involved in making up his or her identity."[22] Glory boxes and the often ordinary objects they contained should not be dismissed for their gendered, domestic materiality. A crocheted doily or china milk jug was selected, made, kept, and used in an evolving process of the individual creation of selfhood.

The choosing of items for the glory box was an assertion of taste, ownership and autonomy. For some women, it represented the betterment of their lives, the conscious improvement of their standard of living in the period between their mothers' generation and their own. It was an expression of aspirational projection articulated through material objects, and, as Judy Giles has argued, "the women who dreamt of a better life running their own homes, with a companionable and caring husband … were as 'modern' in their way as the flapper … These women saw in the realisation of their material aspirations a sense of self-worth and dignity."[23] Ruby, collecting during the early 1950s, deliberately selected

[21] Grant McCracken, *Culture and Consumption: New Approaches to the Symbolic Character of Consumer Goods and Activities* (Bloomington and Indianapolis: Indiana University Press, 1990), 86.
[22] Mihaly Csikszentmihalyi and Eugene Rochberg-Halton, *The Meaning of Things: Domestic Symbols and the Self* (Cambridge: Cambridge University Press, 1981), 17.
[23] Judy Giles, "Class, Gender and Domestic Consumption in Great Britain 1920–1950," in *Gender and Consumption*, ed. Casey and Martens, 26–7.

FIGURE 9.2 Glory box purchased by Kath Davis, Victoria, late 1930s. It contains a drawer full of her needlework Museum Victoria. Photographer: Jon Augier.

more luxurious and less practical items for her box, consciously aiming to improve her lot. She believed that these items would influence her future home life and reflected:

> For me it was probably to have pretty things that I hadn't seen through my early life and at the same time I was going to use those things for me … I was doing this in view of escaping from all of those things that [I] had to do from an early age … it was sort of like I'm not going to live like this all of my life, there's going to be something a little better at the end of the tunnel.[24]

The material culture of glory boxes also documents the varied experiences of first and second–generation post-war migrant women, who brought, adapted and maintained cultural traditions from their homelands in an increasingly commodified Australia. Collections represented what could be transported and what had to be left behind; they acted as

[24] Interview with Ruby Kwijas, recorded by Moya McFadzean, Melbourne, 2003.

touchstones with distant families and cultures, and were a material means of surrounding women with the artefacts of home; or they were simply and pragmatically the foundations for an independent marital household. For these women, from such countries as Italy, Greece, Holland and Ireland, their glory boxes were inextricably linked to the very act of migrating. Their trunks, or even shipping containers, became vessels of miniature dreams of utopia, encompassing simultaneously the universal hopes of the migrant for a better life and the specific dreams of the wife and homemaker.

Thus glory-box collections reflected women's cross-cultural economic priorities, their skills, their ability to save and select wisely. They maintained women's identified ultimate destiny as inextricably connected to a domestic marital environment. The glory box was their property, over which they had ultimate control, but with a socially sanctioned and defined outcome. These social expectations often commenced when women were teenagers, before marriage had even become a real consideration. Take as examples three glory boxes, each from a slightly different time and owned and filled by three different Australian-born women. One was created in the 1930s during the Depression, made for Ester by her father. She recalled:

> It wasn't an official glory box, it was a box which used to hold kerosene in those days. And my father put a lid on it, hinges and a lid, and that was my box. He painted it and lined it … with packing paper.[25]

She filled it almost entirely with the needlecraft of her own hands. The second box was purchased during the Second World War by a young woman and her boyfriend; they selected and paid for it together. It was a veneer sideboard, not branded as a glory box, and she filled it with her needlework as well as purchased manchester and other household goods. The third was purchased around 1950 by the young woman herself; it was a veneer glory box with sections to store linen and breakables. She filled it with a mix of purchased kitchenware and linen, gifts and inherited items, but little needlecraft.

Without making sweeping generalisations, there are already evident here revealing patterns regarding the decline over time in handmade production, and the impact of economic climates on the boxes obtained. The artefacts demonstrate changing styles and popularity of types of glory boxes, or techniques of making do for those who could not afford a

[25] Interview with Ester Rose, recorded by Moya McFadzean, Melbourne, 1992.

"proper" box. They illustrate which items were fashionable to collect and items that, when compared to a number of collections, may be regarded as more unusual or peculiar to a particular collector. They demonstrate wartime rationing, income-related frugality, the decline of handmade production, and increasing mass production and consumerism. They reveal hopes for a future home independent of parents and a hint at the promise of sexual activity, as well as a forthcoming domestic identity as wife, mother and homemaker. As Gwenda, who was collecting during the 1940s, observed: "If you were going to hope to have a boyfriend, subsequently get engaged and then married, well of course you started collecting things. It was just the natural thing to do."[26]

Conclusion

Economy is inextricably linked to materiality—the objects that are created, bought, sold, accumulated, used, treasured and discarded. Glory boxes were by their very nature material; they reflected mass and individual production and consumption, as well as social and cultural change, all of which continued to develop within the thirty years between 1930 and 1960. In particular, the linking of consumerism, domesticity and femininity from the late 19th century had a lasting impact upon the way women in Australia shopped, what they were encouraged to buy, and the way modern identity for women came to be wrapped up in an actual or projected home. It was an environment in which the glory-box tradition flourished.

Glory boxes were as much about economy as they were about skill and creativity—the work of manual labour and hard-earned cash. Women collecting during the pre-war, wartime and post-war years in Australia grew up in times of restriction and regulation. They were informed by a life ethic of work, thrift and the value of domestic security. But they also witnessed, and to varying degrees participated in, a new culture of consumerism, a wave of commodity production that had gathered momentum in 19th-century industrialised Europe and expanded in a post-war environment of burgeoning manufacturing, new materials and gendered marketing strategies. Women were accumulating domestic property, encouraged by manufacturers and retailers who identified them as the key future arbiters of taste and spending in the family household.

---

[26] Interview with Gwenda Mutimer, recorded by Moya McFadzean, Melbourne, 2003.

There are also parallel and occasionally intersecting stories of post-war migrant women, on whose cultural traditions the very act of migration had a significant impact, both prior to leaving and once settled in Australia.

Thus glory boxes came to represent a cult of conservative consumerism—considered, careful and contained—as the nature of collecting gradually shifted from an emphasis on women's own handmade production to the purchase of the ready made. Glory boxes represented for many women their aspirations for a husband, a family and a home filled—at least initially—with the combined work of their hands and pay packets. Glory boxes were a tangible expression of female transition from single to married state and all that entailed.

CHAPTER TEN

CONSUMER GOODS, HOUSEWIVES AND TIME USE IN THE SUBURBAN HOME FROM THE 1920S TO THE 1980S

TONY DINGLE

During the 1960s, or perhaps the early 1970s, a staff photographer at the *Age* newspaper in Melbourne took a black and white photograph that was titled "Resident of Hibiscus Avenue." In it we see a suburban housewife, smartly dressed in a summer frock, perching somewhat uncomfortably on the edge of a large sofa with an enigmatic smile on her face reading the *Women's Weekly* (open at the page containing a crossword puzzle). She is clearly posing self-consciously for the photographer. Her backdrop is the lounge room of her modern suburban home. There is a shag-pile carpet on the floor, and floor-to-ceiling drapes are pulled back from the windows to allow sun to flood into the room. In the corner is a large console television switched on to the cricket (the cricketer on the screen appears to be Jeff Thompson and, if so, dates the picture in the 1970s). Beneath it is a record player and a collection of long-playing records.

There are six Hibiscus Avenues listed in the *Melway* street directory for Melbourne, all of them located in the vast tracts of post-war suburbia that encircle the city. However, location is unimportant, for this image is intended to capture some of the universal elements of post-war suburban living. It depicts comfort, leisure and recreation through material possessions designed to entertain. This chapter seeks to provide a historical context for this image as a means of assessing its validity. Did housewives during the sixties have time to relax and read magazines or watch the television? If so, what made this possible? In searching for an answer, the chapter examines the acquisition of a new generation of consumer goods that either saved labour in the home or offered time-using recreational possibilities. How these commodities were used by housewives

FIGURE 10.1 At home in suburban Hibiscus Avenue, circa mid 1970s. Tony Dingle Collection. Photographer: Unknown

shaped the nature and the extent of their unpaid work in the home. The main focus of this chapter is on the three decades after 1945, during the long economic boom, for this appears to have been a period of transition in the lives and work of married women. Nevertheless, the periods before and after these decades provide a context within which to assess the changes taking place.

The spread of consumer goods

It is now more than three decades since Ruth Schwartz Cowan in her 1976 paper, "The 'Industrial Revolution' in the Home: Household Technology and Social Change in the 20th Century," argued that modern consumerism came to the United States during the 1920s. It was then that electrically powered household appliances replaced increasingly scarce and expensive domestic servants in middle-class homes.[1] Electric light, irons, washing

[1] Ruth Schwartz Cowan, "The 'Industrial Revolution' in the Home: Household Technology and Social Change in the 20th Century," *Technology and Culture* 17 (1976): 1–23.

machines, hot water systems, refrigerators all reduced the physical exertion involved in housework. However, it has been widely accepted that similar levels of consumerism did not come to Australia until the 1950s and 1960s. Greg Whitwell, in his influential *Making the Market: The Rise of Consumer Society,* argues that this was when "Australia emerged as a modern consumer society."[2] With a sustained rise in incomes, more households enjoyed increasing levels of discretionary purchasing power. They possessed both the ability and the inclination to spend more on consumer durables. Between 1951 and 1975, the proportion of incomes spent on food, cigarettes and tobacco, public transport, clothing and footwear all fell, while expenditures on household durables, gas and electricity, and especially cars, rose markedly.[3] Elsewhere, I have examined the case for an earlier onset of consumerism in Australia and concluded that, while there was a massive increase in the amount of electrical energy used in the home from the 1920s, it did not constitute a "domestic revolution" of the same magnitude as was taking place in the United States. The technology that was adopted was for the most part not the most labour saving. It consisted of electric irons, electric radiators and fans, but not items such as washing machines or vacuum cleaners that were being adopted so rapidly in the United States.[4] It would appear therefore that, before the end of the Second World War, only the foundations of consumerism had been laid in Australia.

The growth of spending on household appliances can be traced through periodic estimates of appliance purchases. The first published estimate that I have unearthed is for 1923. This indicated that 75 per cent of all electrically wired homes had acquired an electric iron, 20 per cent an electric radiator and 7 per cent a fan, but only 2 per cent a vacuum cleaner.[5] The next survey is for 1955. This indicates significant changes, with 84 per cent of all homes possessing a radio, 40 per cent a washing machine, 99 per cent an iron, 30 per cent a food mixer, and three quarters of homes in Melbourne and Sydney, but only just over a half of all homes in Brisbane, possessing a vacuum cleaner. Two thirds of all upper income homes possessed a phone but only 16 per cent of households on below average incomes had one. The take-up of fridges varied with average city

---

[2] Greg Whitwell, *Making the Market: The Rise of Consumer Society* (Melbourne: McPhee Gribble, 1989), 3.
[3] Whitwell, *Making the Market*, 4–5, 30.
[4] Tony Dingle, "Electrifying the Kitchen in Interwar Victoria," *Journal of Australian Studies* 57 (1998): 124–5.
[5] *Electrical Times*, June 27, 1925, 745.

temperatures, with three quarters or more of all homes in Brisbane and Sydney possessing one but only two thirds in Melbourne. These figures are lower than in the United States but far higher than in the United Kingdom for the same period. This evidence raises the question of whether the shifts between the two survey dates came before or after the war. National income data strongly suggests the latter, as does the survey, which indicates that it was younger housewives forming post-war households who were responsible for most of these purchases.[6]

By the start of the 1960s, an Australia-wide McNair survey indicated further advances in the range of consumer goods in most homes; 94 per cent had a fridge, 60 per cent a washing machine, 55 per cent a television, 73 per cent a vacuum cleaner, 50 per cent a telephone. In addition, most households had acquired a car.[7] Perhaps the most dramatic shift was in home ownership, which rose from half of all homes in the 1940s to almost three quarters by the beginning of the 1960s.[8] In the rapidly growing suburbs of double- and triple-fronted cream brick veneers, home ownership had become almost universal. Families were now filling their own homes with a range of consumer goods unknown to most of their parents. Consumerism had come into full bloom in the suburbs.

Sue Bowden and Avner Offer have looked at differential rates of appliance take-up in Britain and the United States since the 1920s and have offered explanations for the patterns that they have identified. They draw a distinction between time-saving technologies such as vacuum cleaners, washing machines, dishwashers and telephones, and time-using technologies such as home entertainment in the form of radios, televisions, gramophones and video recorders. Time-saving technologies can increase the amount of discretionary time available to housewives who previously performed these functions without the aid of appliances, while time-using technologies promise to enhance the quality of discretionary time spent in the home. They demonstrate that, in both the United States and Britain, the latter technologies diffused far more rapidly than the former, even though

---

[6] *Real Estate and Stock Journal*, October 1955, 190.

[7] Graeme Davison, *Car Wars: How the Car Won our Hearts and Conquered our Cities* (Sydney: Allen & Unwin, 2004), 22–4.

[8] Patrick N. Troy, "The Benefits of Owner Occupation," *Urban Research Program Working Paper* 29 (1991): 2, 10; Tony Dingle, "'Gloria Soame': The Spread of Suburbia in Post-War Australia," in *Changing Suburbs: Foundation, Form and Function*, ed. Richard Harris and Peter J. Larkham (New York: E & F.N. Spon, 1999), 193–4.

some of them were initially very costly. While the patterns of diffusion were similar in the two countries, there was a considerable time lag between the United States and Britain because incomes in the latter lagged about thirty years behind the former. Their explanation for the differential diffusion of the two kinds of technologies is twofold. On the demand side, "consumers have apparently given greater priority to enhancing the quality of discretionary time than to increasing its quantity." On the supply side, it has proved easier to "increase the attractions of leisure than to reduce the burden of housework." Consequently, the development of time-using technologies has been highly innovative, with new products being developed frequently to offer new forms of stimulation and arousal. In contrast, continuous economies in housework have been much more difficult to achieve and new products have emerged far more infrequently.[9]

The historical rates of diffusion of household technologies in Australia have not yet been subject to similar analysis; however, there is no reason to suppose that the take-up of technologies in Australian homes has followed patterns different from those observed in the United States and Britain. The scattered surveys of appliance purchases already quoted above support this view. Furthermore, average incomes in Australia have been somewhat lower than those in the United States but significantly higher than those in Britain, so adequate purchasing power has been available to make purchases. The new technologies also appear to have diffused quickly from their places of origin through the efforts of the multinational companies that developed them. Many such companies established Australian branches to get under Australian tariff barriers and sell in the local market.

Energy use in the home

The massive increase of consumer goods in the home required energy to power them. When Ruth Cowan referred to the "Industrial Revolution" in the home, she was drawing an explicit parallel between what happened in Britain and many other countries as their economies industrialised from the late 18th century onwards, and what happened in American homes during the 20th century. As she explained:

---

[9] Sue Bowden and Avner Offer, "Household Appliances and the Use of Time: The United States and Britain since the 1920s," *Economic History Review* 47, 4 (1994): 725–48.

> Changes of a similar dimension [to what happened in the home], either in the fundamental technology, or in the routines of workers, would have long since been labeled an 'industrial revolution.' The change from the laundry tub to the washing machine is no less profound than the change from the hand loom to the power loom.[10]

The conventional story of the first Industrial Revolution in Britain emphasises the role of new machines, especially in textile manufacture, in transforming industry from a handicraft base to the factories.[11] This view disguises the most fundamental transformation, which was to replace human and sometimes animal energy in the production process with energy from fossil fuels. People had discovered how to break into nature's bank of stored energy in the form of coal and later oil and convert it into useful work.[12] The first converter was the steam engine. It could power banks of spinning machines or looms in a factory, and it was rapidly adopted to perform a wide range of functions. British coal output increased more than threefold in the half century from 1850, largely to power these new converters.[13] There was an even greater increase in the output of the economy. Some of this resulted from a growth in population but labour productivity rose at an unprecedented rate also. Workers produced far more, not because they were bigger or stronger, but because they could use more steam power to help them produce.

This early phase in the use of fossil fuel–derived energy had little direct impact on what went on in the home. For all its advantages, the steam engine did not prove to be an energy converter that could be adapted for domestic use. What was needed was something that was more flexible, did not give off steam and oil and smells, and could be used in smaller converters. Electricity generated at a central point, often by steam power, and then distributed into homes by means of cables proved far cleaner and more efficient than gas. When combined with the small electric motor, which was perfected in the years before the First World War, the technical components required for an energy revolution in the home were

---

[10] Schwartz Cowan, "The 'Industrial Revolution' in the Home," 8–9.

[11] See, for example, the classic account by Paul Mantoux, *The Industrial Revolution in the Eighteenth Century* (London: Methuen: 1961), 5–528.

[12] Carlo M. Cipolla, *The Economic History of World Population* (London: Penguin Books, 1965), 48–59.

[13] B.R. Mitchell and Phyllis Deane, *Abstract of British Historical Statistics* (Cambridge: Cambridge University Press, 1962).

available.[14] It then became feasible to replace the expenditure of human energy in at least some of the tasks undertaken in the home with machinery powered by electricity, just as had happened with steam power in the factory.

It is possible to trace the speed with which this happened in Victoria by charting domestic electricity consumption. The average household in 1929–30 used 338 kWh per year. A decade later, that figure had nearly doubled to 627 kWh. By 1949–50, it had more than doubled again to 1,521 kWh and, a decade later, it was 2,580 kWh—not a doubling, but a massive increase of more than 1000 kWh over the ten years, and a far bigger absolute increase than in previous decades. By 1968–69, the figure was 3,750, an increase of 1,200 during the decade.[15] Overall, during the four decades from 1929, electricity consumption in the average Victorian household had increased tenfold. This represents a far greater percentage increase in energy use than the British economy had managed in the second half of the 19th century, so we are indeed looking at a domestic revolution in terms both of the speed and of the magnitude of the change.

Given this massive increase in energy use to power consumer durables, it is inconceivable that the hourly productivity of the housewife (compared with the factory worker) did not rise—at least in performing those tasks that had been electrified. One person using a vacuum cleaner for an hour does more cleaning than the same person with a pan and brush. There was not a direct substitution of electrical energy for human energy in all activities. Some of the electricity was powering machines such as radios and televisions that had never been human powered. Furthermore, they were recreational rather than productive. Some electricity use replaced other energy sources such as wood for heating or gas for lighting, but, even here, there could be some savings in human work because electric heating and lighting were far cleaner than their predecessors; therefore, there could be saving on preparatory and cleaning chores.

---

[14] Penny Sparke, *Electrical Appliances* (London: Unwin Hyman, 1987), 37–44; Fred E.H. Schroeder, "More 'Small Things Forgotten': Domestic Electrical Plugs and Receptacles, 1881–1931," *Technology and Culture* 27 (1986): 525–43.

[15] Cecil Edwards, *Brown Power: A Jubilee History of the State Electricity Commission of Victoria* (Melbourne: State Electricity Commission of Victoria, 1969), 296.

Using the productivity gains—conflicting interpretations

There have been conflicting interpretations of how these productivity gains were utilised. In her pioneer analysis, Ruth Schwartz Cowan argued that, in middle-class homes in the US, electrically powered household appliances replaced increasingly scarce and expensive domestic servants from the 1920s. Electric lights, irons, washing machines, hot water systems and refrigerators all reduced the physical exertion involved in housework. However, instead of taking these gains out in increasing leisure—as advertisements for the new appliances urged women to do—they worked longer hours, did more cleaning and washed clothes more often, increasing the levels of home cleanliness. They were spending as much time on their housework as women without these conveniences. In her words, "housework, like so many other types of work, expands to fill the time available."[16]

Cowan's interpretation, which is largely based on home time-use surveys in the United States from the 1920s onwards, has been widely accepted. These indicate that, in the 1920s, housewives not in paid employment were spending more than 60 hours a week on housework, with little difference between city and country. A survey just after the end of the war found that urban housewives had increased their time allocation to around 80 hours but farm housewives had not.[17] Surveys in Britain and France after the war and up to the beginning of the 1970s also indicate figures fluctuating between 60 and 80 hours.[18] It appears that, in some instances, new technologies such as washing machines relocated work back to the home and to the housewife, at least in middle-class homes that might have formerly used a commercial laundry. However, overall, this evidence forms a persuasive underpinning for Cowan's thesis. Despite increasingly widespread use of labour-saving devices, the hours of housework were not declining; so, if housewives were more productive with the vacuum cleaner and washing machine, they must have been achieving higher states of cleanliness in the time that they were spending on housework.

---

[16] Schwartz Cowan, "The 'Industrial Revolution' in the Home," 15.

[17] Schwartz Cowan, "The 'Industrial Revolution' in the Home," 15.

[18] Carolyn Allport, "Women and the Built Environment," *Sydney Gazette: Organ of the Sydney History Group* 6 (1986): 40–1; Sue Bowden and Avner Offer, "Household Appliances and the Use of Time," 734.

There has been a tendency to extrapolate Cowan's thesis to Australia, although there is no Australian data to compare with the 1920s US data on household time use on which it is based.[19] I have argued elsewhere that the adoption of household electrical appliances, as opposed to electric light, was much slower here in the inter-war years, even though the decline in the availability of domestic servants had accelerated between 1933 and 1947. Consequently, there were probably too few labour-saving devices in most middle-class Australian households before the 1950s to adequately substitute for a domestic servant.[20] This interpretation is supported by the series of household equipment expenditures compiled by Graeme Snooks.[21] These decline fractionally during the 1920s and only show a decisive upward movement in the decades after the Second World War. Nevertheless, Cowan's interpretation can still be seen as valid for Australia in the years after 1945. Unfortunately, there is little Australian data on time use in the home until the 1970s but what is available indicates a similar pattern of 60 or more hours spent on housework despite the availability of labour-saving devices.[22]

Using a different approach, Snooks has offered a very different explanation of how productivity gains were utilised but one that still gives a leading role to technological change. He has identified two revolutions impacting on the household. The first, the Industrial Revolution, broke up the household as an integrated labour unit. A gendered division of labour forced husbands into factories and left wives as houseworkers. Then, what he has called a New Economic Revolution after the Second World War saw technological changes in the market economy that reduced the

---

[19] Raelene Frances, "Never Done But Always Down," in *Making A Life*, ed. Jenny Lee and Verity Burgmann (Melbourne: McPhee Gribble, 1988), 126; see also the careful discussion in Raymond Evans and Kay Saunders, "No Place Like Home: The Evolution of the Australian Housewife," in *Gender Relations in Australia: Domination and Negotiation*, ed. Kay Saunders and Raymond Evans (Sydney: Harcourt Brace Jovanovich, 1992), 183–5.

[20] Tony Dingle, "Electrifying the Kitchen in Interwar Victoria," 125.

[21] Graeme D. Snooks, *Portrait of the Family within the Total Economy: A Study in Longrun Dynamics, Australia 1788–1990* (Cambridge: Cambridge University Press, 1994).

[22] Australian Sales Research Bureau, "The Housewife's Day" (Melbourne: typescript report,1960), 1–15; Jean Blackburn and Ted Jackson, *Australian Wives Today* (Melbourne: Fabian Society Pamphlet No. 7, 1963); Duncan Ironmonger and Evelyn Sonius, "Household Productive Activities," in *Households Work: Productive Activities, Women and Income in the Household Economy*, ed. Duncan Ironmonger (Sydney: Allen & Unwin: 1989), 21–5.

premium on strength and greatly expanded the work that women could do in the paid economy. This then stimulated the adoption of labour-saving technologies in the home as a means of releasing housewives to take up jobs in the paid economy. In this scenario, there are no hours of discretionary time available in the home as a result of new technologies.[23]

The difficulty with this interpretation as it relates to the decades of the 1950s and 1960s concerns the causal links. We know from the evidence quoted earlier that most homes had acquired an extensive range of labour-saving consumer goods by the early 1960s, but this could hardly have been stimulated by large numbers of housewives taking up paid employment, for, at this time, only around 15 per cent of married women worked for wages. The trend from then onwards was upwards but still only 40 per cent of housewives were in the paid workforce by the mid-1970s. It seems clear in retrospect that, while these technologies did make it feasible for married women to work for wages, that was not the initial motive for acquiring them. Household consumer goods were a necessary condition to allow housewives to engage in paid work but not a stimulus to seeking it.

Time use in the home

A striking feature of Australian time-use surveys of the 1960s and 70s is the extended periods of time housewives without a paid job spent in the home. Surveys indicated that in both Melbourne and the rural city of Albury-Wodonga, this time spent at home amounted to more than 21 hours out of every 24 on weekdays.[24] What was even more notable was the extent to which other members of the household were spending more time at home as well. Male wage earners were benefiting from a progressively shorter working week. From 1947, the 40-hour week became standard and Saturday work progressively less common, although overtime work was widespread and lucrative because of higher hourly rates of pay. By the 1960s, the standard working week was down to 39 hours. The arrival in the home of the barbecue, the fridge containing cold beer and the TV from 1956 provided a range of home-based recreational facilities for husbands that competed successfully with the pub and the cinema. By the early 1970s, television watching alone absorbed more than 11 hours a week of

[23] Snooks, *Portrait of the Family within the Total Economy*, 14–17.

[24] Cities Commission, "Australians' Use of Time. A Preliminary Report" (Canberra: typescript report, 1975), 40; Australian Sales Research Bureau, "The Housewife's Day" (Melbourne: typescript report, 1960), 6.

the recreational time of working men.[25] Children, too, were remaining longer at school before entering paid employment and, with shorter school hours and long holidays, probably spent more time in the home than they would in paid employment. Generally, the recreational capabilities of the home were expanding through the rapid adoption of time-using recreational technologies. Recreation was becoming increasingly privatised and domesticated. In these years, consumerism was in fact working to keep the family together and ensconced in the household.

Domesticity can be defined in many ways but, if one takes a literal interpretation of it as pertaining to the home, there are grounds for arguing that the post-war decades of the 1950s and 60s represent a high tide of domesticity for Australian households. During these decades, more members of the household were physically together than before or since, and this only changed once married women joined the paid workforce in large numbers from the 1970s. This, of course, implies nothing about harmony, but it does mean that, for some of the time, women putting in their long hours of housework with time-saving appliances were clearly sharing the space of the home with other members of the family who were recreating with time-using technologies.

In retrospect, it is clear that the time-use patterns that emerged in the four decades after 1945 were transitional. While the evidence for Australia is too scanty to allow for precision, it does appear that a decline in hours devoted to housework began in the late 1960s. Some of this was due to the growing proportion of married women entering the paid workforce—and working women had always spent less time on housework, so there was no gain in leisure for them. The other factor was the arrival of television in most people's homes, a time-using as opposed to a time-saving technology. It seems that, for women who remained at home, the reduction in hours of housework corresponded very closely to hours spent watching the box. So, did the gains of the energy revolution in the house at this stage come down to a couple of hours a day of daytime soaps? When questioned in 1975, only 14 per cent of Melbourne women could claim that they gained "much" satisfaction from their viewing, with two thirds claiming "some" satisfaction.[26] These were similar to the levels of

[25] Michael Bittman, *Juggling Time: How Australian Families Use Time* (Canberra: Commonwealth Government, 1991), 28.
[26] Cities Commission, "Australians' Use of Time," 443–50.

satisfaction they derived from housework. Housewives in Britain and the United States were responding in the same way.[27]

More recent studies of time use at home in the US and the UK as well as in Australia during the 1970s and the 1980s indicate that there have since been much more significant reductions in the amount of time housewives (both wage-earning and non-wage earning) spend on housework; in Australia, this amounted to an average decline of 21 hours a week between 1974 and 1987.[28] This has provoked claims from the older generation (who have not reduced time spent on housework as much as have their daughters[29]) that standards have slipped. As one observer noted, "my mother is right, my housekeeping skills leave a lot to be desired. But ... I am not alone in my belief that life is too short to windex the pool fence."[30]

---

[27] Bowden and Offer, "Household Appliances and the Use of Time," 734.

[28] Bittman, *Juggling Time*, 29, cf. Bowden and Offer, "Household Appliances and the Use of Time," 737–9.

[29] Australian Bureau of Statistics, "Unpaid Work: How Couples Share Domestic Work," Australian Social Trends: 1999, http://www.abs.gov.au/websitedbs/D3310114.nfs/home/home?/opendocument?utm_id=GT.

[30] Cathy Sherry, "The Truth about Housework, Motherhood and Grooming," *Age*, June 27, 2006, 13.

CHAPTER ELEVEN

FROM WAREHOUSE TO YOUR HOUSE: PRODUCTION, CONSUMPTION AND THE REINVENTION OF INNER MELBOURNE, 1906–2006*

SEAMUS O'HANLON

Introduction: reinventing the inner city

In March 1997, property developers MAB Corporation began marketing the "Red Tulip warehouse apartments" created within and around the shell of a former factory in High Street, near its intersection with fashionable Chapel Street, in the inner Melbourne suburb of Prahran. The advertising campaign for these new apartments deliberately targeted a new type of urbane, wealthy and hedonistic inner city resident.[1] Location in "fabulous Prahran," "the hottest spot in Melbourne," was a central component of a sales strategy focused on "special person[s] looking for a unique lifestyle close to Chapel Street's" restaurants, cafés, bars, nightclubs and clothing stores.[2] If, as urban historians have long argued, cityscapes can be read as a historical documents—palimpsests upon which multiple stories of the past are layered one upon the other—then the redevelopment of this former industrial site as upmarket housing can perhaps be seen as a physical outcome of the transformation of inner Melbourne from a place of industry and production before the 1970s to one of post-industrial activity and conspicuous consumption today.

---

* My thanks to Tony Dingle, Tanja Luckins and Simone Sharpe for their invaluable comments on earlier versions of this chapter.

[1] Advertisement: "Hillingdon Place" File, Stonnington Archives, Malvern. My thanks to Stonnington archivist David Tuck for this source.

[2] "Mind's the Limit in Warehouse Plan," *Age*, March 15, 1997, "Property Age," 6.

As the Australian economy has been restructured away from its heavy reliance on tariff-protected manufacturing and industrial production in the post-war years, to one based on services and consumption in the contemporary period, our cities have been significantly reshaped, both physically and demographically. In common with the experiences of many other Western countries, Australian cities have seen factories close and new businesses, new structures and new residents move into and reinvent what were formerly landscapes of production into regions of high-status jobs, new globalised models of leisure and consumption, and expensive housing. These changes have been most notable in inner city areas, which since the 1970s have both been gentrified and seen their traditional industries closed or radically restructured. What were once landscapes of production are increasingly places of upmarket residence, recreation, tourism, spectacle and, above all, shopping.[3]

These processes of deindustrialisation and the reinvention of inner city regions as sites of consumption and leisure have been extensively documented by social scientists in recent years. More than 25 years ago sociologist Sharon Zukin alerted us to the impacts of urban deindustrialisation, and the social and cultural significance of the emergence of "loft- [or in Australian parlance 'warehouse'] living" in New York's SoHo district in the 1970s. As she suggested, loft-living represented a short-lived "historic compromise" in which the interests of art and capital came together to create a new type of relatively inexpensive dwelling option for low-income artists that in turn saw new patterns of economic activity—based on leisure, consumption and culture—become the basis of the urban economy. Following Zukin, geographer Julie Podmore has recently argued that since the 1980s loft-living has become ubiquitous, an international phenomenon common to most Western post-industrial cities. For Podmore, loft-living, or the "SoHo Syndrome," is a "socio-cultural process that involves a complex web of relationships between place, identity, and the media, that is diffused to, and (re)produced in divergent inner-city locations" across the globe. Australian geographer Wendy Shaw has similarly noted that, in the contemporary

[3] On the transformation of Melbourne's inner city economy over recent decades, see Tony Dingle and Seamus O'Hanlon, "From Manufacturing Zone to Lifestyle Precinct: Economic and Social Change in Inner Melbourne, 1971–2001," *Australian Economic History Review* 49, 1 (2009): 51–68; see also Seamus O'Hanlon, "The Events City: Sport, Culture and the Transformation of Inner Melbourne, 1977–2006," *Urban History Review/Revue d'histoire urbain* XXXVII, 2 (2009): 30–9.

period, residence in a former industrial building has become one of *the* symbols of international, post-industrial, cosmopolitan urban sophistication.[4]

As yet, few Australian historians have undertaken research into the economic and social impacts of the emergence of post-industrialism, or sought to historicise the cultural meanings of warehouse apartment living and conspicuous consumption for contemporary city life. This is possibly because these changes and what they represent may still be too recent, too much of an unfolding story, to be genuinely the stuff of History. Internationally, however, we are beginning to see some movement on this front, and, in recent years, a number of scholars have sought to bring historical methods and practices to studies of post-industrialism and its effects on the urban landscape. Steven High and others in Canada have been at the forefront of this trend, producing a series of highly politically and socially informed visual and textual studies of the de-industrialisation of the Ontario region of their own country and of the north-eastern states of the USA in the 1970s and 1980s. Jefferson Cowie and Joseph Heathcott's edited collection, *Beyond the Ruins: The Meanings of Deindustrialization*, provides a more culturally focused analysis of the same processes across a variety of geographical locations and periods in the USA in the second half of the 20th century.[5]

---

[4] Sharon Zukin, *Loft Living: Culture and Capital in Urban Change* (Baltimore: Johns Hopkins University Press, 1982); Julie Podmore, "(Re)Reading the 'Loft Living' Habitus in Montréal's Inner City," *International Journal of Urban and Regional Research* 22 (1998): 283; Wendy Shaw, "Sydney's SoHo Syndrome?: Loft Living in the Urbane City," *Cultural Geographies* 13 (2006): 182–206. On similar trends towards "loft-living" in London in the 1980s and 1990s, see Tom Dyckhoff, "Higher and Higher: How London Fell for the Loft," in *London: From Punk to Blair*, J. Kerr and A. Gibson ed. (London : Reaktion Books, 2003), 229–35; and Chris Hamnett and Drew Whitelegg, "Loft Conversion and Gentrification in London: From Industrial to Post-industrial Land Use," *Environment and Planning A* 39, 1 (2008): 106–24.

[5] Steven High, *Industrial Sunset: The Making of North America's Rust Belt, 1969–1984* (Toronto: University of Toronto Press, 2003); Steven High and David Lewis, *Corporate Wasteland: The Landscape and Memory of Deindustrialization*, (Ithaca and London: ILR Press, 2007); Jefferson Cowie and Joseph Heathcott ed., *Beyond the Ruins: The Meanings of Deindustrialization* (Ithaca and London: ILR Press, 2003). See also the special edition of *Urban History Review/Revue d'histoire urbain*, "The Memory and Politics of Deindustrialization in Canada" XXXV, 2 (Spring 2007) for a series of responses to restructuring, deindustrialization and abandonment across Canada from 1900 to the present.

The main focus of these studies and similar investigations into deindustrialisation and economic restructuring in Australia have, however, been industrial cities or towns, rather than the inner regions of large metropolitan areas.[6] And all have been concerned with the unemployment, trauma and despair caused by the collapse of old industries, rather than with the reinvention of these formerly industrial zones as sites of post-industrial activity in the years since the onset of economic crisis in the 1970s and 1980s. In light of this, historian Jenny Gregory has recently suggested that the transformation of Australia's inner cities from sites of low-cost housing and manual jobs to areas of high-cost accommodation and high-status employment must now be fully analysed by historians.[7]

This chapter, which uncovers the 20th-century history of the buildings that are now the Red Tulip Apartment complex, begins that task. In narrating the multiple histories of this one factory site across the course of the last century, the chapter also seeks to uncover a wider story of almost 100 years of economic, social and cultural change in inner Melbourne, the metropolis as a whole, and across Australia more generally. By utilising urban history techniques, including the reading of landscapes as historical sources, the chapter charts the transformation of this one site from a place of industry, employment and production in the first half of the 20th century to one of residence, leisure and consumption today. I argue that the experiences of this one site can be read as a tangible record of the wider changes that have affected Australia's economy and society over the course of the century. Finally, the chapter argues that, while the most recent transformation of the inner city is an important historical fracture and a major reorientation of its economic role, this should be seen as but one step in a series of such changes that have affected the region over the last 100 years as a result of the emergence of new modes of production and new patterns of residence and consumption.

Production, 1906–1989

The suburb of Prahran is located just to the south-east of central Melbourne, about five kilometres from the General Post Office. From

---

[6] Mark Peel, *Good Times, Hard Times: The Past and the Future in Elizabeth* (Melbourne: Melbourne University Press, 1995); Erik Eklund, *Steel Town: The Making and Breaking of Port Kembla* (Melbourne: Melbourne University Press, 2002).

[7] Jenny Gregory, "Obliterating History?: The Transformation of Inner City Industrial Suburbs," *Australian Historical Studies* 39, 1 (2008): 91–106.

1855 until 1994, Prahran was the name of both a suburb and a municipality. As Sally Wilde ably demonstrated in her 1993 municipal history, Prahran is a place that cannot be readily classified socially, culturally or economically. The former municipality included the wealthy enclaves of Toorak and South Yarra, as well as the much poorer working-class area of Windsor at its southern tip. Presently, the suburb of Prahran itself includes well-to-do pockets, bordering the upmarket inner city suburbs of South Yarra to the north and west and Armadale to the east, as well as streets of 19th-century working-class cottages and terraces in the flatter central areas. Like its neighbouring municipality, St Kilda, Prahran has long been home to some of Melbourne's wealthiest citizens as well as its poorest. In the 1960s and early 1970s, much of central Prahran was rebuilt as high-rise public housing by the Housing Commission of Victoria.[8]

For more than a century, Prahran has been a major retail hub, with its main thoroughfare, Chapel Street, serving as Melbourne's second most important shopping destination from the late 1880s until the coming of the drive-in suburban shopping complexes in the 1960s. In the early 20th century, a number of grand department stores, including Maple's, Foy and Gibson, Love and Lewis, the Colosseum and Charles Moore Read's six-storey Emporium, were established in Chapel Street, most notably in the central section between Commercial Road and High Street. But while Chapel Street remains an important retail zone, none of the grand retail emporia survived beyond the 1970s. Throughout the 20th century, Prahran was also an important centre of clothing and other manufacturing industry, as well as a major site of food and drink production. As Sally Wilde has noted, there "used to be literally hundreds of factories in Prahran, particularly in the central and western areas." Most were small in scale, "each employing a couple of dozen people or less," but, until the 1970s, between them they provided manufacturing employment to almost a third of the local population.[9] Food production was perhaps the most employment-intensive of Prahran's industries, with major employers such as Henry Jones IXL being an important provider of seasonal jobs, especially for women and new migrants.[10] While few of Prahran's

[8] Sally Wilde, *The History of Prahran, Volume II, 1925—1990* (Melbourne: Melbourne University Press, 1993).
[9] Wilde, *The History of Prahran*,145–6.
[10] On the history of the "Jam Factory" and its reinvention as a shopping centre in the late 1970s, see Feodora Fomin and John Spierings, "The Recovery and Transformation of the Jam Factory," *Melbourne Historical Journal* 16 (1984): 48–59.

secondary industries survived economic restructuring in the 1970s and 1980s, most of the major retail and industrial complexes remain in-situ, and both Chapel Street and the major east–west streets running off it retain substantial buildings and structures that date from the industrialisation of the suburb in the first half of the 20th century.

One of the largest employers in early 20th-century Prahran was OT Limited, a cordial and drink manufacturing company founded in the late 1890s in Alfred Street, by John Dixon, an English immigrant. As Betty Malone narrates in her *Discovering Prahran* series, "OT was a very hot [chilli] punch used to spice up beer in winter or in soft drinks."[11] OT was immediately popular, locally and internationally, and, by 1909, Dixon had incorporated the company in both London and Melbourne. A year later, he took it public. From 1905, Dixon began to construct what later became the Red Tulip Apartments as a production and distribution complex that straddled High Street, just to the east of Chapel Street. By the 1920s, a number of factories and distribution businesses had also been established in England, Europe, the USA, South Africa and elsewhere.[12] Other than the chilli punch, OT's most famous product, and one that is still sold today, was Kia-Ora cordial. Like many other similar businesses in inner Melbourne at this time, OT produced and sold a range of products, and was what we would now call a vertically integrated enterprise. In addition to making cordial and punch, the company preserved and canned fruit, as well as manufacturing its own glass bottles, paper cups and wooden bottle crates. From 1931, it even began to manufacture its own shipping containers. It would appear that most of these products (bar the shipping containers) were produced on-site in the Prahran factories, although, by the 1940s, the company also owned a tomato-canning operation in North Bendigo as well as a production and distribution facility in Alexandria, Sydney.[13]

---

[11] Betty Malone, *Discovering Prahran: Area Four* (Prahran: Prahran Historical and Arts Society Inc., 2001), 33.

[12] *Local* (Prahran) "Centenary Issue," April 22, 1955.

[13] Defunct Company Records, Kia Ora Ltd, VPRS 932/0/221/4446, VPRS 932/P/221, Public Records Office Victoria (PROV).

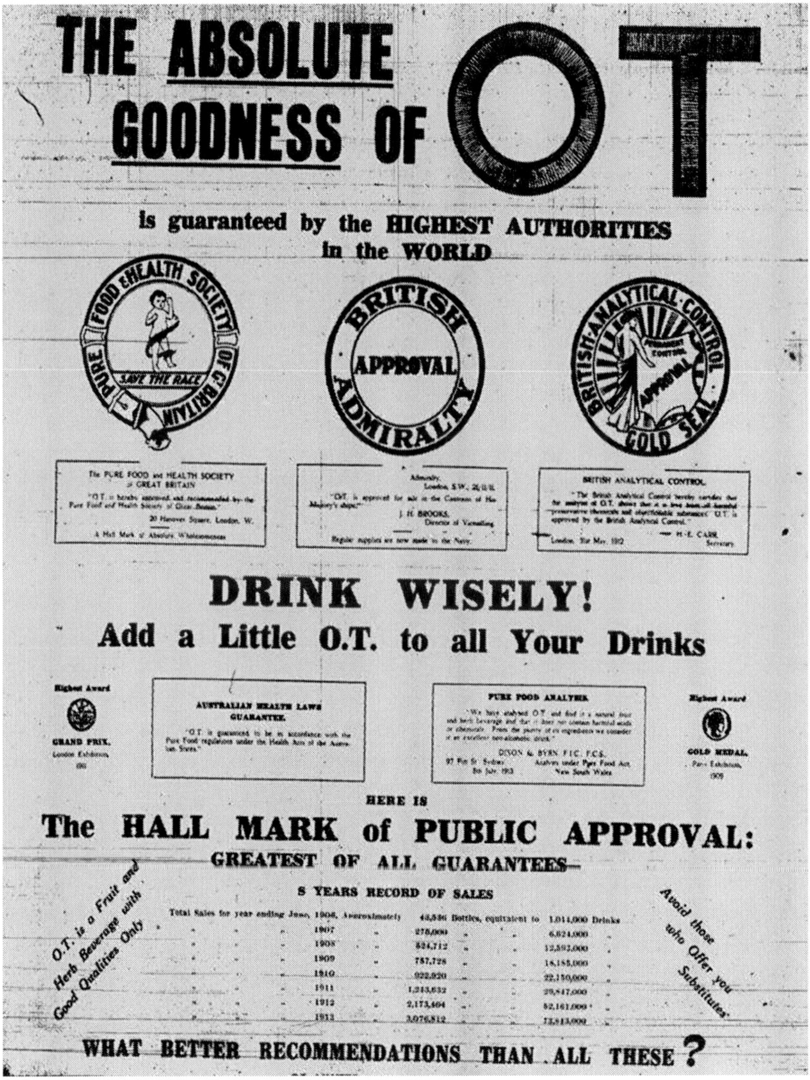

FIGURE 11.1 More than a drink. An advertisement for OT beverages. *Argus*, 23 August 1913. Image courtesy of the State Library of Victoria

John Dixon died in 1942, leaving an estate valued at almost £38,000, including Moana, a grand mansion in Orrong Road, Armadale, that was valued at nearly £10,000.[14] He was succeeded as managing director of OT by his oldest son Roland, who in turn died in 1949, aged only 48. Roland was succeeded by his younger brother, John Leonard (or Jack), who had until then been in charge of the company's Sydney operations. While the war years had seen the company's operations come under the strict control of the Department of Labour and National Service's Food Services Branch, the post-war years saw major investment and expansion.[15] In August 1951, Jack Dixon travelled to the United States on a study and fact-finding trip sponsored by the Commonwealth Ministry of National Development as part of its efforts to modernise the Australian economy after the war.[16] In the same year, the name of the company was changed to Kia Ora Industries Ltd, possibly reflecting the increasing prominence of cordial and foodstuffs as the company's major product lines, rather than the chilli punch, which was becoming less popular as public tastes changed.

Profits remained strong throughout the first half of the 1950s, and were reported at £540,736 for the twelve months to 30 June 1956. In March 1957, a prospectus seeking to raise £200,000 was issued to pay for planned expansion and new investment.[17] But, as with many other local companies, the late 1950s were not kind to Kia Ora. In 1959, the name of the company was again changed, this time to Johnell Ltd (presumably after John Leonard), and, in 1960, the "food trade names, formulae, inventories, plant and equipment and certain freehold property in Bendigo" were sold to Campbell's Soups (Australia) Pty Ltd. The Prahran properties, as well as those in Alexandria, were leased to Campbell's "for a short term," but, at the expiration of this lease, the Prahran properties were to be sold.[18] While Jack Dixon was appointed to the board of the new Campbell's company, the Dixon family's ties to the High Street premises were severed after more than 50 years when the headquarters of Johnell were relocated to

[14] Will and probate of John Dixon, died 28 March 1942, VPRS 28/P3/3711/336/850, PROV; see also Malone, *Discovering Prahran*, 23.

[15] Department of Labour and National Service, Foods services Branch, Industrial Welfare Division Area Two files, Kia Ora Products Pty Ltd Bendigo and Prahran, National Archives of Australia (NAA) 153/1/159.

[16], Kia Ora Industries Ltd—Sponsorship for Travel, NAA 5/60/5313.

[17] Defunct Company Records, Kia Ora, PROV.

[18] Johnell Ltd, Annual Report, 1960.

Box Hill in 1961.[19] Jack Dixon resigned as a director of Campbell's in late 1963.

Campbell's did not stay in the Prahran factories for long, opting instead to integrate the Kia Ora operations into a new production facility located in Shepparton in northern Victoria. The OT buildings were, however, to remain a major site of manufacturing and food production for almost another thirty years. In 1963, they were sold to another Prahran local success story, Red Tulip Chocolates, which had been founded in a Chapel Street shop by a Jewish refugee couple from Czechoslovakia, Geza (George) and Clara (Claire) Gorog, in 1943. In 1945, the company moved to a small factory at 266 High Street and, in the same year, took up some space in the Kia Ora buildings in High Street, opposite the main complex. In 1952, Red Tulip became a public company when the Gorogs, along with Roy and Edith Sanders—both born in Austria, and again presumably refugees from Hitler—took one quarter each of the 200 shares in a new company, Red Tulip Ltd. Like Kia Ora, Red Tulip prospered throughout the early 1950s, but it too began to lose its way as the decade wore on. From 1958, the company increasingly came under the influence of the Port Melbourne–based Henry Berry food and agribusiness group. Clara Gorog retired as a director of Red Tulip in 1959, along with Edith Sanders. George Gorog stayed on until 1962 when William Sanders became a director of Henry Berry. In the same year, Red Tulip purchased the entire OT complex and, from 1963, began manufacturing chocolate there. In 1968, the company was purchased by Beatrice (Australia) Pty Ltd, the Australian arm of the giant Chicago-based food conglomerate. Beatrice maintained control until 1987 when its Australian operations were sold to Cadbury Schweppes. Production of chocolate ceased at the factory in the late 1980s and "Red Tulip's last link with Prahran [was] severed in June 1990 when the offices in High Street" were closed.[20]

Consumption, 1990–2000

"Under instructions from Cadbury Schweppes," the Red Tulip factories were offered for auction in October 1993. Advertised as a "rare renovation or redevelopment site" suitable for "residential, commercial, retail or industrial development," the entire site was bought by the Royal Victorian Institute for the Blind (RVIB) for use as an education facility and

[19] Johnell Ltd Annual Report, 1961, 1963.

[20] Prahran Historical and Arts Society, *Newsletter* (September 1989): 40.

administrative centre.[21] The inner city was changing at this time, however, and factory buildings like the OT/Red Tulip complex had not only exhausted their use and economic value as production facilities but also their potential as secondary office space.[22] Instead, former factory spaces had emerged as highly fashionable residential sites. Following in the footsteps of New York's SoHo and London's Docklands and Clerkenwell, by the 1990s, Melbourne's inner city factories were being reinvented as chic industrial warehouse apartments, marketed to cashed-up young professionals. While RVIB retained a small portion of their holdings and continue to be based there, most of the former buildings were bought by property developers the MAB Corporation in 1996 and redeveloped into what was described in a series of newspaper and other reports as "a $16 million, New York-style warehouse apartment complex."[23] More than 100 apartments and townhouses were created in and around the old factory complex, and, in the spirit of the new consumption-oriented inner city, these were variously marketed as offering "the most exciting lifestyle in history," "fabulous balconies [with] city views," and all "the features of warehouse living," within walking distance of the "cafes, cinemas and shopping" of nearby Chapel Street, Greville Street and Toorak Road. A later advertisement suggested that these apartments saw "Prahran meet New York" and offered a "total lifestyle package ... ideally suited to the new millennium."[24]

In creating the Red Tulip apartments, MAB not only sought to appeal to a new generation of urban-oriented young professionals but also to attract another emerging niche market that was seeing industrial heritage increasingly recycled as living space. The overtly industrial architectural style of the Red Tulip building thus became an important part of the marketing campaign, with the site's past uses actively celebrated as adding historical authenticity and heritage value to the new development. Publicity for the apartments noted that there were "few buildings remaining in Prahran that offer the potential of this project and none have the history and location of Red Tulip."[25] So, rather than hide the industrial origins of the redeveloped complex, the desires of this new market niche saw

---

[21] *Age*, October 2, 1993.

[22] On the intermediate uses of former industrial spaces as secondary offices, see Hamnett and Whitelegg, "Loft Conversion."

[23] Bruce Dunlevy, "Chocolate Factory Boxed," *Australian*, March 15, 1997; "Mind's the Limit in Warehouse Plan," *Age*, 15 March 1997. 6.

[24] Stonnington Archives File: "Hillingdon Place."

[25] Dunlevy, "Chocolate Factory Boxed".

FIGURE 11.2 Red Tulip Warehouse Apartments, Prahran, 2008. Photographer, Seamus O'Hanlon

them actively celebrated, albeit in a fairly sanitised way that privileged architecture over humanity, and technology over toil. "From warehouse to your house," read one advertisement, while another extolled the building's industrial heritage by noting that its "historic chimney" would remain a feature of the new development. New sections of the complex would feature a "steel profiled façade" and "steel frame and glass" design in keeping with the building's industrial aesthetic. "Lifestyle" was on sale here, but so too was "authenticity," or perhaps what United States economist and urban commentator Richard Florida likes to call "edginess."[26] As Julie Podmore has argued, in the 1980s and 1990s architectural commentators, lifestyle magazines and design-focused journals "contributed to the re-coding of inner-city industrial buildings ... as potential live/work or domestic spaces" with particular appeal for those in the new or "creative" industries then emerging.[27] In the post-industrial consumption-based economy, then, former sites of production and industry have become valued as residential sites not only because of their location adjacent to the employment and leisure opportunities of the restructured and reinvented inner city, but for their heritage links to an increasingly romanticised industrial past.

Continuity and change

It is, of course, easy to be cynical about the latest reinvention of the former OT/Red Tulip complex and to see the transformation of this once productive facility into a place of conspicuous consumption in the form of highly-priced residential apartments as a travesty of industrial history and heritage. Yet, as historians, we must be aware that urban landscapes have always changed in response to new economic and social pressures. As we have seen in this chapter, the adaptation and reuse of land and structures has long been a feature of Melbourne's urban form. And, while the reuse of this former factory complex for residential purposes might at first appear to be a profound break with the past, in reality these new uses are entirely appropriate given the site's historical association with the founder of OT, John Dixon. In addition to being a successful soft drink and food products entrepreneur, Dixon was also a property developer, and, like many other entrepreneurs throughout Australia's past and present, he and

---

[26] Zukin, *Loft Living*; Richard Florida, *The Rise of the Creative Class: And How It's Transforming Work, Leisure, Community and Everyday Life* (New York: Basic Books, 2002).

[27] Podmore, "(Re)reading," 285.

his family sought to reinvest excess profits from their main business into the relative safety of the residential property market, especially in the wake of the 1929 sharemarket crash and the ensuing Great Depression.

As with a number of other business people in the 1930s, Dixon found that the most appropriate and profitable avenue for property investment at this time was in the newly emerging market for self-contained flats in Melbourne's inner suburbs. The family's private company, Kia Ora Investments, thus became a prolific developer of flats across the inner city region in the 1930s and 1940s. The best known of their blocks is the 60-flat Kia Ora, developed in 1936 and one of the few remaining Art-Deco flat blocks left in St Kilda Road. Kia Ora Investments also owned or developed a number of other blocks of flats in South Yarra, Toorak and East Melbourne. By the late 1930s, this activity had become a highly profitable sideline to the Dixon family's main food and drink business. In January 1938, for example, they earned more than £1000 in rents from a number of properties managed by the South Yarra real estate firm Williams and Company.[28] These are significant earnings at a time when the basic wage was about £4 per week. And, of course, this income is quite aside from the profits derived from shares in OT.

Conclusion: new residents, new cultures, new desires

As I have argued elsewhere, it is possible to see the demand for Melbourne's inter-war flats as evidence of the forces of change and the relative personal freedoms and new employment opportunities associated with industrialised production techniques and "modern" ideas and attitudes in the first decades of the 20th century. Jill Matthews has recently suggested that the dance halls, picture palaces and apartment blocks of early 20th-century Sydney should similarly be seen as tangible reminders of a period when new forms of work, leisure and social attitudes were rapidly altering lifestyle and consumption patterns, especially for young women and other previously economically marginalised individuals and groups. As she argues, we should see these places as representative of a time when young women's lives began to be reshaped by "modern culture and the possibilities of life in the modern city."[29] The fact that

---

[28] Seamus O'Hanlon, *Together Apart: Boarding House, Hostel and Flat Life in Pre-war Melbourne* (Melbourne: Australian Scholarly Publishing, 2002), 161.
[29] Jill Julius Matthews, *Dance Hall and Picture Palace: Sydney's Romance with Modernity* (Sydney: Currency Press, 2005).

contemporary warehouse apartments such as Red Tulip are deliberately marketed to young, single, professional women and men, and that some of the advertising for these places overtly targets gay men and lesbians, suggests that today, as in the early decades of the 20th century, the inner city is again being remade in ways that cater to the needs, desires and tastes of new residents and new social and cultural groups. The emergence of new dwelling types and new patterns of consumption in the reinvented inner city may also mean that, while the effects of deindustrialisation and economic restructuring have been traumatic for many, for some individuals and groups, these changes have brought social liberation and new opportunities inconceivable in a society dominated by older patterns of production and employment.

CHAPTER TWELVE

POSSESSION ISLAND: COLONIAL AND CONTEMPORARY VISIONS OF AUSTRALIAN CONSUMERISM

KIM HUMPHERY

Consumerism is not an abstract, academic concept; it is for many people a much utilised and often negative descriptor of a western—and increasingly global—zeitgeist. While a perceived right to consume goods and services, to unrestrictedly spend one's hard-earned money, has become accepted by many as a marker of personal freedom, power and expression and as the flag bearer of democracy, excessive consumption presents itself as a social and moral problem; and, historically speaking, it has always done so.

Consumerism is persistently spoken of in everyday conversation and in social commentary as an attitude and a behaviour that, while it waxes and wanes with the economic times, remains somehow definitive of historically rising levels of a western, cum global, affluence. Attitudinally, consumerism is routinely understood by both the public and the social critic as an individual, generational or cultural obsession: an obsession with continually wanting, acquiring and discarding stuff—and with both evaluating others and seeking existential meaning through this process. Behaviourally, this propensity towards abundance is apparently all too clearly demonstrated in boom-to-bust cycles of non-stop shopping and unconstrained spending, and in the mounting levels of refuse left behind as we tire of one product and opt for another. Consumerism, moreover, is often indeed to be coupled with an ethos of materialism, generally understood as an overvaluing of things and money, and an exaggerated concern with their accumulation, ownership and display. Paradoxically, in the contemporary West, these two phenomena seem to both converge and diverge in that purchasable things have come to be promoted not as objects to be hoarded and cherished but as items to be transiently experienced and quickly discarded. In this sense, the West has seemingly perfected a form of consumerism that has buckled and twisted almost out of recognition the possessive materialism of which it was born.

If we understand affluence, particularly in the West, as bound up with these contradictory notions of possession, and as expressed through what has vaguely become known as consumer culture, then where does Australia fit in this narrative? Historians and social observers have long claimed that Australia fits here all too well: that a materialism and, in the post–Second World War period, a vigorous consumerism must be taken as partially, even largely, definitive of an Australian set of cultural values. In this short chapter, I move between the colonial and the contemporary in order to explore this contention. In particular, I trace some of the lines of reiteration to be found in colonial and contemporary social commentary on Australia as a consumer nation.

The stuff of colonialism

I begin with a glance at the colonial history of a very current notion in relation to contemporary materialism and consumerism. This notion is that of consumption as pathology and of a love of things as somehow particularly definitive of an Australian version of the good life. Students of Australian history will recognise the deliberateness of this chapter's title. It refers to James Cook's key and final act before leaving sight of the east coast of Australia on 22 August 1770. On that day, sensing that his voyage of discovery was complete and that New Holland was separate from New Guinea, Cook named a small island lying off the coast of Cape York, "Possession Island," and on its shore he hoisted the English flag, laying claim to New South Wales in the name of George III.[1]

This occasion as an event of the historical past has now been largely forgotten, but that was not always the case. At one time, 22 August rivalled, for some, 26 January as a suitable "Australia Day." Indeed, in the early 1900s, a so-called "Possession Day" was mooted by the Australian Natives Association as a nationalist alternative to the conservative-led

[1] C.M.H. Clark, *A History of Australia: From The Earliest Times to the Age of Macquarie, Volume 1* (Melbourne: Melbourne University Press, 1963), 50. See also Greg Dening, "Living With and In Deep Time," in *The Historian's Conscience: Australian Historians on the Ethics of History*, ed. Stuart Macintyre (Melbourne: Melbourne University Press, 2004), 46–7.

invention of "Empire Day."[2] The naming of Possession Island was, in the literal sense, an act that symbolised, more than any other, an ethos of colonial expansion. Yet, as Paul Carter has argued, Cook's sophisticated understanding of the act of naming—and his seemingly odd decision to plant the British flag on a tiny island rather than on the Australian mainland—spoke of the complex process through which Cook's very journeying was involved in the naming of space as vaguely characterised place. For Cook, Carter carefully insists, the task was not in fact to claim the world, but to chart and document it.[3] Cook's process of naming this island certainly marked a land grab; but, even more so for Cook, it marked a task of exploration properly completed. We can, however, add yet another layer to this story. Cook's planting of the King's colours on and naming of Possession Island announced a moment of cultural transmission in relation to understandings of the material world. It metaphorically brought to the edge of a continent a mentality of possession: a mentality that Cook himself famously observed seemed absent on the continent itself.

Cook, as is well known, lauded what he saw as the non-materialism of the Australian "natives," commenting in the noble savage vein on their lack of covetousness towards material possessions. Cook did, of course, stick fast to his own worldview, yet throughout his travels he was no deliberate spoiler of other cultures. When it came to the Antipodes, Cook was thus driven to admire, and to heavily romanticise, the fact that the Aborigines, in his much-cited words, "live in a Tranquility which is not disturbed by the Inequality of Condition."[4]

Here, in these moments of possession and of ethnographic observation on the apparent "thinglessness" of Indigenous culture, Cook set in motion what would become a particularly Australian way of grappling with the western dilemma about how to relate to and live through the material world. The themes of possession, materialism and, more recently, consumerism have woven themselves through Australian history. So too have the contrasting dreams of a tranquil life lived without things—on the

---

[2] Stephen Alomes, *A Nation at Last: The Changing Character of Australian Nationalism 1880–1988* (Sydney: Angus & Robertson, 1988), 54. Empire Day was observed in Australia on May 24, from 1905 on.

[3] Paul Carter, *The Road to Botany Bay: An Essay in Spatial History* (London: Faber & Faber, 1988), 27–8.

[4] Captain James Cook, cited in Manning Clark, *A Short History of Australia* (New York, Mentor, 1969), 19 (Cook's capitalisation).

beach or in the bush. This push and pull between the excessive and the simple has long been identified as shaping an Australian identity. Yet covetousness, it seems, has always ultimately been the winner.

Overwhelmingly, the Australian historian and social critic has taken the new world history of exploration, settlement and nation-making in a distant and physically tough land as the basis of portraying Australian society as fundamentally materialistic: one far more geared to acquisition than to a frugal, uncluttered life. An Australian material acquisitiveness has rarely, if ever, been explored in detail within historical work and social commentary; yet this has not detracted from a sense that the present is mechanistically produced by the past by way of a linear continuity. Somehow, the historical development of Australia, marked by long periods of economic prosperity in the 19th and 20th centuries and underscored by a brash, go-ahead entrepreneurialism, has simply conditioned Australians into being one of the most consumption-oriented peoples in the world.

In fact, there is only thin evidence of an Australian exceptionalism here. White Australia, in its formative first century, largely mirrored rather than magnified what Karl Polanyi so well identified as what *was* exceptional: the fact that Britain in the 19th century was the first society in history to elevate the concepts of gain and economic growth to a general principle of action and meaning in everyday life.[5] Australia, in so many respects, simply followed suit. Discursively, however, a yearning for things and a propensity to buy them was certainly envisaged by colonial observers themselves as somehow more vociferous in the colonies than elsewhere, and as thoroughly definitive of the historical development of the Australian life-world.

In no uncertain terms, Australia has thus long been considered a veritable experiment in materialism—and early social observers were more than quick to portray the new antipodean society as essentially pecuniary and acquisitive. In 1835, for example, the *Van Diemen's Land Monthly Magazine*, reflecting on the character of free emigrants, intoned: "To make a fortune, therefore, or at least to better themselves in a pecuniary point of view, is the aim of all." Such a "money-making and illiterate population," such an "engrossing desire of wealth," did not, the

---

[5] Karl Polanyi, *The Great Transformation: The Political and Economic Origins of our Time* (Boston: Beacon Press, 1992 (1944)), 31.

author lamented, make for "a high standard of National character" and was "considered as affecting the morals of the community." This article, in fact, prefigured the work of the American sociologist, Thorstein Veblen, who was to coin the term "conspicuous consumption" in the 1890s. In such a "money-making community," the 1835 article went on, individuals were driven to "a display of opulence" that disguised the harsh and frugal economic realities of a new country.[6]

Similar concerns had been earlier voiced by the likes of David Collins, who noted that already, in 1798, settlers in the new colony were prone to debt, attracted by "the enjoyment of articles which they could do without," and prone as well to "throwing away their money in purchasing, at every public auction, rags and trifles."[7] Collins recognised that, in part, such "consumerism" (as we now would call it) was due to a shortage of European articles. Nevertheless, these kinds of observations in relation to the Australian colonies were *de rigueur* by the 1840s—and, unbeknownst to the colonial critic, would set the tone for two centuries of Australian social commentary on our propensity to buy.

For the more astute of colonial observers, the stark contrast between European and Aboriginal society was not forgotten, and the colonial representation of an Australian love of wealth, material things and consumption was to be re-embedded in cross-cultural comparison. As Alexander Harris intimated in his *Settlers and Convicts*, published in 1847, an Australian materialism could from the very beginning be construed as a kind of social pathology: "Avarice and covetousness," Harris wrote, "are vices unknown to the savage: and he can only regard the man labouring under them as one infected with some shocking and mysterious disease."[8] Harris's very early discovery of that condition now rather glibly known as "affluenza" must surely be credited here, despite

[6] Anonymous, "The Australian Character," *Van Diemen's Land Monthly Magazine*, 3 (1835), 112–14, cited in *Select Documents in Australian History: 1780–1850*, ed. C.M.H. Clark (Sydney: Angus & Robertson, 1969), 435–46.
[7] David Collins, *An Account of the English Colony in New South Wales, Volume II* [1802] (Adelaide: Australian Facsimile Editions No. 76, Libraries Board of South Australia, 1971), 97.
[8] Alexander Harris, *Settlers and Convicts or Recollections of Sixteen Years' Labour in the Australian Backwoods / by an Emigrant Mechanic* [1852] (Melbourne: Melbourne University Press, 1964), 232.

the unsurprising racism of his language.[9] In fact, this recourse to the notion of consumption as illness was soon to become even more apposite. The "gold fever" of the 1850s was to do little but cement the portrayal of the colonial citizen as wildly avaricious in outlook. William Howitt's *Land, Labour and Gold*, published in 1855, was filled with stories of a population drunk on speculation and the promise of riches. Indeed, Howitt—not unlike Harris—identified a sort of early pathological desire for wealth and material prosperity in the colonies and was not the first or last social commentator to equate the Australian with the "Yankee," identifying the same unswerving, money-making urge.[10]

Colonial commentators, of course, were generally not, in articulating a distaste for a rampant antipodean materialism, budding proto-socialists. Their class-based complaints were inherently conflicted, with most observers in fact praising a colonial prosperity and industriousness, but insisting vigorously that it be well governed and accompanied by the development of civilities and high culture. A desire for and display of capitalist advancement and comfort was not the problem; it was that, in the colonies, the getting of wealth and material goods was seemingly open to all and sundry—and was thus debased. This was a theme well plundered by the colonial observer such that, by the 1880s, the promise of Australia had become the promise of a mass, increasingly bland, consumer culture.

R.E.N. Twopeny's *Town Life in Australia*, published in 1883, signalled fully this apparent rise of a crass Australian consumer mentality, no longer simply embedded in an obsession with trifles, but now the very *raison d'être* of colonial life. Twopeny in fact identifies what we might call a dull materialism, rather than an emulative consumerism; he writes of, and has much fun lampooning, a bland, anti-aesthetic practicality in the Australian consumer marketplace. In this reading, Twopeny is not unlike the reading critics of the 1950s who were so utterly disillusioned with mass-consumer

---

[9] This until recently somewhat over-used term has been playfully defined as "a painful, contagious, socially transmitted condition of overload, debt, anxiety, and waste resulting from the dogged pursuit of more." See John de Graaf, David Wann and Thomas H. Naylor, *Affluenza: The All-Consuming Epidemic* (San Francisco: Berrett-Koehler, 2001), 2.

[10] William Howitt, *Land, Labour and Gold or, Two Years in Victoria: with Visits to Sydney and Van Diemen's Land* [1855] (Kilmore: Lowde, 1972), 190.

suburbanism.[11] Long before them, however, Twopeny discovers an Australian mass consumer culture involving, not a love of luxury and style, but a love of sheer profit and easily available goods.[12] What Twopeny finds in the colonies is a homogeneous society of relative abundance in which the cheapness of colonial life makes for a taken-for-granted acceptance of a plethora of ordinary everyday commodities. When Twopeny's colonists spend, they thus do so vigorously, not stylishly. "In everything," Twopeny writes, "the colonist likes quantity."[13] "Like the stock from which they spring," he observes, "their ideas of pleasure are still limited."[14] In many respects, then, Twopeny chides Australians for being heightened materialists but, worse, incompetent, tasteless consumers. In many respects, too, he would, in articulating these views, have felt somewhat at home among contemporary Australian social critics.

The contemporary material

Australia remains, many contend, a country of myopic, materialistic pleasures; and, far from diminishing as a thematic of Australian social criticism, consumption has over the past decade or so regained the topicality it enjoyed not only in the colonial period but also in the 1950s, 60s and 70s. We have for a number of years now been experiencing the reinvigoration of a critique of consumerism within public intellectual work in Australia. This is embedded in—and provides echoes of—the genre of Australian social observation sampled above; but it is connected also to a somewhat differently inflected international rejuvenation of anti-consumerist politics.

Over the past decade or more, especially within a number of "Rich World" countries, a new vibrancy and urgency has been evident in relation to an, albeit long, ongoing debate about the causes, ramifications and future of dominant modes of affluent consumption. Targeting western populations in particular, a resurgent left and liberal opposition to consumerism has focused on what has succinctly, if somewhat vaguely,

---

[11] For a discussion of this post-war critique, see Kim Humphery, *Shelf Life: Supermarkets and the Changing Cultures of Consumption* (Cambridge: Cambridge University Press, 1998), Chapter 8.

[12] R.E.N. Twopeny, *Town Life in Australia* [1883] (Sydney: Sydney University Press, 1973), 111.

[13] Twopeny, 64

[14] Twopeny, 202.

been called overconsumption.[15] Social commentators, journalists, religious leaders, political activists and academics across the sciences, social sciences and humanities have voiced often impassioned resistance to what is seen as a hitherto increasing, and increasingly global, obsession with the consumption of material goods and commodified experiences.[16] This obsession may well have taken a substantial hit through economic downturn, but, in Australia, more so than most affluent countries, a vigorous western consumerism remains.

Overwhelmingly, this resurfaced opposition to consumer abundance has been characterised by an environmentalist ethos—questions of resource usage and waste have been central to this debate. But the latest desire to challenge western (cum global) consumerism—and any return to its pre-2008 heights—is also social, cultural and emotional in focus. While almost all contemporary critics and activists talk of the need for an environmentally sustainable mode of living, many also focus intently on how the consumerism driving overconsumption undermines our sense of wellbeing and happiness; contributes to a culture of overwork, haste and instantaneous gratification; underscores a bland cultural homogenisation of life; and fragments communities and social relationships.

This most recent of critical waves has found a ready home in millennial Australia, not least because, of all western nations, Australia has experienced one of the most vigorous of consumer booms over the two

---

[15] Overconsumption has been variously conceptualised but refers essentially to a tendency to consume goods and services at a level over and above that which is necessary to maintain a reasonable standard of living and at a rate that is greater than can be environmentally sustained in terms of resource provision and the handling of waste.

[16] For a taste of this work see: Juliet B. Schor, *The Overspent American: Why We Want What We Don't Need* (New York: Harper Perennial, 1999); Barry Schwartz, *The Paradox of Choice: Why More is Less* (New York: Harper Collins, 2005); de Graaf, Wann and Naylor, *Affluenza*; Kalle Lasn, *Culture Jam* (New York: Eagle Books, 1999); Robert Frank, *Luxury Fever: Why Money Fails to Satisfy in an Era of Excess* (New York: Free Press, 1999); Paul R. Ehrlich and Anne H. Ehrlich, *One With Nineveh: Politics, Consumption, and the Human Future* (Washington: Island Press/Shearwater Books, 2004); Tim Kasser, *The High Price of Materialism* (Cambridge MA: MIT Press, 2002); Benjamin R. Barber, *Consumed: How Markets Corrupt Children, Infantilize Adults and Swallow Citizens Whole* (New York: Norton, 2007). See also, from France, Christian Comeliau, *The Impasse of Modernity* (London: Zed Books, 2002); and from Britain, Oliver James, *Affluenza: How to be Successful* and *Stay Sane* (London: Vermilion, 2007).

decades to 2008. In the face of this, the opportunity for biting social observation has not been overlooked. By the mid-1990s in Australia, there was a discernable increase in the number of reflective and critical media articles on shopping and consumerism: articles that both rehearsed and reformulated an entrenched genre of critical social commentary.[17] In 1993, for example, Gary Foley, writing on the state of Indigenous/non-Indigenous relations in Australia (and in part resurrecting Cook's original observations), made a point of defining his own Koori culture as non-materialistic and as standing in contrast to the increasingly dominant myths of a free enterprise system "motivated by a desire for wealth and material possessions."[18] In a not dissimilar vein, Richard Neville, in a 1994 feature article in the *Age*, wrote of the need to challenge the sacred cow of consumer choice and pursue a new ecologically oriented commerce.[19] A few years later, Pamela Bone introduced Australia to the US concept of affluenza in another *Age* article in 1997, and Phillip Adams in 1998 pitched in with a piece on the horrors of the shopping mall as a gulag with muzac.[20] The theme of wellbeing, or rather its absence through the rampant pursuit of national and individual monetary wealth, was also taken up. By the late 1990s, Australians were being characterised as both hyper-consumerist and also inherently emotionally conflicted, not least because, as Hugh Mackay insisted, we were obsessed with getting and spending but cognisant as well that the meaning of life and the source of

---

[17] Indeed, this is characteristic of the western media generally, as a search of a number of western daily newspapers indicates. This search, spanning 1990 to 2007, was undertaken as part of a broader Australian Research Council–funded project on anti-consumerism in the West. The search indicated that, from the mid-1990s onwards, there was a notable, though by no means overwhelming, upsurge of interest in topics related to consumerism and its critique within a sample of western newspapers, including the *Guardian* in Britain, the *New York Times*, and the *Age* in Melbourne. Since 2000 especially, there has, across all of these newspapers, been a steady flow of detailed articles and commentary published on a range of themes, particularly "luxury fever" and "affluenza," "downshifting" and "voluntary simplicity." For a more detailed discussion of these concepts and responses, see Kim Humphery, *Excess: Anti-consumerism in the West* (Cambridge: Polity, 2010).

[18] Gary Foley, "White Myths Damage Our Souls," *Age*, July 21, 1993, 15.

[19] Richard Neville, "Who Challenges the Real Sacred Cow," *Age*, March 17, 1994, 15.

[20] Pamela Bone, "A Measure of Happiness Lost in a Time of Measured Wealth," *Age*, November 6, 1997, 15; Phillip Adams, "Born to Shop in the Gulag," *Weekend Australian*, August 1–2, 1998, "Review," 32.

happiness resides outside the materialistic.[21] Notwithstanding this conflicted consciousness, by 2003 consumerism had apparently all but triumphed. In returning to the metaphor of affluenza, Anne Manne announced that the Great Australian Dream had, after year upon year of unconstrained shopping, "turned into an empty crypt of consumption."[22]

Undoubtedly, it has been the work of analysts such as Clive Hamilton and, to a lesser extent, Richard Eckersley that has most effectively reinstated consumption in Australia as socially (and environmentally) problematic. By the mid-2000s, both analysts had written engaging and provocative "best-sellers" on the consequences of affluence and materialism, giving particular attention to the depletion of wellbeing through emulative hyperconsumption, overwork and overspending. Both writers also marked Australians as particularly pathological in their approach to the commodity, with Eckersley commenting—in strikingly "colonial" terms—that: "Once we have met our basic needs, most consumption today is located within the vices, little within the virtues—feeding off envy, to say nothing of greed, lust and other moral hazards."[23]

Ironically, by late 2008, this output of polemic slowed in tandem with the global economy. Opponents of consumerism scrambled, like everyone else, to rejig their analysis in face of a boom gone pear shaped. There is no reason to assume, however, that these various writers would now, in face of an uncertain economic future, disavow an understanding of overconsumption as damaging to society, culture, nature and the individual. Taking a longer-term view, most critics would no doubt insist that, although consumerism in its most rampant guise may have been in retreat for time, it remains an essential propensity of affluent societies—and, as such, must continue to be challenged, particularly as it gears up once more. They would, I would argue, be absolutely right in articulating such a position; and, here, I declare my own allegiance to anti-consumerist politics.

---

[21] Mackay cited in Jane Faulkner, "Everybody's Happy Nowadays?" *Age*, September 14, 1999, 1.

[22] Anne Manne, "Why We're Richer but Feeling Poorer," *Age*, April 12, 2003, 11. See also, Denise Cullen, "In the Grip of Affluenza," *Age*, April 21, 2003, 3.

[23] Richard Eckersley, *Well & Good: How We Feel & Why it Matters* (Melbourne: Text, 2004), 51. See also Clive Hamilton, *Growth Fetish* (Sydney: Allan & Unwin, 2003); Clive Hamilton and Richard Denniss, *Affluenza: When Too Much is Never Enough* (Sydney: Allen & Unwin, 2005).

Yet, in terms of the present chapter, what is of interest about much contemporary anti-consumerist critique in Australia is the ease with which Eckersley and others can invoke a relatively "timeless" sense of why Australians consume—and what our apparent yearning for things says about an Australian life-world. There is, in fact, an almost effortless recourse by contemporary Australian critics to an assumed material continuum extending back two centuries: one rendering the Australian citizen, always already known as an inveterate consumer, as materialistic *par excellence*. It must be conceded that this is only a partial echo of colonial concerns; a long tradition of mass culture critique—in which modern consumption is construed as a straightforward product of attitudinal manipulation and cultural degeneration—has been far more influential on how contemporary Australian observers interpret the consumer present. But Australian social commentary is inevitably overlaid also with a perennial concern about the essentially pecuniary nature of the Australian dream, and of the somehow greater propensity here than elsewhere for acquisition at all costs.

The question is, what do we make of this trace of the colonial in the contemporary? In part, it must certainly be recognised as tired repetition based on the bland assumption that the past reproduces the present: that Australia is, through its very formation and economic development, inescapably riven with a crass materialism that continually "infects" each new generation. But there is also something more conceptually interesting going on here. As Elizabeth Grosz has observed, although the present does not contain the past, "they coexist and function simultaneously."[24] This is well put, and is particularly the case in relation to the imaginary of Australian material life. If contemporary Australia is enmeshed with a "consumer culture," then this is not because our history irrevocably makes it so. It is because current economic arrangements and social frameworks continue unrelentingly to animate a particular form of exchange. Yet the constant return in Australian social criticism to the theme of a national—and historically entrenched—love of stuff does in some constructive sense keep the material world, and how it comes to be understood over time, in full view. It provokes us into grappling with how the values placed on material things are formed and transformed in a deep historical realm: a realm that does not so much mechanistically create the present as reverberate alongside it.

---

[24] Elizabeth Grosz, *The Nick of Time* (Sydney: Allen & Unwin, 2004), 250.

If we are, then, to be sensitive to the physical and cultural context of place, it may well have been the case that the materialism of an early industrial era was likely to take on quite different forms in different lands. That is, it was apt to permutate and to exhibit changing levels of intensity as it travelled the globe. In the case of early colonial Australia, a lived relationship to objects was to be shaped through the very act of exile and emigration. This is why we cannot entirely dismiss colonial social commentary, however elitist, blinkered and wildly overgeneralising it seems in relation to pronouncing the colonist utterly materialistic in mentality. The early colonists, after all, were a people who had left a commodity-laden Europe for a land where such commodities were, at least for many decades, in short supply. From very early on, part of the loss of exile and emigration was a "commodity loss," and part of the remedy was acquisition. But these were people, as well, who had traversed the globe, who had had their senses literally bombarded with new physical and social realities, and whose mind-set was thus turned with a new intensity to the *material* in terms of the natural wonders and sheer potential of new places, and in terms of everyday physical survival.[25] And, finally, these were people who were confronted with a cultural tableau of Indigeneity that, however savage and decrepit they portrayed it, stood as a reminder of a quite different relationship to the object world, one that needed to be vigorously rejected (if occasionally romanticised).

So, has this heritage, in almost socio-biological terms, proved to be the cultural bedrock of a white, commodified nation, rendering generation after generation instinctually acquisitive? And is this an acquisitiveness that has been reconfirmed rather than challenged through successive waves of emigration, the triumph of "Australia Incorporated" in the early to mid-20th century, and the most recent decades of extraordinary, export-driven prosperity? Contemporary commentary on Australian consumerism—in its modernised repetition of colonial observations—implicitly nudges at such a proposition. In doing so, it courts the banal. But, equally, it tantalisingly suggests that the shadow of a past is somewhere there in the material practices that characterise the life-world we now inhabit—practices that remain still to be confronted in transforming the economy as presently lived.

---

[25] Mukerji, drawing on the work of J.H. Elliot, makes a similar point about the impact of encountering new physical realities on the reformulation of a western materialism. See Chandra Mukerji, *From Graven Images: Patterns of Modern Materialism* (New York: Columbia University Press, 1983), 20–1.

CONTRIBUTORS

MATT BAILEY

Matt Bailey works in the Department of Modern History, Politics and International Relations at Macquarie University. Matt is writing a PhD thesis on the history of shopping centre development in Sydney. He has an ongoing research interest in urban and oral history, as well as histories of consumer culture.

NATASHA CAMPO

Natasha Campo holds a PhD from the History Program at La Trobe University. Natasha has published and presented widely in academic forums as well as in the mainstream press on Australian feminist history, and has a particular interest in the way feminism has been represented and remembered in the popular media. She currently works in the School of Journalism and Australian Studies at Monash University and is an editor of *Lilith: A Feminist History Journal*. Her latest book, *From Superwomen to Domestic Goddesses: The Rise and Fall of Feminism*, is published by Peter Lang International Academic Publishers (2009).

ROBERT CRAWFORD

Robert Crawford is Senior Lecturer in Public Communication at the University of Technology, Sydney. Robert is the author of *But Wait, There's More...: A History of Australian Advertising, 1900–2000* (2008) as well as various articles on the history of Australia's advertising and media industries appearing in national and international journals. He is also an editor and contributor to *Australians in Britain: the Twentieth Century Experience* (2009) and co-edits *Public Communication Review*.

TONY DINGLE

Tony Dingle recently retired from the Faculty of Business and Economics at Monash University where he was Associate Dean Education. He is an economic and urban historian and has researched and published extensively in Australian and British economic, social, urban and environmental history. He has written or edited ten books as well as many journal articles. His recent projects include studies of the growth of consumerism in Australia, urban transformations in old inner city industrial areas, the evolution of miner's houses and a history of the relationship between Melbourne and the River Yarra.

DAVID DUNSTAN

David Dunstan is Senior Lecturer and Deputy Director at the National Centre for Australian Studies at Monash University. David is the author of *Better than Pommard: A History of Wine in Victoria* (1994 and second edition forthcoming) and has written extensively about the wine industry in Australia. He is an editor and contributor to *Australians in Britain: The Twentieth Century Experience* (2009). His first work experience was in the cellar and home delivery with a well-known Melbourne licensed grocery and for many years he wrote about wine for the Melbourne *Age*, the Sydney *Sun-Herald* and other publications.

KIM HUMPHERY

Kim Humphery is Associate Professor and Deputy Head of the School of Global Studies, Social Science and Planning, RMIT University. Kim has written widely on histories, practices and theories of consumption, particularly in Australia, and more recently on the nature of Western materialism and a renewed politics of overconsumption. *Shelf Life: Supermarkets and the Changing Cultures of Consumption*, Cambridge University Press, Melbourne, was published in 1998, while *Excess: Anti-Consumerism in the West*, Polity, Cambridge, was published in 2009.

SUSIE KHAMIS

Susie Khamis is a Lecturer in Macquarie University's Department of Media, Music & Cultural Studies. Susie's research interests include Australian consumerism, advertising and branding. Her work has been published in *Australian Cultural History*, *Journal of Australian Studies* and *M/C: A Journal of Media and Culture*.

MOYA MCFADZEAN

Moya McFadzean has been Senior Curator of Migration in the History and Technology Department at Museum Victoria in Melbourne since 1995. She has curated and co-curated exhibitions at the Immigration Museum and Melbourne Museum and has delivered numerous conference papers in Australia, the UK, Sweden and Taiwan on representing migration histories in museums. In 2009 Moya completed her PhD in History at the University of Melbourne on a cultural history of glory boxes in mid–20th century Australia.

AMANDA MCLEOD

Amanda McLeod is a writer and historian with a particular interest in social, consumer and commercial life. Amanda holds a PhD in history from Monash University (2004) and has worked on a wide range of projects both inside and outside the academy. Her first book, *Abundance: Mass Consumption in Postwar Australia*, was published in 2007. Between 2007 and 2009 she was Williamson Postdoctoral Research Fellow in the Australian Centre at the University of Melbourne. She is currently writing an historical and philosophical analysis of Consumer Affairs Victoria—*A Fair Deal* and blogs at http://gettingawayfromthejoneses.blogspot.com/.

SEAMUS O'HANLON

Seamus O'Hanlon is the Director of the International Studies program at Monash University where he teaches contemporary and public history in the School of Philosophical, Historical and International Studies (SOPHIS). Seamus is the author of *Together Apart: Boarding, House, Hostel and Flat Life in Pre-war Melbourne* (2002) and co-editor of *Go!: Melbourne in the Sixties* (2005). His latest book is *Melbourne Remade: The Inner City since the Seventies*, published by Arcade in August 2010.

JOHN SINCLAIR

Professor John Sinclair is Honorary Professorial Fellow in the Australian Centre at the University of Melbourne, researching the role of advertising in the globalisation of media in Australia. Other ongoing work covers various aspects of the globalisation of the media and communication industries, with a particular focus on Asia and Latin America. John's books include *Latin American Television: A Global View* and the edited work *Contemporary World Television.* He has held visiting professorships at leading universities in Europe and the United States, is on the editorial advisory boards of a number of international journals, and is active in communication organisations.

JUDITH SMART

Judith Smart is a principal fellow at the University of Melbourne and an adjunct professor at RMIT University. Judith has published on Australian women's organisations in the first half of the 20th Century, as well as on women and political protest, women and religion, the Miss Australia beauty contest, and the Billy Graham Crusade. She is a past editor of *Australian Historical Studies* and present editor of the *Victorian Historical Journal.* Her major current project (with Professor Marian Quartly,

Monash University) is a history of the National Council of Women of Australia 1931–2006.

INDEX